Published under the auspices of
The Center for Japanese Studies
University of California, Berkeley

POLICE AND COMMUNITY IN JAPAN

Police and Community in Japan

Walter L. Ames

UNIVERSITY OF CALIFORNIA PRESS

BERKELEY . LOS ANGELES . LONDON

University of California Press
Berkeley and Los Angeles, California

University of California Press, Ltd.
London, England

© 1981 by
The Regents of the University of California
Printed in the United States of America
1 2 3 4 5 6 7 8 9

Library of Congress Cataloging in Publication Data

Ames, Walter L.
    Police and community in Japan.

    Bibliography: p.
    Includes index.
    1. Police—Japan.   2. Japan—Social conditions—
1945–   I. Title.
HV8257.A2A47   363.2′0952   80-12642
ISBN 0-520-04070-8

To the late RICHARD K. BEARDSLEY
respected scholar, sensitive teacher, considerate friend

CONTENTS

PREFACE

The data for this book were collected during eighteen months of anthropological field research in Japan for my doctoral dissertation, from January 1974 until July 1975.[1] I used participant-observation and the case-study method by working directly with police officers in the police station of the Tokyo suburb of Fuchu for five months as a preliminary study, and in the Kurashiki and Mizushima police stations in the city of Kurashiki, Okayama prefecture, for the year-long main study. I also studied a *chūzaisho* ("residential police-box") in rural Takamatsu Town, Okayama prefecture, incorporating the hamlet of Niiike, which was studied from 1950 to 1956 by the University of Michigan's Center for Japanese Studies as a representative farm hamlet. I spent a final month in Tokyo gathering additional police and crime information, and making a study of the Tokyo Seventh Riot Police.

The police were my "tribe," and in the anthropological tradition, I tried to do everything they did as much as possible. I had an office in the Kurashiki police station for over a year and worked with nearly all types of policemen: I walked the beat with policemen, worked shifts in patrol cars, accompanied juvenile police as they counseled delinquents, and went to crime scenes with criminal investigators and to traffic accidents with traffic police. I trained and went to demonstrations with the riot police in both Okayama and Tokyo. I was dressed in police uniform on several ceremonial occasions.

The National Police Agency gave me official permission for and facilitated my study in every reasonable way in Tokyo and Okayama. The

1. See Walter L. Ames, "Police and Community in Japan" (Ph.D. dissertation, University of Michigan, 1976).

Okayama Prefectural Police Headquarters supplied information and ordered the Kurashiki and Mizushima police to assist me in the research. The police were generally open and cooperative except concerning some security matters. The length of my stay in Kurashiki allowed me to form personal bonds with a number of police officers, and they were candid about many of the informal as well as formal aspects of police work and police relations with the community. Most of my data on the police were gathered through documents supplied by the police, observation of police methods, and extensive interviews with police officers, ranging from bureau heads in the National Police Agency to patrolmen in "police-boxes" (kōban) and chūzaisho. Since I speak and read Japanese, all research was done without the aid of an interpreter.

I gathered data on the community by interviewing representatives of groups involved with the police, by observing citizens' reactions to the police, and from a survey of 421 residents in selected neighborhoods in Kurashiki. The Kurashiki City Office was very helpful in supplying information and introducing me to individuals I wanted to meet. The Kurashiki branch manager of a large bank introduced me to many of his fellow Rotarians, who wield considerable influence in the city, behind the scenes. These men, mostly doctors, invited me to their homes frequently to eat sushi and discuss the hidden workings of the Kurashiki power structure. They were invaluable in enlightening me concerning many of the informal relationships of the police and the community. Our neighbors and friends in Kurashiki also provided helpful insights regarding the police and Japanese society in general.

I studied Japanese gangsters (yakuza) through occasional direct contact with them. The police have a uniquely Japanese relationship of cordiality and mutual understanding with gangsters, and they introduced me to gangster bosses and took me to gangster offices in Kurashiki and Mizushima. I went to bosses' homes and to a gangster funeral, and even found myself at a gangster fight one evening while working at a kōban. I never felt personal danger when I was with gangsters. The police supplied me with information and documents on gangsters, while friends, including the medical Rotarians, pointed out informal gangster relations with the police and the city and prefectural administrations.

Gaining access to the police was the most critical factor in the success or failure of my research in Japan. My efforts began long before my arrival in Tokyo in January 1974. An American law professor introduced me to the director of the prestigious Asia and Far East Institute for the Prevention of Crime and Treatment of Offenders (UNAFEI) (an institution jointly operated by the United Nations and the Japanese Ministry of Justice and located in Fuchu) when he visited Ann Arbor. We discussed my research project, and he made some helpful suggestions. After he returned to Japan, we corresponded, and I asked if I could be informally affiliated with the institute as a springboard for my study of the police. He not only agreed to my affiliation but, on his own initiative, requested a high official of the National Police Agency to secure official police permission for my study. This official, in the first criminal-investigation section of the National Police Agency, approached the general-affairs section, which issued a document granting permission for the study and assured me of assistance in every possible way, including introduction to officials of the Okayama Prefectural Police Headquarters.

After arriving in Japan, I paid my respects to the director of UNAFEI, and he arranged a meeting for me with his contact man in the National Police Agency. I visited the official in the criminal section, who introduced me to the chiefs and other key officials in the general-affairs section and other sections that I would be dealing with. He also introduced me by telephone to the chief in the Fuchu police station so that I could begin my preliminary Fuchu police study. When I went to Okayama, the general-affairs section of the National Police Agency telephoned the police administration division of the Okayama Prefectural Police Headquarters and gave me letters of introduction to the prefectural police officials. A high elite-course police officer whom I met in Tokyo and who had served in the Okayama Prefectural Police Headquarters also gave me a letter of introduction to the headquarters. Top officials of the prefectural police headquarters telephoned the Kurashiki and Mizushima police stations and asked them to assist me in my study. I met the chiefs and assistant chiefs in these stations, and they assigned a section chief to serve as liaison for my study (the patrol section chief in Kurashiki and the security section chief in Mizushima). The police station officials then introduced me to the police officers in the *kōban* and *chūzaisho* and in the different specializations that I observed, interviewed, and worked with for over a year.

The key to my access to the police was the official permission for the study which I secured from the supreme authority—the National Police Agency. Thereafter, my introductions descended from the top (the general-affairs section of the National Police Agency) to the bottom (*kōban* and line officers in various police station sections) of the command structure. If I had attempted to approach the police from an outside source to a point intermediate in the police hierarchy (such as through an influential local in Kurashiki to the police chief), or had simply befriended the police officers in the local *kōban* in an attempt to study them, my access would have been limited and localized. The fact that I went from the top to the bottom legitimized my study and reassured police officers at the level in which I was most interested—the local level—that I could be trusted.

Having been to Japan on several occasions, I was aware of the various ways one can validate interpersonal relations and express gratitude and indebtedness for assistance. I exchanged traditional New Year's and mid-summer greeting cards and gifts (called *o seibo* and *o chūgen*) with police officers and others who had helped me; I brought back souvenirs (*omi-yage*) to my main benefactors whenever I went on a trip; and my wife made cookies and other American treats, which I occasionally gave to various police officers to express my friendship. I also carefully followed the command structure by securing permission of section chiefs before interviewing people in their sections, and by notifying the assistant police chief whenever I was in the police station to talk to men of certain sections or to work at my desk. Because I was able to fit myself into the Japanese system of reciprocal obligations, police officers were able to relate to me more comfortably. Yet there are certain trade-offs required by this approach. An American often feels burdened or even trapped by the binding obligations.

The police were very helpful, as were Kurashiki City officials whom I met through a college professor in Tokyo. When I moved my family from Tokyo to Kurashiki, our furniture arrived before we did, whereupon persons from prefectural police headquarters and the Kurashiki police station, as well as police officers from the local *kōban* and officials from the city office, took a hand in moving our furniture into the house and setting it up before our arrival. I was soon given an office in the Kurashiki police station on request and was there daily. I became close friends with several policemen, such as the old sergeant from the nearest *kōban* who dropped by our home constantly and who eventually likened me to his son. I met and interviewed officials as high as the chiefs of the Okayama Prefectural Police Headquarters, the Shikoku Regional Police Bureau, the Tokyo Metropolitan Police Department, and the National Police Agency. The police extended every possible courtesy, and the Kurashiki police seemed to accept me as one of themselves.

I wanted to conduct a survey of police officers in Kurashiki and Mizushima to ascertain attitudes and to obtain data on their backgrounds. I saved this for the last month or two of my stay in Okayama, sensing the potential sensitivity of this request and wanting not to risk the souring of relations prematurely. Several line police officers in Kurashiki helped me prepare a questionnaire by candidly suggesting problem areas that could be surveyed. The top Kurashiki police officials, with whom I had developed deep personal bonds while using my office in the police station and through informal and recreational contacts, approved my survey. The Mizushima police chief was more cautious, however (I was always more of an outsider in Mizushima), and wanted prior prefectural police headquarters approval. I assumed headquarters would approve the survey because they had granted all my other requests, so I went to Okayama City and asked permission. Headquarters refused, saying it was unalterable policy to deny all requests made by nonpolice researchers to administer questionnaires to police officers (they said it would be "proof they could not deny"). I appealed to my contacts in the National Police Agency, but they were ineffectual because of the autonomy of the prefectural police in such routine decisions. If I had been content to survey only the Kurashiki police station, the prefectural police headquarters would never have needed to say no. My relations with the prefectural police headquarters became somewhat chilly after this, but in part for two other reasons as well: the chief and assistant chief of the headquarters with whom I had established rapport were transferred and, I believe, headquarters had begun to fear that perhaps I knew too much about the police.

Our stay in Kurashiki ended on an upbeat, however. The day we left the city, the police chief, several section chiefs, patrolmen from *kōban* I had studied, as well as a member of the prefectural public-safety commission (a total of thirty-six people, including other friends), came to the train station to see us off. They presented us with gifts and flowers and arranged to have a recording of "Auld Lang Syne" played over the loudspeakers as the train pulled out.

The year that I began my study—1974—was a uniquely historical time to be making a study of the Japanese police. Besides being the hundred-year anniversary of the creation of the modern Japanese police system modeled after those on the continent of Europe, it also marked the twenty-year anniversary of the return of the Japanese police to a more centralized organizational structure after a period of radical decentralization on an American model that was imposed on Japan during the occupation after World War II. The heritage of the postwar American influence lingers to an extent, and the present police establishment is a sometimes unevenly mixed amalgam of the prewar European and the overlaid American type of police system. I felt that it was an entirely appropriate time for an American researcher to be studying the police system of Japan. It will be evident in the book that, in a number of ways, the Japanese police system may be operating more effectively than many of its foreign counterparts. The Japanese, who for so long have borrowed from the West, may have something that they can teach us about policing and crime control.

There are many people and institutions without whose assistance this book would not have been possible. I wish to thank the late Richard K. Beardsley, my adviser and doctoral committee chairman at the University of Michigan, for suggesting the project and guiding me during the research and writing of the dissertation and the book. I had the unique advantage of having Professor Beardsley within the distance of a local telephone call during a portion of my fieldwork in Kurashiki while he made a restudy of Niiike in 1974. I am indebted to Professor B. James George, Jr., former Director of the Center for the Administration of Justice, Wayne State University, for advising me on strategy for gaining access to the police, and for introducing me to UNAFEI. I also wish to thank the faculty of the School of Criminal Justice, Michigan State University, especially Professors Louis A. Radelet and Ralph F. Turner, for allowing me to sit in police-related classes before I left for Japan, and for advising me on the study.

I am indebted to numerous people and institutions in Japan, not all of whom it is possible to mention. I am particularly grateful to the director, Tokoi Zen, and the staff of UNAFEI for securing police permission for my study and introducing me to key officials in the National Police Agency, as well as for providing me with a desk in the Institute during my stay in Fuchu and giving me much encouragement. I wish to single out for thanks the following National Police Agency officials: Watanabe Masaro, Fujimaki Seitaro, Nitta Isamu, Ito Kazumi, Suzuki Kuniyoshi, and Tachibana Masao. I am indebted to the two successive chiefs of the Fuchu police station during my study, Hirose Haruyori and Seshimo Kennosuke. I am especially grateful to the former head of the Tokyo Seventh Riot Police, Shibata Isao. I am also indebted to the following Supreme Court and Justice Ministry officials: Justice Dando Shigemitsu, Kamiya Hisao, Tamura Yataro, Tsuchimoto Takeshi, and Takayasu Kikuyoshi. Numerous scholars and researchers assisted me, including the following: Hirano Ryuichi, Miyazawa Koichi, Mugishima Fumio, Nakahara Hidenori, Nakano Takashi, and Yonemura Shoji.

Police officials and officers in the Okayama Prefectural Police Headquarters and the Kurashiki and Mizushima police stations who assisted me are too numerous to mention, so I will offer a heartfelt thank you to all of them collectively. I also wish to single out citizens of Kurashiki who provided me with invaluable assistance: Akagi Motozo, Akamatsu Akira, Maeda Akira, Muroyama Takayoshi, Otani Akira, and Uno Otohei.

The overseas portion of the research, as well as part of the dissertation write-up period, was funded by a generous grant from the Social Science Research Council, and the writing of the dissertation in Ann Arbor was additionally supported by Grant No. 76NI–99–0065 from the Law Enforcement Assistance Administration, U.S. Department of Justice, and also by a grant from the University of Michigan Center for Japanese Studies and a Rackham Dissertation Grant.

I want to give special thanks to Professor Ezra Vogel, who read the manuscript in an earlier version and gave extended and invaluable comments. I should also like to thank Professors Lloyd Ohlin, Frank Upham, Tanaka Hideo, Inoue Masahito, Fujikura Koichiro, and Dr. Matthias Scheer for their comments and encouragement on the manuscript. Many of their suggestions have been incorporated into this final version of the book.

I wish to acknowledge my sincere gratitude to Professor Jerome A. Cohen, Director of East Asian Legal Studies and Associate Dean of the Harvard Law School, for providing me with an office and for his financial assistance and unfailing encouragement while I rewrote the dissertation into its present book form during my second and third years at Harvard Law School. I also gratefully acknowledge a generous grant (Grant No. 78–38–0.888.8.91310.412) from the Japan–United States Friendship Commission during my third year at the Law School (1978–79), without which the final revision would not have been possible. The dissertation was expertly typed by Joan Oldroyd, and the book manuscript, by Karen Mark and Bonnie Garmus. Expert editing by Gladys Castor was an invaluable asset, and I wish to thank Phyllis Killen and others at the University of California Press for unfailing pleasantness and assistance.

I should like to express gratitude, affection, and appreciation to my wife, Evelyn, my daughter, Kimberly, and my son Byron, who accompanied me to Japan and made the research period an unforgettable family experience. I deeply appreciate their (and my subsequently born son Darren's) love, patience, support, and active assistance during the writing of the dissertation and rewriting of the book manuscript. Their endurance while I simultaneously earned a law degree and wrote a book was truly remarkable. And I thank my parents and my wife's parents for their interest and encouragement throughout this project.

When I was organizing my data I faced the dilemma whether or not to make the book explicitly comparative. I chose not to do so, for two reasons: First, I have had less direct experience with police work in the United States than in Japan, and my comments would be essentially derivative from secondary sources and thus of a different quality than my firsthand data on Japan. Second, I felt that my primary responsibility as an anthropologist was to report accurately the observations I made and the data that I gleaned, and to explain police phenomena within the structure of Japanese society and in the context of Japan's cultural heritage. I therefore trust that the reader will use this book along with the sociology of police literature to confirm or refute the theoretical arguments made by others.

Finally, I have wanted to express my observations and conclusions frankly, although I recognize the risk of embarrassing the police and disappointing the many fine police officials who so kindly assisted me. In most instances, I have chosen to be forthright on potentially sensitive topics, and I apologize to the Japanese police and the individuals who helped me for any problems which my comments may cause. My purpose has been not to criticize but merely to explain the realities of the Japanese police system as I see them. Any errors in this book are, of course, entirely my own responsibility.

INTRODUCTION

The Japanese police pride themselves on being the world's best. Their confidence is apparently well founded, for Japan has the lowest crime rate in the industrialized world, and its crime totals have actually followed a downward curve since 1955. Japan is one of the few major nations—perhaps the only one—where one can walk the streets of its large cities late at night and feel in no danger. This stems not only from an efficient and strong police organization, but from general cooperation by the community in fighting crime. Japanese society itself maintains a remarkable level of order and control.

Previous studies have indicated that the Japanese police are very successful.[1] There is a need, however, for greater knowledge about the wide variety of situations to which the police adapt themselves—not just patrol behavior in the Tokyo context. This study examines how the police develop their approach in different kinds of communities and in response to various problems and complexities in Japanese society. Their adaptation has not been static, for the strategies of the police have shifted over time as Japanese society has changed. But the police have not been molded in a vacuum. Rather, they fit Japanese society like a glove fits the hand, and the societal hand has determined the form of the glove.

Part One will deal with the adaptation of the police to the community viewed in a larger sense as the whole of Japanese society. It will initially look at how the police fit into the tightly knit rural community, where the usually high degree of closeness to the people becomes an ideal or model

1. See David H. Bayley, *Forces of Order: Police Behavior in Japan and the United States* (Berkeley and Los Angeles: University of California Press, 1976), and William Clifford, *Crime Control in Japan* (Lexington, Mass.: Lexington Books, 1976).

for police-community relations for all police officers. It will then examine
the techniques of policing urban areas, where the rural ideal of police-
community intimacy is more difficult to attain because of greater social
complexity, and the problems the police encounter as they adjust to a rapidly changing and evolving society. Attention will then shift from socially
conforming clienteles of the police in rural and urban neighborhoods to
clienteles that are more-or-less socially nonconforming. These include
youth, the Korean minority and *burakumin* (a group subject to severe social and economic discrimination), and, finally, gangsters. The mode of
police adaptation varies with each of these different clienteles. Part One
concludes by considering how the police adapt to certain special problems,
including the investigation of crimes, maintenance of public security, and
regulation of businesses affecting public morals (*fūzoku eigyō*).

Solidarity and loyalty among police officers is essential to the strength
and effective operation of the police system as it interacts with the community. The inculcation and maintenance of these qualities is the subject
matter of Part Two. Recruitment into the police involves an almost total
remaking of individuals and usually a lifetime commitment to the police
profession. Solidarity among the ranks and absolute loyalty to the organization are instilled and kept up, both on the job and in the private lives of
police officers, through extensive training and other formal and informal
mechanisms. Loyalty and solidarity are crucial to the police and are primary tools in their mission of protecting society from various "enemies."
Yet there remain stresses and latent seams in the police structure despite
intensive socialization efforts.

The book places emphasis on the *actual* operation of the Japanese police, not merely the ideal; on the informal aspects of policing rather than
the formal. This is the level at which cultural and societal adaptation is
most manifest. The distinction between what is really occurring and what
is professed to be occurring is aptly expressed in the Japanese dichotomy
of *tatemae* and *honne*. A *tatemae* is a ground rule or principle that spells
out the way things should be ideally but ignores the fact that in reality they
are not that way at all. The contrasting *honne* is the real intention, the
essence or the substance. The first is a superficial form or formalism, the
latter is reality. The two are always linked in the Japanese mind "like two
sides of a piece of paper."[2]

2. Nieda Rokusaburo, *Tatemae to honne* [Form and essence] (Tokyo: Daiyamondosha,
1973), p. 8.

A *tatemae/honne* sort of distinction is not unique to the Japanese. Such a dichotomy is found everywhere, but it plays a vital role in Japanese society. An awareness of this is essential to an accurate understanding of a topic as potentially sensitive as the police relationship to the community and the nature of the police organization. Formal *tatemae* are probably given emphasis in the homogeneous and closely knit Japanese society in an attempt to bring order to existence and to smooth interpersonal relations by not subjecting awkward realities to open scrutiny. Usually, no one is deceived by the *tatemae*, because everyone involved understands without making explicit the *honne* that underlies it. The Japanese often distinguish between *tatemae* and *honne* by ignoring the façade and adapting to reality according to the situation.

In the real world confronted by the police, the theme of adaptation often conflicts with that of solidarity and loyalty. Adaptation to differing local communities or clienteles can hinder police solidarity and a consistent police structure. Conversely, the maintenance of a solid front to society and various perceived enemies can thwart the meshing of the police with the community. The distinction between *tatemae* and *honne* prevents adaptation from dominating solidarity and loyalty, and vice versa, by maintaining a balance between them. For example, the *tatemae* of solidarity and loyalty within the police is never fully achieved (the *honne*), hence the police enjoy a degree of individual flexibility that enhances adaptation to varying clienteles. Likewise, the *tatemae* of a well-adapting police structure masks the *honne* of a powerful police system that, in many ways, stands apart from the people and is at times even feared by them. This interplay of *tatemae* and *honne*, which recurs throughout the book even though it is not always explicitly expressed, results in a sometimes confusing picture of police images that do not precisely mesh and of contrasting public reactions to the police.

RESEARCH LOCATIONS

The main study took place in the rapidly urbanizing and industrializing prefecture of Okayama. (A five-month preliminary study was made in Fuchu, a suburb in western Tokyo.) I chose Okayama because it is more representative of Japan as a whole than Tokyo or Osaka. I focused my study on one location to see the various textures of police adaptation to the community, instead of taking a superficial look at a number of disparate locations. Okayama is located about seventy-five miles west of Osaka

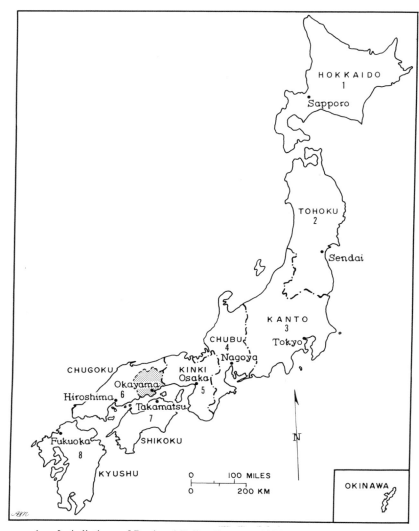

MAP 1. Jurisdictions of Regional Police Bureaus, 1974
    1   Hokkaido Prefectural Police Headquarters, Sapporo
    2   Tohoku Regional Police Bureau, Sendai
    3   Kanto Regional Police Bureau, Tokyo
    4   Chubu Regional Police Bureau, Nagoya
    5   Kinki Regional Police Bureau, Osaka
    6   Chugoku Regional Police Bureau, Hiroshima
    7   Shikoku Regional Police Bureau, Takamatsu
    8   Kyushu Regional Police Bureau, Fukuoka
SOURCE: National Police Agency, ed., *The Police of Japan*, pp. 67–68.

TABLE 1. *Okayama Prefecture Compared with Forty-seven Others*

Category	Okayama's Rank
Land area	17
Population	20
Population density	24
Business firms	20
Farm households	10
Manufacturing firms	16
Shops	25
Elementary and junior high schools	19
Automobiles	18

SOURCE: Okayama Prefecture, ed., *Okayama-ken tōkei nempō, 1971* [Okayama prefecture statistical yearbook] (Okayama: Okayama-ken Tokei Kyokai, 1974), pp. 288–293.

on the main island of Honshu facing the Inland Sea. It is a traditionally rich agricultural region famous for its rice, fruit, and mat-rush production.[3] It has industrialized rapidly since the mid–1950s, mainly through land reclamation by filling in the Inland Sea. The northern portion of the prefecture is bounded by the Chugoku mountain range and is still very rural. The extension of the Shinkansen ("Bullet Train") to Okayama in 1972 and the completion of the eastern Okayama portion of an expressway from Osaka in early 1975 have greatly increased Okayama's contact with the metropolitan areas of Tokyo and Osaka. This has hastened its social and economic integration with the large urban centers of Japan.

Okayama is an average or slightly above average prefecture in most comparisons (see table 1). Its relatively high ranking in number of farm households (10) and manufacturing firms (16) reflects the fact that Okayama is an agricultural prefecture in the process of industrialization.

I concentrated my study in Okayama on three localities: Kurashiki City, the Mizushima industrial complex on the coast of the Inland Sea a few miles from "old Kurashiki," and Takamatsu Town, inland from Kurashiki. These three locations afforded me a three-way comparison that incorporated on a small scale and within close proximity three of the major situations into which the police everywhere in Japan adapt: a stable urban residential and business center, a major industrial complex, and a rural farm area. We shall take a brief look at these three areas.

3. A rush (*igusa*) used in the weaving of tatami-mat covers.

Kurashiki.

Kurashiki is the second largest city in Okayama prefecture, with a population of 393,800 in 1974. (Okayama City is the largest, with a population of 501,200.) The present city was formed by the amalgamation of the cities of Kurashiki, Tamashima, and Kojima in 1967. The jurisdiction of the Kurashiki police station, out of which I worked, is varied. It covers the center of the city, "old Kurashiki," which is lined with Edo-period (1600–1867) rice granaries and old samurai houses with thickly plastered white walls and black-tiled roofs. This enchanting area has become a tourist center with art and archaeological museums, and retains much of the flavor of Edo and prewar days. The neighborhood social structure is relatively intact because the old city was not bombed during the war. The jurisdiction also includes shopping malls, bar and restaurant districts, workers' neighborhoods, villages of former outcastes (*burakumin*), apartment complexes, farm areas, and new residential neighborhoods built within the last fifteen years to accommodate the influx of white-collar workers.

Mizushima.

The Mizushima area became a part of Kurashiki City in 1953 and directly borders on the Inland Sea. The jurisdiction of the Mizushima police station, in which I also worked, is separate from the Kurashiki police station jurisdiction, covering the mammoth industrial complex built since 1953 on land reclaimed from the sea. The concentration of industry is very dense on the reclaimed land: there are thirty-one major industrial facilities, including a huge steel mill, a large oil refinery, an automobile plant, and several petrochemical plants, all crowded into 7.2 square miles.[4] The Kawasaki Steel Corporation's apartment complex located in Mizushima is the largest in the prefecture, with over fifteen thousand people. The jurisdiction also includes slum neighborhoods of day laborers, the largest grouping of Koreans in Okayama prefecture, farm areas, old fishing villages, bar districts, and shopping malls. There are several groups of gangsters,

4. Kurashiki City Office, ed., *Mizushima no tenbō* [A view of Mizushima], a pamphlet published by Kurashiki City, 1971.

active labor unions, and Communist organizations in both the Mizushima and Kurashiki police jurisdictions.

Takamatsu.

Takamatsu Town is located twenty miles west of Okayama City in the heart of ancient Kibi, a prehistoric culture center and a rich agricultural region, and was incorporated into neighboring Okayama City administratively in 1971. It follows the national pattern of farm areas bordering on cities in that many of the residents commute to work in Okayama City and Kurashiki City, leaving most of the farming to wives and the old people. I studied the Kamo *chūzaisho* in Takamatsu in detail because its jurisdiction is the most agricultural of the two *chūzaisho* in the town, and because it includes the hamlet of Niiike. A *chūzaisho*, or residential police-box, is a police building, usually located in a village or rural town, in which one policeman lives with his family and polices the surrounding area. I briefly studied several other *chūzaisho* as well, one in a rural and isolated mountain area, to provide contrast with Takamatsu Town.

Although this is essentially a case study of the police in Okayama, the generalizations that emerge can be extended to the Japanese police as a whole. Okayama is an ideal place to study the police because in most aspects of crime and police work it is much more representative of the entire country than is an atypical location such as Tokyo. The jurisdiction of the Tokyo Metropolitan Police Department is one of the smallest in land area (forty-fourth out of forty-seven prefectures), yet has the largest population, and is ranked first in numbers of police officers, reported crimes, criminal arrests, and traffic accidents. Okayama is slightly above the national average in each of these criteria (see table 2). The Kurashiki and Mizushima police jurisdictions cover mixed urban-rural areas, yet are essentially urban. This is reflected in their police forces (see table 3). The land areas of their jurisdictions are among the smallest in the prefecture, but their populations, numbers of police officers, crimes, arrests, and traffic accidents are among the highest of the prefecture's twenty-three police stations.[5]

5. The twenty-three Okayama prefecture police stations are Okayama Higashi, Okayama Nishi, Okayama Minami, Saidaiji, Ōtsū, Seto, Bizen, Ushimado, Tamano, Kojima, Kurashiki, Mizushima, Tamashima, Kasaoka, Yakake, Ibara, Sōja, Takahashi, Niimi, Katsuyama, Tsūyama, Shōei, and Kami.

TABLE 2. *Comparison of Police Work in Okayama and Tokyo, 1973*

	Population	Area (sq. miles)	Police Officers	Reported Crimes	Criminal Arrests	Traffic Accidents
Tokyo Rank (among 47 prefectures)	11,506,800 1	823.4 44	38,420 1	208,188 1	108,236 1	42,357 1
Okayama Rank (among 47 prefectures)	1,811,200 20	2,735.8 17	2,470 19	18,806 13	12,282 14	11,789 16

SOURCE: Police White Paper, pp. 380, 432–435 and 480–483.

TABLE 3. *Comparison of Police Work in Kurashiki and Mizushima, 1973*

	Population	Area (sq. miles)	Police Officers	Reported Crimes	Criminal Arrests	Traffic Accidents
Kurashiki Rank (among 23 police stations)	157,718 2	39.8 19	146 3	1,926 3	1,158 3	1,283 2
Mizushima Rank (among 23 police stations)	98,380 7	24.5 22	99 4	1,334 4	656 7	904 4

SOURCE: Documents from the Okayama Prefectural Police Headquarters, 1974.

HISTORICAL BACKGROUND OF THE POLICE

It was noted above that the Japanese police have assumed various forms and strategies 'as they have adapted to a changing society.[6] Before the Edo period (1600–1867), formal social control was performed essentially by the military and by groups of citizens organized for mutual defense. During Edo, an elaborate police apparatus was developed. Magistrates (*machi bugyō*) with samurai status served as the chiefs of police, prosecutors, and judges in criminal as well as civil matters in Edo and in most castle towns. These magistrates were covertly assisted by inspectors (*metsuke*), who ferreted out cases of misrule by officials and spied on samurai or groups who were thought to be menaces to the government. The police responsibilities of the magistrates were delegated to police sergeants (*yoriki*) and police officers (*dōshin*), both sword-carrying samurai, the former mounted and the latter unmounted. Semiofficial detectives (*meakashi*, or *okappiki*, as they were called in Edo) were at the lowest level, carrying only a short metal truncheon (*jitte*) to neutralize the slash of a criminal's sword. Detectives, of low class or outcaste origin, were often former outlaws who had turned to serving the government to save themselves from execution. The shogun's private rural domains were administered by local intendants (*daikan*), lower-level officials in the shogunal hierarchy whose duties included law enforcement and judicial functions. The Edo government's social-control mechanisms were augmented by mutual-responsibility groups of citizens, such as the *gonin gumi* (a "five-family association"), composed of neighbors who assisted each other and who were collectively liable to the government for any crimes or disorder caused by members. This was a direct precursor to present neighborhood organizations that aid the police.

A period of transition in police organization followed the fall of the Edo government and the beginning of the Meiji period (1868–1912). Kawaji Toshiyoshi, a former samurai from Kagoshima, was sent to Europe in 1872 to study police systems. On his return he recommended a series of measures for police reorganization that were heavily influenced by France and Prussia. The result was the establishment of the Home Ministry (Naimushō) in 1873, which directly controlled prefectural administrations by appointing governors. It also controlled the police through the police bu-

6. This section of the history of the Japanese police is adapted from a chapter of my doctoral dissertation: Walter L. Ames, "Police and Community in Japan" (Ph.D. dissertation, University of Michigan, 1976), pp. 28–73. It will also appear as part of an article entitled "Police," in *Encyclopedia of Japan* (Tokyo: Kodansha, 1980).

reau (*keishikyoku*, later *keihokyoku*) under its jurisdiction, although routine management of police activities was handled at the prefectural level. The Tokyo Metropolitan Police Department (Keishichō), the police force in the capital, was organized in 1874 with Kawaji as head. In 1875 the Administrative Police Regulation (*gyōsei keisatsu kisoku*) clarified the separation of judicial functions from other functions of the police, giving primary responsibility for adjudication to the new Ministry of Justice (Shihōshō) and for law enforcement to the police. The police retained the authority to issue ordinances and perform quasi-judicial functions, however. For example, the Law of Summary Procedure for Police Offenses (*ikeizai sokketsu rei*) of 1885 provided chiefs of police stations with authority to summarily prosecute and adjudicate "police offenses" (*ikeizai*), punishable with detention for less than thirty days and fines of less than twenty yen. *Ikeizai* were light offenses usually dealing with public morality or matters of daily life.

The centralized police system had a range of responsibility that went far beyond the three essential police duties of crime prevention and arrest of criminals, protection of life and property, and the maintenance of public peace. It regulated public health, factories, construction, and businesses, and issued permits, licenses, and orders mandated by law to achieve these functions. For instance, police doctors periodically checked prostitutes for venereal disease, and police officers saw to it that people received their preventive inoculations, and checked sanitation in such public establishments as restaurants and barber shops. When the stringencies of war increased after the outbreak of fighting in China in 1937, the police were given the added responsibilities of regulating business activities for the war effort, mobilizing labor, and controlling transportation. Even fire-fighting activities were under police direction. The police also had the duty to regulate publications, motion pictures, associations, political meetings, and election campaigns, as well as to control thoughts and political crimes. The Special Higher Police (*tokubetsu kōtō keisatsu* or *tokkō*) were established in all prefectures in 1928 for this purpose, reporting directly to Tokyo, not to the prefectural police headquarters. Assisting the police (who were far less numerous than at present) in cases of proscribed political activities was the Military Police (*kempei*), who also performed judicial functions and operated under orders from the army, navy, justice, and home ministers. With the ascendancy of the military, especially after the Manchurian Incident of 1931, the *kempei* began to assume normal police functions, leading to friction with police officers.[7]

After Japan's surrender in September 1945, American occupation officials commissioned Lewis J. Valentine of the New York City Police Department and Oscar G. Olander, Commissioner of the Michigan State Police, to study the police system. On their recommendation, occupation officials urged the Diet to enact a new Police Law in December 1947. The Home Ministry was abolished, and the police were shorn of their fire protection, public health, and other administrative duties, as well as their authority to issue ordinances or adjudicate minor offenses. The police system was decentralized, and autonomous police agencies were established in all cities and towns with a population of 5,000 and over, resulting in about 1,600 independent municipal police forces. Towns and villages of less than 5,000 population, too small for the financial burden of an autonomous force, were policed by the National Rural Police (*kokka chihō keisatsu*), which was organized prefecturally and centralized at the national level only in police standards, identification, communications, training, scientific crime detection, and crime statistics. Popular control of the police was to be insured by the establishment of politically neutral public-safety commissions (*kōan iinkai*) to control and supervise the police, appointed by the prime minister, prefectural governors, or mayors, subject to Diet or local assembly consent.

The drastic decentralization ran into immediate problems. It was simply not adapted to the centralized Japanese society, economy, and polity that had evolved since the Meiji period. Small municipalities did not have the financial capacity to support police departments, and frequent accusations of undue influence on the police by local community bosses and gangsters were heard. Morale and effectiveness in maintaining law and order in the chaotic period after the war sank to an alarming low. When fighting broke out in Korea in 1950, occupation officials hurriedly ordered the formation of the National Police Reserve (*kokka keisatsu yobitai*) to fill the gap left when the occupation forces were sent to Korea.[8] Supplied with American weapons and military uniforms, it was later renamed the Self-Defense

7. Daikasumikai, ed., *Naimushōshi* [History of the Home Ministry], 4 vols. (Tokyo: Chiho Zaimu Kyokai, 1970), 2:602.

8. The National Police Reserve, like an army from its inception, never performed the peacekeeping function of police officers. It was justified under the postwar Japanese constitution (which forbids the maintenance of a standing army) as a "peace preservation" force.

Force (*jieitai*). In June 1951, the Police Law was amended to allow smaller communities to merge their police forces with the National Rural Police. Eighty percent of the communities that had autonomous forces surrendered their independent status in that year. The Police Law creating the more centralized police organization of the present passed the Diet in June 1954, after extraordinary leftist opposition. Leftists feared that a re-centralized police system would prove to be oppressive of political liberties obtained after World War II. The immediate postwar experience showed that the structure and operation of the police could not be radically altered at will but had to conform to the vertical and centralized structure of Japanese society to operate effectively.

PRESENT STRUCTURE

The Japanese police system is based on prefectural police units. They are autonomous in daily police operations within the prefectures, yet are linked into a national system through the supervision of the National Police Agency. This agency supervises police education and training programs, procures police equipment, compiles criminal statistics, and furnishes nationwide services on criminal identification. Information on nationally significant crimes and incidents is forwarded to the National Police Agency by the prefectural police. The agency also coordinates interprefectural police affairs, such as the movement of police officers to other prefectures during large-scale mobilizations. Seven regional police bureaus (*kanku keisatsu kyoku*), plus the prefectural police headquarters of the prefecture of Hokkaido, are the lowest level of the National Police Agency and serve as liaison with the prefectural police. The National Police Agency is not a separate police force, and the police officers who staff it perform only supervisory functions.

Public-safety commissions supervise the police at the national and prefectural levels through consultation with the director general of the National Police Agency and the chiefs of the prefectural police, who exercise actual control. Prefectural commissioners are appointed by prefectural governors with the consent of the prefectural assemblies, and national commissioners are appointed by the prime minister with the consent of both houses of the Diet. The chairman of the national commission is minister without portfolio in the cabinet. The public-safety commission system is one of the main remnants from the postwar period of police decentralization and is supposed to guarantee democratic control of the police.

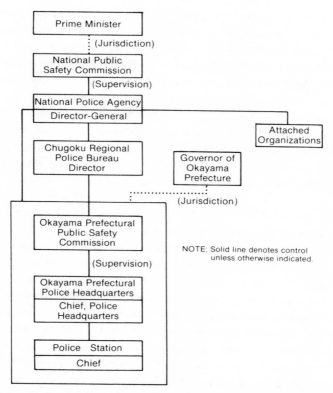

FIGURE 1.   National Police Organization as It Relates to Okayama Prefecture
SOURCE: Adapted from Ralph J. Rinalducci, *The Japanese Police Establishment*
(Tokyo: Obun Intereurope, Ltd., 1972), p. xvi.

Members of the commissions, however, both national and prefectural, are usually elderly and conservative men who almost always defer to police decisions. In reality, the police are totally independent of effective formal external checks on their power and operation. However, the weight of public opinion serves this function informally.

Prefectural police headquarters (*kenkei hombu*) control everyday police operations in each prefecture. The chief, the assistant chief, the security division chief, and several of the other highest officials are National Police Agency employees. All other officers are employed by the prefecture. The national government provides the prefectural police with funds for the salaries of national employees, police educational facilities, criminal-statistics expenses, purchase of police vehicles, boats, weapons, and other police equipment, expenses incurred in escort and guard duty, disasters, and riot control, and expenses involved in investigating offenses against the internal safety of the state or serious offenses affecting several prefectures. The prefectural police finance all other expenses, mainly salaries of police officers who are not national employees, police buildings, uniforms, and gasoline for patrol cars. The financial arrangement is of particular interest because of the independence it gives the National Police Agency in the sensitive area of internal security. The prefectures, in effect, pay for the patrolman on the beat, traffic control, criminal investigation, and other daily police functions. They have little or no control over the public security units. Finances and the transfers of high police personnel are the most important factors in police operations, and the National Police Agency controls the critical aspects of both.

Each prefecture is divided into districts, and a police station (*keisatsusho*) exercises jurisdiction over each district. Police station boundaries are not necessarily city boundaries, and larger cities usually have several stations. Police stations are under the direct control of the prefectural police headquarters and have no formal administrative ties to the governments of the towns or cities in which they are located. The area within each police station is further divided into the jurisdictions of urban *kōban* (more correctly *hashutsusho*, a police-box manned by several officers on a shift system) and *chūzaisho*. Thus, every square foot of Japan is under the direct jurisdiction of a police station and a *kōban* or a *chūzaisho*. These latter two form the primary units of police organization and provide close and frequent contact between police officers and citizens. We shall now turn to a consideration of the *chūzaisho* as the ideal form of police adaptation to the surrounding community.

ADAPTATION TO THE COMMUNITY

one

POLICING THE RURAL COMMUNITY: THE *CHŪZAISHO*

Policing the countryside, though it is less complex than policing urban areas, requires adaptation to a variety of situations. Okayama prefecture is typical in its range of physical and social variation. Widely scattered and isolated farming hamlets are found in small river valleys and basins deep in the rugged Chugoku mountains in the northern part of the prefecture. Farm areas adjoining the larger urban centers along the coastal flood plain of the Inland Sea in the south, often incorporated within the administrative limits of cities, give evidence of encroaching urbanization—apartment houses surrounded by rice fields, and the blight of gas stations and small factories lining main roads. The valleys and small plains are filled with irrigated fields, and low hills are covered with dry fields. Scattered hamlets with closely packed houses are nestled at the foot of hills. The more isolated hamlets retain their traditional social structure and patterns of daily life to a greater extent than those in transition near cities, but even in the most mountainous areas villages are changing as roads and communications improve and more farmers find work in factories.

Police presence in these different rural settings is maintained through *chūzaisho*, or "residential police-boxes." A *chūzaisho* is a police residence with an office attached to its front. A police officer lives in it with his family, surrounded by the village or rural town. The characters for *chūzai* connote an official who is sent to be a resident. The relationship between the policeman in the *chūzaisho* (he is called a *chūzai san* by the Japanese) and the local villagers or townsmen epitomizes the ideal relationship of the police and the community in Japan, in the eyes of both the police and the citizenry.

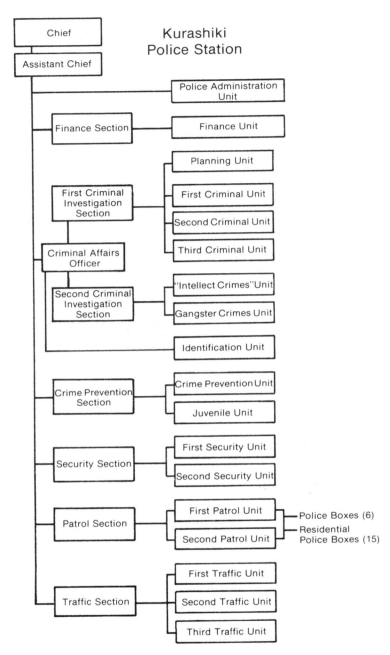

FIGURE 2. Organization of the Kurashiki and Mizushima Police Stations, 1974

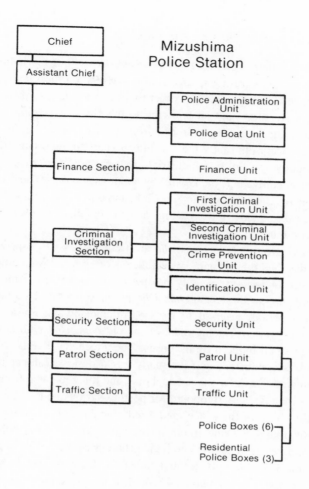

Mizushima
Police Station

Chief

Assistant Chief

Police Administration Unit

Police Boat Unit

Finance Section — Finance Unit

Criminal Investigation Section
- First Criminal Investigation Unit
- Second Criminal Investigation Unit
- Crime Prevention Unit
- Identification Unit

Security Section — Security Unit

Patrol Section — Patrol Unit

Traffic Section — Traffic Unit

Police Boxes (6)

Residential Police Boxes (3)

In 1974, there were 10,239 *chūzaisho* throughout the nation.[1] There were 15 in the Kurashiki police station jurisdiction the same year, and 3 in Mizushima. This reflects the fact that the Kurashiki jurisdiction incorporates more rural land area, owing to the city's expanding boundaries. One-time villages are fewer in Mizushima because much of its land came into existence within only the last fifteen years through land fill that was subsequently developed in industrial-urban fashion. *Chūzaisho* outnumber their urban equivalent, the *kōban*, by about two to one. There were 5,858 *kōban* in 1974 (including 6 in Kurashiki and 6 in Mizushima). The number of *chūzaisho* is slowly decreasing, and the number of *kōban* is rising as Japan continues to urbanize.

The living quarters in *chūzaisho* are frequently small, especially in the older ones, and their general appearance is often run-down compared with the homes of farmers recently prosperous from Japan's rising economy. The neighbors of the Kamo *chūzaisho* in Okayama that I studied, built in the Meiji period, referred to it as a "dilapidated old house" (*boroya*). Okayama is now replacing most of the old *chūzaisho* with new ones resembling small modern rural houses. The attached office is where police business is conducted, and it usually has a desk, a cabinet for holding police materials, and a police telephone, and it is separated from the living quarters by a door. A signboard for posting various notices and slogans is located in front of the office, and a red globular light denoting the police is always found over the entrance (see figure 3). A similar light is placed over the doorway to *kōban* and police stations as well.

Chūzaisho are usually located rather far from the police station, the main link being the telephone. The *chūzai san* goes into the police station about three or four times a month for meetings and other business. He is essentially on his own in policing his jurisdiction and must rely on the cooperation of the community to an even greater extent than the policemen in urban *kōban*. The nature of police work in the countryside demands an especially close relationship with the rural populace.

HISTORICAL DEVELOPMENT OF POLICE BOXES

Before examining the role of the police in rural settings, we should take a brief look at the development of police-boxes, both *chūzaisho* and *kōban*. There are no direct historical precursors of the *chūzaisho* in Japa-

1. National Police Agency, ed. *Keisatsu hakusho, 1974* [Police white paper] (Tokyo: Okurasho Insatsukyoku, 1974), p. 53.

FIGURE 3. *Chūzaisho* in Fuchu

nese history. Social control in the countryside was maintained informally among neighboring farm families and through neighborhood units organized by feudal authorities for collective responsibility, such as the *gonin gumi* of the Edo period. Local families of influence (*shōya*) were sometimes enlisted by the government to assist in controlling the rural populace, but they were unlike the modern *chūzai san*. In larger cities, order was maintained by several types of watch-points, indirect precursors of the present *kōban* (literally "alternating watch"). *Tsujiban* were established throughout Edo, Kyoto, and Osaka by the Edo government, the feudal lords (*daimyō*), and "bannermen" (*hatamoto*, direct retainers of the shogun). There were five or six hundred located at intersections of large roads in Edo, and they were usually staffed by assistants hired by the

A *chūzai san* and his wife in front of their *chūzaisho*, Fuchu, Tokyo. The motor-bike is used for patrolling the jurisdiction. The sign next to the door notes the number of traffic accidents that occurred the day before in Tokyo and in the *chūzaisho* jurisdiction.

warrior class (*bushi*).[2] *Jishinban* were originally set up by landlords in each artisan and merchant neighborhood to prevent crime and incidents, but local family heads and hired men eventually assumed the responsibility. They were supported by neighborhood funds, and watch duty was

2. Based on an interview with a police historian at the National Diet Library, Tokyo, 1974. See also Takeo Yazaki, *Social Change and the City in Japan* (Tokyo: Japan Publications, Inc., 1968), p. 226.

rotated among the neighbors. There were 990 *jishinban* in Edo in 1850.[3] *Kidoban*, or guard posts, were set up at the entrances to commoners' neighborhoods and were staffed in shifts by the local residents, or more commonly by hired guards. *Tsujiban* supervised the *jishinban* and *kidoban* that were staffed by commoners.

The system of *chūzaisho* and *kōban* was begun at the suggestion of a foreigner. A captain of the Berlin Metropolitan Police, Heinrich Friedrich Wilhelm Höhn, served as an adviser to the Home Ministry from 1885 until 1891. He toured Japan eight times and recommended the establishment of police residences throughout the country. Accordingly, in 1888, the Home Ministry ordered the police divided into two types: indoor-duty (*naikin*) and outdoor-duty (*gaikin*) police. The *gaikin* police were then distributed in *chūzaisho*, with one policeman for every 500 to 1,500 people in small towns and for every 1,500 to 3,000 people in the more remote countryside. All police station jurisdictions were divided into areas, and one *chūzaisho* supervised each area. *Chūzaisho* were usually established near village and town offices where possible, to concentrate governmental facilities in one location. *Kōban* were set up in cities where it was not feasible to establish a residential *chūzaisho*. By 1912 there were 13,353 *chūzaisho* and 2,473 *kōban* in Japan.[4] The establishment of *chūzaisho* and *kōban* marked the end of the system of gathering police officers into one location, which had been the practice in Japan until that time, and the beginning of the present system of distributing them evenly over the land area.

Chūzaisho played a special role in the early development of Japanese industry. Officials of large factories would request that the police establish a *chūzaisho* immediately adjoining their plants on company land. These were called *seigan chūzaisho* ("petitioned" *chūzaisho*). The company paid for the building of the *chūzaisho* and even paid the policeman's salary. The *chūzai san* was, in effect, a paid guard for the company, who protected nearby company housing from burglars and helped thwart strikes and calm labor unrest. Gangsters were also employed to handle labor problems. In the jurisdiction of the Kurashiki police station, two such *chūzaisho* were built by the mammoth Kurashiki Spinning Company, the

3. *Nihon rekishi daijiten* [Dictionary of Japanese history], 1969 ed., s.v. "Jishinban," p. 299.

4. Daikasumikai, ed., *Naimushōshi* [History of the Home Ministry], 4 vols. (Tokyo: Chiho Zaimu Kyokai, 1970), 2:608.

major industry in prewar Kurashiki. One is now a *kōban*, and although the prefecture pays the officers' salaries, the buildings and land are still owned by the corporation. A *kōban* and a *chūzaisho* in Mizushima are also still owned by large companies.

An early identity of rural citizens with the police is seen in the fact that some *chūzaisho* were built by villagers because they wanted a police presence. A *chūzaisho* I visited deep in the Chugoku mountains of Okayama, for instance, was built by the village on its own land in the late Meiji period. The villagers did not pay the *chūzai san*'s salary, as some corporations did, but the entire community used to pitch in yearly to repair the building. The police repair it now, and when it is rebuilt in the near future the prefecture will pay for the building and perhaps even buy the land.

ROLE OF THE *CHŪZAI SAN* IN THE COMMUNITY

The *chūzai san* traditionally holds high prestige, which is an important aspect of his idealized relationship with the rural community. The three prestige positions in villages (*mura no san'yaku*), each personifying an aspect of the distant central government in the modern period, have been the village head (*sonchō*), the school principal (*kōchō*), and the *chūzai san*. The *chūzai san* and the school principal are appointed by the government and come into the village from the outside. The village head is always a local resident.

The prestige of the *chūzai san* is linked to the power of the police and was highest before the war. The *chūzai san* embodied the entire weight of the Home Ministry and was entrusted with enforcing all its regulations in the village—economic, health, and administrative. He was thus viewed somewhat ambivalently by the villagers. They sometimes referred to him as *okami* ("one who is above," a term for a powerful official) and feared him, yet they were friendly and tried to be close to him because he could help them in time of need. Some farmers saw him as allied with the landlord strata, as was evident during tenant riots in Okayama in 1918. Tenant farmers derisively called rural policemen *jinushi no inu* ("dog of the landlords") and were said to spit at them during those riots.[5] The *chūzai san* is not usually feared now, but he is still seen as the representative of the police establishment and the government.

The *chūzai san* is usually invited to village events such as school ath-

5. Related to me by a police historian, Okayama, 1974.

letic meets (*undōkai*), concerts, and graduations, and village festivals. He also often attends weddings and funerals. He is a frequent guest at meetings of the village residents' organization (*burakkai*), especially those with dinners, and is often asked to speak on some police-related topic, such as crime prevention or traffic safety. The *burakkai* also serves as the crime-prevention association (*bōhan kumiai*) in the village, and when the *chūzai san* speaks on crime prevention, the *burakkai* is meeting in its capacity as a crime-prevention association.[6] Most crime-prevention associations were formed at the request of the police, and village leaders rotate in serving as chairman, often held as a concurrent position by the head of the *burakkai*. There are few crimes in most rural areas, but more traffic accidents, so the *chūzai san* is often asked to speak on traffic safety.[7] In those instances, the *burakkai* meets as the village branch of the nearest town's traffic-safety association (*kōtsū anzen kyōkai*). Traffic-safety associations are also usually formed at police behest, and the headship rotates similarly among village leaders. Invariably, the *chūzai san* is given a seat of honor at village events along with the village head and the school principal.

A story that shows the traditional status of the *chūzai san* in rural villages is told about former Prime Minister Tanaka when he returned to his native village in remote Niigata prefecture after being elected prime minister. All of the village notables turned out to greet him at the village meeting hall, and the new prime minister walked up to the head of the table and promptly seated himself in the place of honor. The story has it that Prime Minister Tanaka's elderly mother quickly reprimanded him, telling the national leader that the place of honor was reserved for the *chūzai san*. Laughing, Tanaka then changed places with the *chūzai san*. This story points to traditional notions of police prestige that are held even now by many elderly people with prewar educations.

The pace of police work in a truly rural *chūzaisho* is quite leisurely, which affects the *chūzai san*'s ability to become close to the community. A *chūzai san* is usually only assigned the day shift and works a forty-four-hour week of eight hours a day for five days, plus another four-hour day. The shift in Okayama prefecture is officially divided into four hours of patrol, two hours of visiting homes in the jurisdiction (called *junkai ren-*

6. Crime-prevention associations are usually called *bōhan kyōkai* throughout Japan, and Okayama's term is atypical.
7. One *chūzaisho* that I visited in the Chugoku mountains reported about one crime of some sort, usually minor, and about two traffic accidents a month. These both usually increase if a major highway goes through the jurisdiction.

A *chūzai san* helping a farmer clear a ditch during patrol of his jurisdiction. Spontaneous assistance from the *chūzai san* while on patrol or during a visit endears him to the local farmers.

raku, described more fully in the next chapter), and two hours of sitting on duty in the *chūzaisho* office (*keikai*, "watch"). *Chūzai san*, like policemen in *kōban*, are required to pay a *junkai renraku* visit to every home in their jurisdiction twice a year to update records that they keep about the people and any valuables in the households. They also use the visits to pass on suggestions about crime prevention or traffic safety and, significantly, to hear complaints or rumors about what is occurring in the neighborhood. Most people readily provide the information. This practice creates for the police a wealth of raw data about the locality, which proves beneficial when travelers inquire at the *chūzaisho* or *kōban* about an address or when a crime occurs. Besides homes, the *chūzai san* also visits the post office and the Farm Cooperative (Nōkyō), the only places in the village with substantial amounts of cash, on the twentieth day of every month—crime-prevention day—to see if they are handling their money safely.

Patrol for a *chūzai san* is not much different from *junkai renraku*, except that formal police record keeping is not involved. The *chūzai san* travels by motorbike, going to the most distant and isolated hamlets six or seven times a month and nearby ones almost every day. The purpose of patrol is simply to visit homes, and if something happens while he is out, he handles it. He usually visits the homes of those who are most cooperative with him, spending hours chatting about all sorts of things. Households that tend to be receptive to the police are often formally designated by the police as "crime-prevention checkpoints" (*bōhan renrakusho*), which are discussed in the next chapter. Those who seem to welcome the *chūzai san* most are small-shop keepers and the more wealthy or long-established households in the village. Many are former landlords and tend to be the informal village leaders. They know much of what is happening in the village, especially the shopkeepers, and are usually willing to share their information with the *chūzai san*.

The important point is that the *chūzai san* relies on his personal knowledge of the people in his jurisdiction in performing his police work, and not on formal police record books. His effectiveness in investigating crimes and other problems when they occur in the tightly knit hamlets stems from his knowledge of all the local residents. This extensive personal knowledge and the ability to elicit information from key village informants when necessary is the essence of the closeness to the community that is considered an ideal by the police. It is an instrumental relationship and does not necessarily imply universal affection by the villagers for the resident police officer.

The *chūzai san* often spends more time in the *chūzaisho* than the formal work schedule calls for, which enhances his relationship with villagers. In the summer months, the *chūzai san* lounges in front of the television with his children in his pajama-like white underwear during the hours he is supposed to be sitting in the office. Because he is available, all sorts of problems are brought to him. One *chūzai san* referred to himself as a *yaoya* ("jack-of-all-trades"). People sometimes come to the *chūzai san* to discuss personal problems, such as plans for a job, schooling, or marriage, or to seek his counsel about marital spats or parent-child quarrels. In one *chūzaisho*, a boy came to ask the *chūzai san* to use his gun to shoot a bird that flew down and took food from him as he was returning from the store. Another *chūzai san* said that students often came to the *chūzaisho* to look at his maps in order to plan outings. It is said that twenty years ago when telephones were scarce in rural areas, local residents would often come to the *chūzaisho* to make calls because it was the only place in the village with a telephone. The personal counseling function performed by police officers occurs most often in the most traditional and isolated rural areas and was more frequent in the past, but it still takes place in virtually all *chūzaisho*, and even in *kōban*, to some extent.

ENFORCING THE LAW IN THE *CHŪZAISHO*

There is a certain amount of tension in the role of a *chūzai san* enforcing the law within a social setting that stresses closeness between him and the surrounding community. Police officers by the nature of their job must formally intervene occasionally and invoke legal sanctions when violations of the law occur. Yet this can be at odds with the idea of rapport and understanding between the *chūzai san* and his tightly knit village neighbors. His dilemma is solved by the distinction between *tatemae* and *honne* referred to in the Introduction. The formal *tatemae* is that he enforces the law evenhandedly and rigorously, but in reality (the *honne*) the villagers neither expect nor want him to do so.

In the stable rural surroundings of a *chūzaisho*, the way in which the *chūzai san* relates to his neighbors and the people in his jurisdiction is critical to his effectiveness. His manner and the degree to which he enforces the law is a prime factor in his relationship with the villagers. Villagers seem to prefer a *chūzai san* who is not overly zealous in enforcing the law, especially traffic regulations, one who goes fishing occasionally or watches television at home instead of patrolling his jurisdiction constantly. Police chiefs often counsel new *chūzai san* privately to strike a medium and not write too many traffic tickets or clamp down too hard in their jurisdictions, realizing that if they overenforce the law (which itself is a *tatemae*), they will alienate the people by going against the local mores and customs—the unwritten laws (*fubunritsu*)—which are the *honne* that actually govern society.[8] When there is overt and flagrant lawlessness and when property or individuals are endangered, as in a burglary,

8. Told to me by a former chief of a rural police station, Okayama, 1974.

the *chūzai san* is, of course, expected to intervene. The local citizens express their satisfaction with a *chūzai san* who is not overzealous by bringing him gifts of vegetables or sake, and the local leaders (the village association heads), by asking the police chief not to transfer the man.

An example of how a *chūzai san* should not enforce the law occurred in the Kamo *chūzaisho* in Okayama several years ago. The *chūzai san* was very active in enforcing the traffic laws and in stopping and questioning the local residents on trivial matters. The villagers were repelled by his relentlessness, as were his fellow police officers because he consistently had the most traffic arrests. The police chief told him to be less strict so that the people would not resent him, but he apparently did not listen. He eventually became ill and died while working at the *chūzaisho*, and, I was told, few people were sorry to lose him.[9]

When a minor crime does occur, the *chūzai san* is often relaxed in the way he handles it. I once visited a *chūzaisho* which had had a burglary in its jurisdiction reported that morning. Someone had entered a home while the occupants were gone, and a couple of bottles of whiskey had been stolen. The woman living there sent her son to the *chūzaisho* to report the crime, and the *chūzai san* and I went to the scene. He had the woman fill out some forms, and when she could not do it correctly, he did it. He spent a little over three hours there chatting, finishing the forms, eating food and drinking tea the woman brought out, and watching television. This leisurely pace in investigating a crime is in keeping with the low-keyed approach to police work in general in a *chūzaisho*. The infrequency of crimes also gives the *chūzai san* the luxury of time.

It has been noted that villagers often invite the *chūzai san* to dinner parties and drink with him. They do this in order to form what the Japanese call *ningen kankei* ("human relations"). They hope to build up goodwill with him so he will not intervene too frequently in their daily lives. Yet their efforts to create rapport can go too far. *Ningen kankei* is particularly powerful in a country like Japan, which is ethnically and culturally homogeneous and whose people live close together and are bound into the lives of their neighbors and friends through an intricate system of obligations. The closely knit social system in Japan is kept functional through a tradition of ritualized gift-giving and exchanges described as the "oil that keeps the machinery running smoothly" (*junkatsuyū*). Gift-giving to the

9. Related by a resident in the jurisdiction of Kamo *chūzaisho*.

chūzai san can reach a danger point when it shades over into action or restraint on his part concerning a specific incident as a quid pro quo for favors given by the villagers. This is where the traditional system of social exchange leaves off and bribery begins. It would prevent the intervention of the *chūzai san* when it is plainly called for—when even the unwritten local mores and customs are violated, such as when violence or a theft occurs.

The police in Okayama attempt to prevent an excessive buildup of *ningen kankei* and the potential of overt bribery (rare in the Japanese police) by transferring the *chūzai san* about every two or three years. This length of time allows him to become fully acquainted with the villagers, but not too deeply enmeshed in reciprocal obligations. The periodic transfer of the *chūzai san* to another location is a good example of the attempt by the police organization to strike a balance between the potentially conflicting goals of institutional integrity and solidarity within the police and the need to adapt and integrate into the local community.

FAMILY INVOLVEMENT IN POLICE WORK

One of the unique aspects of a *chūzaisho* is the involvement of the family of the *chūzai san*, especially his wife, in police work. A family is so essential to the effectiveness of the *chūzai san* that the few young single police officers assigned to work in a *chūzaisho* often have marriages arranged for them while serving in that position. If the new wife is from the jurisdiction of the *chūzaisho*, however, the police officer is usually transferred to avoid entangling ties. His wife and children help the *chūzai san* integrate into the village through the normal course of daily living and forming friendships. They are a major factor in his degree of closeness to the local community.

The wife of the *chūzai san* must handle the affairs of the *chūzaisho* when her husband is out on patrol or *junkai renraku*. She receives calls from the police station, gives directions to travelers, and has to locate her husband by telephone if there is a traffic accident or a crime. She is sometimes required to be even more centrally involved in policing. For example, one wife told me about the time her husband caught a thief, brought him to the *chūzaisho*, and told her to watch him while he went back to the house that had been broken into. The man said he had to urinate, but since she did not want him in her house to use her toilet, she told him to use the irrigation ditch in front. He fled and was not caught for a month. Another wife said that people would leave their bicycles in a vacant lot next to the *chūzaisho* while taking the train to work, school, or shopping, often not locking them because they considered them safe next to the *chūzaisho*. One day she saw a man getting on a bike that she knew was not his, and when she called out to him, he started riding away. She said she chased him about a mile and a half while holding her one-year-old child. She caught him, questioned him, and then called the police station from a nearby phone. A detective was sent out to arrest the man.[10]

The wives of *chūzai san* receive a monthly allowance of ¥10,000 per month ($33 in 1975) from the police for their services, in addition to occasional recognition from the chiefs of the police station or the prefectural police headquarters. One *chūzai san*'s wife said she was recently given a blanket by the police as a token of appreciation. Wives sometimes complain that the most difficult aspect of life in a *chūzaisho* is the way the husband's work affects the private lives of the entire family, for someone invariably comes or an emergency occurs whenever the children are being fed or bathed. In a survey conducted by the National Police Agency in 1972, the complaint raised most often by wives is that they found it very difficult to leave their *chūzaisho* home for any length of time because of the necessity of having someone there at all times.[11] Frequent moves resulting in changes in schools for his children are also a major drawback for the *chūzai san*. One officer lamented that none of his three sons wanted to be policemen because of the many times they had to be uprooted while growing up.

THE CHANGING *CHŪZAISHO*

The *chūzaisho* system inevitably must alter as Japanese society to which it adapts undergoes changes. Many of these changes may ultimately affect the *chūzai san*'s closeness to the rural community. One of the major forces of change originates in police officers themselves—that is, the stronger notions of leisure and free time evident in younger police officers. A *chūzaisho* is not a glamorous assignment, compared with being a motorcycle policeman or a detective. But an even bigger drawback is the fact that the *chūzai san* never really has a vacation. He cannot hang a sign on his door, as can shopkeepers in the village, saying "Sorry, closed for the

10. National Policy Agency, *Gaikin tsūhō* [Patrol bulletin], vol. 12, no. 3, p. 25, from a survey conducted in 1972.
11. *Patrol Bulletin*, p. 52.

A *chūzai san* standing next to his mini-patrol-car, Okayama. The *chūzaisho* is in the background.

day." If there is a problem or a traffic accident on his weekly day off, or in the middle of the night, he must handle it. In the National Police Agency survey referred to above, the overwhelming response by *chūzai san* to the question of what aspect of *chūzaisho* work they think should be changed most was a request for clarification of the distinction between work hours and free time and days off.[12] Older men, with prewar educations that stressed values different from those of postwar education, do not complain as much about the inconvenience. In Okayama, 80 percent of the *chūzai san* are over forty years old and thus have prewar educations. Older men also tend to make better *chūzai san* because they have more experience and maturity and are better able to give counsel to citizens and to command respect in traditional rural settings. By contrast, 80 percent of the police officers in urban *kōban* are under forty. *Kōban* are on a shift system and allow scheduled free time every week.[13] But the number of *chūzai san* with postwar educations and different notions of mission and

12. Ibid., p. 49.
13. Figures from an interview with a patrol section official in the Okayama Prefectural Police Headquarters, 1974.

leisure will slowly increase each year, which will intensify the pressure for changes in *chūzaisho* work patterns.

Another factor in the trend toward change is that the individual burden of police work in a *chūzaisho* is relatively high compared with that in a *kōban*. In Okayama prefecture, *chūzaisho* have heavier burdens in jurisdictional area and population per police officer than *kōban*, and are very close to *kōban* in the ratio of traffic accidents per police officer. Only in the ratio of crimes per police officer are *kōban* higher than *chūzaisho*. This reflects the fact seen earlier that the traffic accident rate, rather than the crime rate, is the major problem faced by the *chūzai san* and for that matter, by the police in general in Japan. Because of the heavy burden on the individual *chūzai san*, the police now tend to phase out *chūzaisho* in areas bordering urban centers and along major traffic arteries and turn them into *kōban*, which have more manpower. Urban encroachment increases the population of the jurisdiction, with an accompanying increase in crime and traffic accidents. Police estimated that within a five-year period from 1974, the 270 *chūzaisho* in Okayama prefecture would be decreased to 200 and the number of *kōban* would rise from 84 to 110.[14] *Chūzaisho* will be retained in mountainous areas with low populations where they are best adapted to effectiveness in police work. *Chūzai san* in these remote areas are being further assisted, however, by the gradual introduction of mini-patrol-cars, which will allow them easier access to remote mountain areas in winter and when roads are muddy.

As an interim measure in rapidly urbanizing areas, the police are introducing two-man *chūzaisho*, in which a *chūzai san* lives with his family, and to which another police officer commutes for work each day. These retain much of the intimate community contact of a regular *chūzaisho* but halve the burden on the *chūzai san*. Yet because of the undesirability of having a family live in an environment of busy police work with other officers commuting in for their shifts, these are considered only a transition to formal *kōban*. The effect of the *kōban* system on police relations with the community in the more complex urban environment is the subject we now turn to.

14. Interview with patrol section official, Okayama Prefectural Police Headquarters, 1974.

two

KEEPING ORDER IN THE URBAN CONTEXT: THE *KŌBAN*

Cities present a range of complexity for police work not found in the country, because of larger and more diverse populations. Despite Japan's often noted societal homogeneity, neighborhoods differ considerably in the types of people that live in them, the degree of neighborhood solidarity, and the willingness of residents to cooperate with the police. The Japanese police adapt to various urban settings primarily through the use of the *kōban* as a deployment system. The police visualize the *chūzaisho* with its resident police officer as the ideal form of police relationship to the community, but it is an ideal that is difficult to achieve in an urban setting. The *kōban* is an adaptation that facilitates police closeness to the community by allowing a constant police presence at the neighborhood level. Instead of just one policeman and his family, as in a *chūzaisho*, a number of police officers work shifts to handle the increased volume of work. The *kōban* provides a flexible basis for policing in a variety of urban situations.

Police officers in *kōban* are affectionately referred to by local residents as *o mawari san* ("Mr. Walkabout"). The *o mawari san* and the *chūzai san* are the mainstay of the Japanese police system. They are the primary mechanism employed by the police in crime and traffic accident prevention. They are the first to handle almost all incidents before other police specialists, like detectives and traffic policemen, are called in. Their duties cover all fields of police activity, channeling information on various incidents to the respective specialized police units for further investigation.

All police-school graduates serve in *kōban* as their first assignment. They work there for a few years before transfer to a specialized police unit, such as traffic, criminal investigation, or the riot police. *Kōban* are usually staffed by young officers, with a few older sergeants as the leaders. Many policemen look back on their first days in a *kōban* nostalgically, as their "birth place as a police officer" (*keisatsukan no furusato*).[1]

THE KŌBAN SYSTEM

The term *kōban* had been used in early Meiji for the dormitory-like buildings in Tokyo in which policemen lived and out of which they patrolled. *Kōban* were renamed *hashutsusho* in 1888 and were used only as police-boxes. All *hashutsusho* in Tokyo were renamed *kōban* in 1909, and were officially changed back to *hashutsusho* later. Most people now call police-boxes *kōban* because it is easier to say and has lost its original meaning as a dormitory.

Kōban in Okayama are now on a grueling three-shift system with the following sequence:

Overnight (*tōmu*)	8:30 A.M. to 8:30 A.M.
Rest day (*hiban*)	8:30 A.M. to 8:30 A.M.
Day (*nikkin*)	8:30 A.M. to 5:15 P.M.

The overnight shift is awake for a total of sixteen hours. Five hours is allowed for sleep at night, two hours for meals during the twenty-four-hour period, and an extra hour's break is given at night. The sleep is broken into two portions, however, with work in between. Emergencies or noisy drunks coming into the *kōban* often prevent any sleep at all for the officers on duty at night. The day shift has an hour's break for lunch. The standard workweek is forty-four hours, plus an additional ten to fifteen hours of overtime each week. Meals are taken in the *kōban* from nearby restaurants that deliver, or police officers change their coats and go to a restaurant. It is against policy to eat in a restaurant in uniform, though many in Okayama do it anyway.

Kōban usually have an office area in front with desks and cabinets, and there are large glass windows in the front wall. A signboard is located in front, full of posters of wanted or missing persons or displaying slogans for crime prevention and other police interests. There is usually a small cooking and storage area in the back, a resting room with a closet and a safe for pistols, and a covered area in the rear for parking bicycles or motorbikes (see figure 4).

1. Takahashi Shoki, *Kōban to seishun* [Police-box and youth] (Tokyo: Tachibana Shobo, 1973), p. 3.

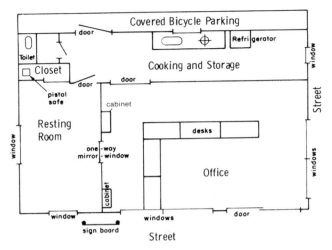

FIGURE 4. *Kōban* in Kurashiki

Police officers in the *kōban* usually spend the morning and afternoon hours visiting homes, patrolling, giving street directions to travelers, and handling lost items—that is, in "service activities." It is the time of maximum community contact with police officers. The pace of police work begins to pick up in the early evening, with an increase in drunks, fights in bars, and other incidents. The peak is from about 10:00 P.M. until 1:00 A.M., and then slacks off abruptly. The early morning hours are spent in sleeping, patrolling, and sitting in the *kōban*. The twenty-four-hour shift is physically taxing, and the police officers are visibly tired by midnight.

One of the problems policemen face is the boredom of spending hours in the same small *kōban* day after day. Yet there are usually visitors and varied activities throughout the shift. The *kōban* serves as a spot where citizens may sit and chat, and some spend hours with the police. These people tend to be shop owners with flexible time schedules, elderly neighborhood leaders, and people whose personalities are attracted to police officers. The *kōban* is also a location where detectives and other police specialists can sit and relax without being under the direct supervision of their superiors. It is significant that *kōban* (and elementary schools) are often called by the names of the old villages that their now-urban jurisdictions once comprised, even though the names are no longer used as addresses. Their jurisdictions frequently match the former village bounda-

Morning meeting in the patrol section office, before going to the *kōban* for duty.

ries. The significance is that the police rely on the long-established cooperation between households in the former villages for crime prevention and investigations. The *kōban*, like the elementary school, thus becomes a hub of traditional village solidarity and identity in a modern urban context.

As we saw in the discussion of *chūzaisho*, a major duty of police officers assigned to a *kōban* is to visit the homes in the jurisdiction regularly (*junkai renraku*).[2] These visits provide police officers with information

---

2. In addition to *kōban* and *chūzaisho*, many police stations, including Kurashiki and Mizushima, have a blue and white van called a "mobile police-box" (*idō kōban*) used for visiting apartment complexes. There were 150 mobile police-boxes throughout the nation in 1973. The police feel that apartment complexes have insufficient contact with police officers, so they make periodic visits in these vans, bringing a folding table, chairs, and crime-prevention and traffic-safety literature for distribution. They announce their presence over loudspeakers, and residents are expected to gather and talk to the police about crimes or other problems. The vehicle is used about twice a week for this purpose in Mizushima, but only once a month in Kurashiki. The effectiveness of the vehicles is open to question; when I went to several apartment complexes in Mizushima in one of them, the police stayed five or ten minutes at each complex, and only a few women and children gathered around it. The police stood near the vehicle and seemed embarrassed. They are considered "soft" and "friendly" vehicles and are used for visiting schools and nursing homes, as well as for hauling police equipment and personnel.

An average-size *kōban* in the jurisdiction of the Mizushima police station.

and contacts that enable them to perform their functions effectively. The jurisdiction is divided into as many segments as there are police officers assigned to the *kōban*. Each police officer is required to visit every home and business establishment in his area twice a year. A record book for each area holds a card for each family or firm. The following information is elicited for families: place of origin, names and birthdays of all members of the family, whether or not they are living in the household, their occupation and employer, and whom to contact in emergencies. Perhaps an even more important purpose of this periodic visit is to gather information and gossip about occurrences in the neighborhood. The police cannot force people to provide the information, yet almost all people do so voluntarily (the police say that "only Communists" refuse to answer).

Junkai renraku is based on the prewar system of information gathering by the police called *tokō chōsa* (household survey), instituted in 1874. The same information was requested, with additional questions about whether the people were receiving vaccinations, whether they had a criminal record, and if they were of an aristocratic lineage. Persons who refused to answer were taken to the *kōban* for questioning.

The police insist that the information for *junkai renraku* is used solely

An elderly neighbor stops for a chat with the sergeant of the local *kōban*. *Kōban* serve as a focal point for neighborhood socializing.

for public service purposes, such as helping an inquirer locate an address. This is certainly one of the main uses of the information, for Japanese streets are usually not named, and houses were not numbered serially until recently. Yet, this statement is a *tatemae* to an extent. The *honne* is that the police frequently use the information in investigations: detectives spend a great deal of time in *kōban* referring to the *junkai renraku* record books. The main difference between *junkai renraku* and the prewar *tokō chōsa* is that the scope of the information requested today is slightly narrower and answers are not compulsory.

The *kōban* has a wealth of other data on the jurisdiction as well, which is helpful to the police in diverse urban areas, such as lists of people working late at night who might be of help as witnesses to crimes, of people who are normally cooperative with the police, of people who own guns or swords, of all rented homes and apartments that might serve as hideouts for fugitives, of people with criminal records, and of people with mental illness; organizational charts of gangs in the police station jurisdiction and in the prefecture (sometimes complete with photographs of all the gangsters); lists of old people in the area living alone who should be vis-

A young *o mawari san* filling out records during a regular *junkai renraku* visit to a home in the jurisdiction of his *kōban*. Most people cooperate and provide the requested information.

ited periodically, of all neighborhood organizations in the jurisdiction and their leaders, and of all bars, restaurants, and amusement facilities in the jurisdiction; a short history of the *kōban*; and a compilation of the total population, area, and number of households in the jurisdiction. Records of all recent crimes in the area, "wanted" posters and bulletins on criminals, and information on left- and right-wing political groups in the area are also kept in the police box.

All police officers in the *kōban* familiarize themselves with the information in their records and thus gain an immense knowledge of their jurisdiction. The records also provide continuity when new policemen are transferred to the *kōban*. Extensive record-keeping is much more important to police officers in *kōban* than to those in *chūzaisho*, though the *chūzai san* keeps similar records, as we have seen. Policemen in *kōban* must rely on their formal records, whereas the resident *chūzai san* usually has intimate personal knowledge of his rural jurisdiction. The records from the *junkai renraku* system are very helpful to police officers in urban areas who must adapt to larger and more diverse populations.

CITIZEN SUPPORT FOR THE *O MAWARI SAN*

The effectiveness of the police in urban areas rests to a great extent on cooperation from citizens organized into voluntary police-support groups. These groups are usually coextensive with neighborhood associations, termed *chōnaikai* in cities and towns, and *burakkai* in villages. As was noted in chapter one, crime-prevention functions are performed by crime-prevention associations (*bōhan kumiai*, as they are called in Okayama prefecture), and traffic safety is encouraged by traffic-safety associations (*kōtsū anzen kyōkai*). The difficulty of keeping order among the large and diverse populations of cities requires institutionalized mechanisms of citizen support, such as extensive police records and neighborhood associations. The police must rely on personal relationships formed with leaders of these associations to provide them with the type of cooperation and information that a *chūzai san* elicits informally from various residents of his surrounding village.

Crime-prevention associations and traffic-safety associations are volunteer citizen organizations. Japan has a long tradition of voluntary citizen involvement in community service activities. Volunteerism covers a wide range of areas, from voluntary welfare-case workers (*minseiin*)[3] and voluntary probation officers (*hogoshi*)[4] to the myriad of citizen support groups that surround the police. Similar types of persons are engaged in all the various volunteer activities, and often the same persons hold several positions simultaneously in different voluntary service organizations. They are mostly elderly men, often over sixty, and usually they either are self-employed shop or small-factory owners or are retired. Unlike office or factory workers, they have free time to spare for engaging in community service activities.

Chōnaikai, on which crime-prevention associations are based, were the basic unit of local government before the war, but their administrative function is now gone. They now perform essentially social and service functions in their respective neighborhoods. Every household in a neighborhood belongs to the *chōnaikai* because of its location within the neigh-

3. Voluntary welfare-case workers (*minseiin*) work under the direction of the city Welfare Office and oversee the elderly, families receiving national welfare, and juvenile delinquents. There were 486 such volunteers serving in Kurashiki in 1975.

4. The probation system in Japan is handled almost entirely by volunteers. Okayama in 1974 had only 12 professional probation officers to supplement 954 volunteers. The volunteers (*hogoshi*) are assigned cases by the prefectural probation office and are paid four dollars (¥1,200) a month for their efforts.

borhood boundaries. Most *chōnaikai* have their own meeting halls, built and maintained by a small monthly fee collected from the residents of the neighborhood. Not all *chōnaikai* are active; the active ones spray for mosquitoes, plan recreational and cultural activities for women, children, and the elderly in the neighborhood, and help prevent fires, traffic accidents, and crime in the neighborhood. Their level of activity, which seems to be correlated with the neighborhood's overall cooperativeness with the police, depends on the general characteristics of the neighborhoods and the motivation of those who head the associations.

Most *chōnaikai* are divided into sections that may include a women's association, a children's association, an old folks club, a sanitation division, a fire-protection division, and a crime-prevention division. Each division or association is headed by a resident of the neighborhood, and these leaders meet periodically under the direction of the head of the *chōnaikai* to plan neighborhood activities. The heads of the association are usually chosen by consultation among the previous heads or prominent families in the neighborhood. They serve for a year or two and may be reappointed to their positions or asked to take other responsibilities within the group. Like the *burakkai* noted in the previous chapter, when a *chōnaikai* meets to discuss crime prevention, it is called a crime-prevention association; at all other times it is simply called a *chōnaikai*. Almost all neighborhoods have crime-prevention associations.There were 233 in Kurashiki in 1974, linked together by a city crime-prevention federation (*bōhan rengōkai*) headed by the mayor.[5]

About one house in every fifty in urban as well as rural neighborhoods is designated as a "crime-prevention checkpoint" (*bōhan renrakusho*).[6] These homes circulate crime-prevention fliers among the surrounding houses and generally serve as a convenient conduit for the police to provide information to neighborhoods. They are supposed to notify the police of crime or trouble in the vicinity, and, in fact, a number of the households so designated do pass on tips informally to the police. Housewives usually perform any duties involved when their homes are designated as checkpoints. *Bōhan renrakusho* are identified by a metal plate near the front door or on the gate, or sometimes by a lighted sign. They are chosen by consultation between the police and the head of the local crime-prevention

5. Figure provided by the Kurashiki police station, 1974.
6. Ibid.

association. The *bōhan renrakusho* system, unified nationally by the police in 1969, had precursors in the neighborhood crime-prevention watchpoints organized spontaneously by *chōnaikai* in various areas during the chaotic period after World War II.

Neighborhood crime-prevention associations assist the police in the semiannual crime prevention campaigns. The year-end campaign is especially active, with the residents of some neighborhoods patrolling at night to discourage thieves and to watch for fires. Sometimes parades are organized to urge citizens to lock their doors. I participated in a "lock patrol" in 1974 in Fuchu, near Tokyo, in which association officers went around with police officers to the houses in their neighborhoods, inspecting the door and window locks. The patrolling of neighborhoods at night by citizens, who clap sticks together as they walk to frighten away thieves and who watch for fires, has a long tradition in Japan that stretches back at least into the Edo period. Traditionally, it made sense to patrol at the year's end because the rice harvest was in storage, money was circulating for debt payment, and honest citizens were partying.

Every police station jurisdiction also has a voluntary citizens' traffic-safety association (*kōtsū anzen kyōkai*) that works with the traffic police in promoting traffic-safety consciousness and in preventing traffic accidents. Branches of the association are organized roughly by *kōban* jurisdictions, which in Kurashiki frequently correspond to old village boundaries, thus focusing the activities on traditionally cohesive local groups. Traffic-safety associations are much more active than crime-prevention associations in regional areas like Okayama prefecture because traffic accidents are perceived by citizens and police as a greater threat than crime.

In Okayama, traffic-safety associations also engage in semiannual campaigns to reduce traffic accidents, campaigns that are much more elaborate than the crime-prevention campaigns. They encompass activities for school children, parades, radio and television messages, distribution of leaflets to drivers stopped at intersections, and sound-cars blaring traffic-safety slogans. At other times of the year, local branches of the associations have occasional meetings for neighborhood drivers at which traffic police officers talk. They also urge neighborhood residents to pledge never to drive while intoxicated and to place a sticker above the door to their home declaring their vow. Some branches distribute fliers about traffic safety to all homes in their area. At New Year's, the police and the associations in Kurashiki set up roadblocks where the police test the breath of drivers for alcohol while the association members distribute traffic-safety literature to the drivers.

Other associations also aid the police in traffic safety. The traffic-safety mothers' association (*kōtsū anzen haha no kai*) has a representative from each *chōnaiki*, who is usually the head of the *chōnaikai*'s women's association. The mothers don yellow sashes and hold yellow flags to help children cross streets near schools, urge pedestrians to use pedestrian bridges over railroad tracks, and actively participate in traffic-safety campaigns. During one campaign in Kurashiki, the mothers lined up along a busy street for the purpose of "glaring at and embarrassing" drivers who violated the law.[7]

Police are also aided by uniformed "traffic assistants" (*kōtsū kyōjoin*), volunteers who stand at busy street corners to help discourage reckless driving and to aid pedestrians. They also help the police during traffic-safety campaigns and when festivals or other events bring large crowds into the area. These citizens are chosen by the police from each *kōban* area on recommendation by the heads of the *chōnaikai*. Many appear in uniform twice a day at street corners during rush hours or when school children are going to and from school. Awarded only about three dollars a year (¥1,000) for their services, they are sometimes ridiculed by drivers.

POLICE INFORMERS AND NEIGHBORHOOD ASSOCIATIONS

One of the primary ways that citizens provide support for the police is by feeding information to them about people or occurrences in their neighborhoods. In the urban jurisdictions of *kōban*, officers of *chōnaikai* and members of police-support groups form the core of the extensive network of police tipsters. They often belong to prominent and stable families, know most things that occur in their neighborhoods, and are usually willing to talk about them to the police.

The police assiduously cultivate their relationships with the officers of neighborhood associations, and reward them when they assist the police. For instance, the elderly head of a *chōnaikai* in Okayama City, two elderly male officers in the association, and the elderly head of the neighborhood women's association were invited to the Okayama West police station and

7. *San'yō shimbun* (Okayama), 28 September 1974, p. 5.

given a framed certificate of appreciation, an expensive wall-plaque, and a gift of money for helping the police solve a murder that occurred in their neighborhood.[8]

Families whose houses have been designated *bōhan renrakusho* are particularly encouraged to volunteer information to the police, and the police present them with small amounts of money (usually less than $5—¥1500) for tips on matters of particular interest.[9] An elderly traffic assistant in Kurashiki, a longtime resident of his neighborhood, told me that he informs the police about families in the neighborhood which have undesirable backgrounds (i.e., *burakumin* and others) so they may be screened out during police recruitment. The daily interaction between members of police-support groups and police officers builds rapport that enables the police to elicit sensitive information more easily.

One of the ways that the police cultivate deep bonds with the members of neighborhood associations and other support groups is to go drinking with them. Some neighborhood crime-prevention associations in Kurashiki hold year-end parties at restaurants in town in honor of the police officers in the local *kōban*. This practice is usually more common with *chūzaisho* than with *kōban*. Only one *kōban* in Kurashiki had such a year-end party sponsored by the residents of its jurisdiction in 1974. Ironically, drinking parties are more frequently held with officers of traffic-safety associations in Kurashiki. For example, the general meeting of the traffic-safety association is usually held in a restaurant, with the police chief, assistant chief, traffic section chief, and other traffic policemen in attendance. A short business meeting is followed by an evening of eating, drinking, and singing. A similar meeting was held by a particularly active neighborhood branch of the association and several traffic police officers in 1974.[10] The police and members of the associations are usually careful to take taxis home after these parties, to avoid the unthinkable embarrassment of causing a traffic accident while intoxicated.

Another aspect of the police relationship to their supporters in neighborhoods is the flow of gifts and favors that pass between them. The heads of the neighborhood organizations or other prominent people often bring cases of beer or bottles of sake to the police officers in the local *kōban*.

8. I was shown photographs of the awards and the recipients in the Okayama Prefectural Police Headquarters, 1975.
9. I was told this by a police officer in Kurashiki, 1975.
10. This information was provided by traffic policemen in Kurashiki, 1974.

Officers I came to know in one *kōban* enjoyed an air conditioner donated by a local company head, and got free lunches every day from a small, box-lunch factory nearby. The owner of a new restaurant in a residential area of Kurashiki, before opening for business, was urged by gangsters to buy pachinko machines and other recreational equipment from them for his restaurant. He refused, then invited the police officers from the local police box to visit his restaurant often for a free meal, in uniform, to keep the gangsters away. His restaurant was soon designated a *bōhan renraku-sho*, and he became very active in various police-support activities. Most gifts by local citizens to police are simply displays of gratitude for services or favors performed, such as a souvenir from a trip for having checked on the house while the occupants were gone, or a flower arrangement (*ike-bana*) for the *kōban* for some past kindness. Sometimes the reciprocation is more substantial, such as when an elderly man (who also served as a traffic assistant) paid for the repainting of the interior of a *kōban* in Kura-shiki because the patrolmen there had befriended him.

ADAPTATION TO VARIOUS URBAN SETTINGS

There is variation from neighborhood to neighborhood in cities in the degree of support, manifest in the various ways noted above, that police officers receive from local residents. The police must adopt somewhat different approaches to different types of neighborhoods depending on the level of support and general neighborhood characteristics.

Police officers in the several *kōban* and *chūzaisho* that I studied in Ku-rashiki and Mizushima, in comparing the neighborhoods of their jurisdic-tions, evaluated some as cooperative and positive, others as uncooperative and negative in their interactions with the police. Descriptions varied somewhat with the police officer, but the overall impression remained that some neighborhoods are more helpful to the police than others. One ex-planation for these variations may lie in the personalities of the police officers assigned to a police box—people of a particular area are able to relate to certain policemen better than to others. The age and sex of the people interacting with policemen also seems to affect their image of po-licemen and the degree to which they will cooperate with them (older people and females seem to have a more positive image of the police and are more cooperative than are younger people and males). The sum of a person's past experiences with policemen, both positive and negative, also undoubtedly influences his or her desire to cooperate with policemen and his or her image of the police.

Perhaps the key factor in the variation of citizen cooperation by neighborhoods is the character of the leaders in the neighborhoods. The officers in the *chōnaikai* and other neighborhood voluntary associations are the ones who most often actively cooperate with the police, whereas others in the neighborhood are essentially passive in their relationship. Some neighborhoods seem to have more people willing to assume leadership roles than others, and these neighborhoods are generally the most cooperative with the police.

We shall examine a sample of neighborhoods in Kurashiki and Mizushima that I studied intensively, to get some notion of the diversity of situations to which police must adapt and the range of community cooperation.[11] The different neighborhoods in Kurashiki and Mizushima are, I believe, typical of most medium-sized cities in Japan, but probably do not reach the extremes in variation of large metropolitan centers like Tokyo or Osaka. They do, however, seem to cover most types of citizen response to the police in Japan.

Hama Machi.

Hama Machi is located in an area that was a village until about sixty or seventy years ago. It is typical of many neighborhoods in the outlying areas of cities in its age and types of buildings. It is located behind the Kurashiki train station and is a mixture of tightly packed old homes of former farm landlords, small shops that are mostly clustered along the street leading to the train station, and long, old buildings that stand close together, each divided into several rather small homes. A few newer homes and some small household factories are also nestled throughout the neighborhood. A small amount of open land remaining behind the string of shops is farmed by old, farm households. The area was almost entirely farming until the Masu factory of the Kurashiki Spinning Company was built in 1915 and transformed it into a densely settled workers' neighbor-

11. I conducted a survey of eleven neighborhoods in Kurashiki and Mizushima in 1975, chosen to catch various qualities observable in Kurashiki City. There were 421 respondents to the survey, ranging from 28 to 60 per neighborhood. The respondents were chosen at random and were given a written questionnaire to fill out by high school girls who volunteered to help me. The description of neighborhoods in this chapter, and their degree of cooperation with the police, is based in part on the results of my survey.

hood and a small shopping area. The families are mostly stable, with only
1.1 percent of the people receiving public welfare assistance;[12] about 60
percent of the residents have lived in the neighborhood between eleven
and fifty years. Few of the residents appear to be wealthy.

The active *chōnaikai* has placed loudspeakers around the neighborhood
to announce activities, which are frequent. The number of *bōhan renrakusho* is low (one for every eighty houses), but the houses are close together, and the neighbors seem to watch out for each others' homes and
property, thus informally performing the function of the checkpoints. Most
of the residents say they interact with a large number of surrounding families or the entire neighborhood. The people are active in many volunteer
activities; for example, the largest number of volunteer firemen for the
volunteer fire company (*shōbōdan*) in the area come from this neighborhood. Shop and small factory owners make up the bulk of the *chōnaikai*
and police-support-group leadership. Burglaries are relatively high in the
neighborhood, partly because it is near the train station, and this probably
influences crime-prevention-association activity.

Police officers in the nearby *kōban* receive extensive support from the
leaders of the Hama Machi *chōnaikai*, and some of the most active members of police-support groups in the entire jurisdiction of the Kurashiki
police station come from this neighborhood. For instance, the traffic-
safety association in the area consistently has the most frequent and elaborate activities. Local leaders often come to the *kōban* to chat with the
police officers, making it a sort of informal neighborhood gathering-place
for people who are attracted to the police. The police receive moderate
cooperation from most of the residents in the form of information on
crimes and occurrences in the neighborhood, but the local leaders seem to
be more forthcoming. People have lived in the neighborhood long enough
to be well acquainted with each other; but they have not lived there for
many generations, which would impede cooperation with the police, owing to deep personal ties with other households. The sergeant in charge of
the local *kōban* spends most of his time visiting his supporters in the
neighborhood, usually the local leaders, much in the style of a *chūzai san*.
His outgoing and grandfatherly manner, as well as the large number of

12. Figures provided by the Kurashiki City Office, 1975. Tax data would have given a
better indication of neighborhood wealth, but they are not available by neighborhoods.

willing neighborhood leaders, accounts to a great extent for the generally cooperative nature of the area.

Hon Machi.

Hon Machi is the old center of Kurashiki, surrounding one side of a hill just north of the old Kurashiki *daikansho* (the administrative center of the town in the Edo period).[13] It was the main shopping area of Kurashiki until the present shopping mall was built nearer the train station in the early 1900s. The houses average several hundred years in age, though many of the families have changed through the years, and they are mostly large with white plastered walls, black tile roofs, storehouses and rice granaries, and are surrounded by large walls with gates. The architecture is typical of Edo-period samurai and wealthy merchants' mansions. Hon Machi residents on the average have lived in the neighborhood much longer than residents of Hama Machi. Most families are moderately well off financially (1.9 percent receive welfare), and many are very wealthy. A large number of the residents of this stable neighborhood are shop owners.

The neighborhood is said to typify the attitudes of traditional Kurashiki (i.e., in being aloof and indifferent to the affairs of others), and this is perhaps confirmed in the lack of a functioning *chōnaikai* and the fewest *bōhan renrakusho* of all the neighborhoods I studied (one for every ninety-six houses). Few volunteer firemen of the area *shōbōdan* come from Hon Machi (four men), even though the headquarters is located almost within the neighborhood. Interaction within the community is slightly below average for a stable downtown neighborhood. Crime victimization is fairly high, probably because of the many shops, yet the residents appear to consult less with their neighbors on how to reduce crime than in any of the other neighborhoods I studied. This also reflects, perhaps, the lack of mutual concern and interaction in the neighborhood.

Police officers state that Hon Machi is not as cooperative with the police as are neighborhoods like Hama Machi. There are fewer neighborhood leaders willing to be involved in police-support activities, and this is reflected in the lack of a functioning *chōnaikai*. Police officers feel that older

13. A *daikansho* was the administrative headquarters of a *daikan*, an Edo-period official who administered lands directly held by the Tokugawa government (*bakufu*). *Daikan* were found in rural possessions of the *bakufu*, and Kurashiki was one such directly held Tokugawa domain, serving as a rice storage and transshipment point.

and long-established neighborhoods in which households have developed strong interpersonal bonds (*ningen kankei*) are less likely to cooperate with police officers in various ways, including the investigation of crimes that occur there, than are more recently formed neighborhoods. Longtime residents may not feel good about talking to police during the routine *junkai renraku* visits or during investigations, because of uncertainty concerning the effects of cooperation on their relations with others in the neighborhood.

Many of the large houses in Hon Machi are surrounded by high walls with gates, and police say that this affects cooperation by the residents. The gates are often locked, with an intercom near the entrance to turn away unwanted callers. Walls prevent easy access to the neighborhood homes, cutting down on the ease of police visits. Another factor is undoubtedly the type of *kōban* serving the neighborhood. Hon Machi is within the jurisdiction of the Chūō Kōban ("Central Police-Box"), the largest in Kurashiki and second largest Okayama prefecture, with thirteen officers assigned to it. It is really a miniature police station covering the areas of several former neighborhood *kōban* that were consolidated. The larger scale of the *kōban* and its jurisdictional area and its resulting increased impersonality must affect the quantity and quality of the interactions of the police officers with local residents.

Funagura Chō.

Funagura Chō is located on the other side of the old *daikansho* from Hon Machi, and during the Edo period it was a neighborhood of boatmen and stevedores who loaded the barges carrying rice from the granaries near the *daikansho* to Osaka. It is still a neighborhood of laborers, but now there are small shops scattered through it. The number of people on welfare is fairly high (5.7 percent), indicating a lower economic level than most of the neighborhoods I studied. The *chōnaikai* is one of the most active in Kurashiki and is the only one with both neighborhood *bon* festival dances and a children's sumo wrestling contest each year.[14] The *chōnaikai* leaders are almost exclusively shop owners and other stable families; few laborer families assume leadership. There is an average number of *bōhan renrakusho* (one for every forty-two houses) in the neighborhood. The number of members of the *shōbōdan* is high (eight men), even

14. *Bon*, or *obon*, is a lively mid-summer Buddhist festival commemorating the dead by dancing, feasts, and cleaning of the ancestral graves.

though the neighborhood is far from the headquarters. The people seem to interact with one another widely because many have been there for generations (nearly 70 percent had lived there from eleven to fifty years, and about 15 percent had been there over fifty years). Crime is about average, though disturbances from drunk laborers used to bring the police frequently into the neighborhood, especially before a nearby *kōban* was merged with the more distant Chūō Kōban in 1971.

Police officers point out that poorer workers' neighborhoods like Funagura Chō tend to have more of an "old townsman esprit de corps" *(shita machi ninjō)* than do richer neighborhoods like Hon Machi—that is, a mutual concern among residents about helping each other, looking out for the children, keeping an eye on the neighbor's house while no one is there, and sharing little luxuries such as special holiday foods. The houses are close together, often joined side-by-side into row houses, and seldom have fences around them to inhibit the comings and goings of neighbors, and this increases interaction among the residents. Neighbors are well aware of what others are doing in such close and intimate settings, and this contributes to a decrease in crime and allows better tips to the police. The lack of fences and gates makes it easier for police officers to stop in and talk to the residents. The neighborhood *chōnaikai* is active in Funagura Chō probably because there are a number of stable families such as the shop owners who are willing to act as leaders. They also serve in police-support capacities. In many respects, Funagura Chō is similar to the cooperative neighborhood of Hama Machi.

Kawanishi Machi.

Kawanishi Machi is in a relatively old section of Kurashiki and, until the outlawing of prostitution in 1956, was the red-light district of Kurashiki *(akasen kuiki,* "red-line district," in Japanese). There were thirty-six brothels in the neighborhood, mostly side by side and lining one street. The brothels now either are inns (said to be infrequently used by bar hostesses for illegal prostitution) or have been converted into bars or restaurants (50 percent of Kurashiki's bars and 24 percent of its inns are in Kawanishi Machi).[15] A former police box located in the brothel area has now been closed and merged with the large Chūō Kōban. Most of the people living in the neighborhood are shopkeepers, and the neighborhood

15. Figures provided by the Kurashiki police station.

is stable financially except for a small slum area behind the old brothels (3.6 percent of the residents received welfare—mostly those in the small slum). A large majority have lived in the neighborhood from eleven to fifty years (almost 80 percent). The *chōnaikai* is active, with shop and former brothel owners usually serving as leaders. There is a large number of *bōhan renrakusho* in the neighborhood (one for every twenty-six houses), and the people seem to have wide neighborhood interaction. The majority of the volunteer firemen for the area *shōbōdan* are from Kawanishi Machi. The crime rate is about average among the neighborhoods I studied.

The police seem to agree that some of the more cooperative neighborhoods are those that were formerly brothel districts. This is said to result from the rather close and cooperative relationship that existed between the brothel owners and prostitutes and the police during the days of legalized prostitution. The police would stop in every evening to check the register of patrons staying in the brothel, and the prostitutes would often inform the police if one of their patrons had an unusual amount of money. Police doctors were in charge of checking prostitutes occasionally for venereal disease before and during the war when the police performed public health functions.

The police told me that many of the people who are most willing to cooperate with them in Kawanishi Machi are the former owners of brothels who now run bars or inns. Bar owners, like brothel owners, need police protection to keep violence down, and they naturally will have a more positive image of the police and will be more willing to cooperate in investigations and other police activities. New bar owners, who had no connection with the legalized prostitution in these neighborhoods, now often have gangster ties and are not very cooperative with the police in investigations. The *chōnaikai* in Kawanishi Machi is active because of the need for neighborhood solidarity to combat violence and other threats.

Kawatetsu Danchi.

Kawatetsu Danchi in Mizushima is the apartment complex (a *danchi* is such a complex) of the Kawasaki Steel Corporation for its employees. It was built in the 1960s as the nearby steel plant was put into operation. It is composed mostly of blue-collar workers, though white-collar employees occupy several buildings. In all, seventy-six buildings with 3,452 apartments house about twelve thousand persons. Because a ten-year limit is set on the length of time people can live in the apartments—to encourage employees to buy a house and become part of some community—there is little sense of a stable and permanent community in this complex. There is virtually no one on welfare, owing to the paternalistic employment policies of the company.

There is no *chōnaikai* or other such volunteer neighborhood association in the apartment complex. The company's apartment management office handles all the usual *chōnaikai* functions, and it selects a representative in each building to act as liaison with the residents. Each building has a household designated by rotation each month for routine functions such as collecting fees for sewage disposal and other such fees, and each stairwell designates a household by rotation to direct stairwell cleaning and other activities. Interaction seems limited mostly to stairwell groups. The parent-teacher associations of the two elementary schools are the main organizations in which people participate, other than hobby clubs organized by the company. Each permanent building representative's apartment is designated a *bōhan renrakusho*, and they jointly form a crime-prevention association. There is little crime, mostly limited to bicycle thefts and vandalism to automobiles. A *kōban* is located in the center of the apartment complex.

The police usually comment that large apartment complexes are rather uncooperative toward the police. This is particularly true in complexes run by the prefectural or city government, which have more diversity in residents than do company apartments. This uncooperative attitude probably stems from a number of factors. For one thing, residents of apartment complexes are usually younger on the average than residents of other types of neighborhoods, and as was mentioned, younger people seem to have a slightly more negative image of the police than do older people.[16] In addition, and what is perhaps more significant, residents of apartment complexes have limited interactions with their neighbors and so they have little information to pass on to police; volunteer neighborhood police associations are practically nonexistent, and neighborhood leaders willing to assist police are scarce. The structure of the living arrangement provides people with little contact with the police, except in formal and frequently negative situations such as renewing a driver's license at the police station

16. This statement is based on personal observations and on conversations with police officers and scholars, and is borne out in the results of the survey I conducted in the eleven neighborhoods.

or being stopped for a traffic violation. As an example, the police officers in the *kōban* located within the Kawatetsu Danchi do not even bother to visit the apartments of residents regularly for *junkai renraku*, unlike policemen in *kōban* located in more normal neighborhoods. They simply go to the management office of the apartment complex and copy from the office records the information they would usually gather during home visits.

People tend to have a more positive image of police officers if they have recently talked to one in a positive context, or if they can recognize by sight the police officers in the local *kōban*.[17] Residents of large apartment complexes seldom have this opportunity. Of all the neighborhoods that I studied in Kurashiki and Mizushima, the large steel company *danchi* was most reminiscent of America in the social distance I sensed between police officers and the local residents. The anonymity of the *danchi* affects community solidarity and, in turn, the willingness of residents to be involved with police.

THE TREND TOWARD CONSOLIDATION

The police began to consolidate small neighborhood *kōban* and nearby *chūzaisho* into larger *kōban* in the early 1970s. Greater manpower was considered necessary as it became desirable to have the *kōban* manned at all times and to have two or more officers on duty in the evenings. The need for increased manpower was occasioned by an increase in incidents and an alarming jump in assaults on lone police officers in *kōban* during evening shifts. The large Chūō Kōban, which covered several of the neighborhoods that I studied in Kurashiki, was formed through the amalgamation of two smaller *kōban* in the center of the city. Consolidation continues: the police consolidated or had plans to consolidate eight small *kōban* or *chūzaisho* into two or three *kōban* in the Kurashiki police station jurisdiction during the twelve-month period of my study (1974–1975).

Consolidation may be a necessity for the safety of police officers and to concentrate police power, but it leads to a concomitant increase in geo-

17. Based on conversations with police officers and citizens and on the results of my survey. Respondents who had talked to a policeman within the past year or who recognize the local police officers by sight had slightly more positive images of the police than those who had not talked to police officers or who could not recognize them. They also indicated slightly more willingness to cooperate with police in criminal investigations and to talk openly with police during a periodic home visit. See Walter L. Ames, "Police and Community in Japan" (Ph.D. dissertation, University of Michigan, 1976), pp. 405–406 and 423.

The Chuō Kōban, the largest police-box in the Kurashiki police station jurisdiction. The second floor is used by the police officers as a resting area.

graphic and social distance between the police and the local community. As *kōban* become more like miniature police stations, citizens feel less personal identification with individual officers simply because there are more officers in the *kōban* and it is farther away. This, in turn, can lead to a decline in their willingness to cooperate in supplying tips to the police on neighborhood occurrences, which would hamper police effectiveness in solving crimes and preventing disorder.

Despite these inevitable changes, the *kōban* system is flexible in adapting to different urban settings. For instance, it can be combined with patrol cars and other vehicles to provide a quick response to emergencies and to meet changes in society and in crime patterns. It still offers extensive citizen contact with the police, even in the larger consolidated *kōban*, when compared with other possible mechanisms of deployment, such as an almost exclusive reliance on patrol cars or police substations, as in many American cities. The *kōban* remains the main police tool in Japan for dealing with a rapidly changing society, the subject of the next chapter.

three

ADJUSTING TO A CHANGING SOCIETY

Social theorists suggest that the imperatives of industrialization and urbanization create pressures in all societies which inexorably propel them toward change, including growing individualism and impersonality.[1] The dislocations caused by social change and increased impersonality are said to be a root cause of crime and disorder in modern urban societies.

Japan has undergone rapid and profound alterations during its more than a hundred years of modernization since the beginning of the Meiji period. The pace of change has in fact quickened to a remarkable degree since the end of World War II. In the two previous chapters we saw that police work in the countryside and in the city is changing as Japanese society evolves. Yet, aside from perhaps only apartment house complexes, the urbanization pattern of the Japanese has not been overly disruptive to the social fabric. On the contrary, individuals seem to urbanize into already existing structures or, as in the new neighborhoods, quickly create face-to-face relationships among most of the inhabitants which are not dissimilar from those found in traditional villages. The *chōnaikai* organized in many neighborhoods, discussed in the previous chapter, are a good example of such networks.

Urbanization and change, however, inevitably lead to a certain amount

1. See, e.g., Clark Kerr et al., *Industrialization and Industrial Man* (Cambridge: Harvard University Press, 1960), and Talcott Parsons, *The Social System* (New York: Free Press, 1951), pp. 51–67. Kerr's theory is dubbed the "convergence theory," in which he suggests that the technology shared by industrialized societies creates increasingly uniform patterns of bureaucracy and rationality, as well as increased individualism. Parsons suggests that in industrialized societies, there are pressures toward "universalism" (obligations irrespective of the social status of the other) and "self-orientation" (norms calling for satisfaction of self-interests).

56

of anonymity and impersonality, even in Japan. There are manifestations of the decline of a tight-knit society, with possibly far-reaching ramifications for police work. This does not necessarily imply a rapidly rising crime rate or urban chaos, for the evidence is mostly to the contrary, but it indicates changes in crime patterns and the resulting necessity for new kinds of police responses.[2] The police must adapt from the traditional small community, where the policeman had close contact with the people, to a more modern and complex structure. Societal changes are manifest in the increasing concentration of crime in urban centers, shifting crime patterns between rural and urban areas, and changing rates of arrest and levels of citizen cooperation. These all presage further challenges for the police.

The primary police reaction to these changes has been similar in some ways to that of police in other parts of the world when faced with new problems—that is, an increasing reliance on technology to solve crimes and keep order as the personal relationships once used by the police continue to weaken. There is, however, the distinct possibility that this response by the police is creating social distance between them and the citizenry, thus aggravating the decline of citizen cooperation. The Japanese police, long expert in involving the community in crime control, are resorting to techniques of police-community relations based on the American pattern to combat growing remoteness from citizens. We shall first look at the effect of increasing urbanization on trends in crime.

URBANIZATION AND TRENDS IN CRIME

In the Introduction it was noted that Japan's crime rate has been dropping or has remained virtually the same every year since 1955.[3] This is a phenomenon unique in the industrialized world. Crime rose sharply after

---

2. Nothing in this chapter should be taken to suggest the probable development in Japan of urban crime problems similar to those in the United States. Impersonality may be presumed to cause changes in crime, but Japanese cities show few of the major crime problems of American cities of comparable size.

3. Japanese crime statistics are thoroughly reliable. They include *all* reported crimes, not merely the seven major crimes covered in the FBI crime statistics in the United States (i.e., criminal homicide, forcible rape, robbery, aggravated assault, burglary, larceny, and auto theft). Studies have indicated that the number of crimes actually committed in Japan was 69.3 percent higher than the total reported in 1974. Specifically, the ratio of unreported occurrences for various crimes were as follows: burglary (46.7%), fraud (164.7%), intimidation (172.9%), vandalism (1,625.4%), assault and battery (12.9%), and trespassing (376.2%). See Criminal Investigation Bureau, National Police Agency, *Shuto ken ni okeru hanzai no ansū nado chōsa kekka* [Survey results on unreported crimes, etc., in the metropolitan area] (Tokyo: National Police Agency, 1974), p. 35.

TABLE 4. *Concentration of Crime and Population within 31 Miles (50 Kilometers) of Tokyo, 1970 and 1975*

	Population	Reported Crimes	Crime Rate (per 100,000 population)
1970	21,263,487 (20.5%)	353,380 (27.6%)	1,659
1975	24,067,925 (21.7%)	348,720 (28.3%)	1,447

SOURCE: National Police Agency, ed., *Keisatsu hakusho, 1976* [Police white paper] (Tokyo: Okurasho Insatsukyoku, 1976), p. 95.

World War II, owing to the economic hardships and social dislocations caused by Japan's destruction and defeat. As reconstruction progressed, crime peaked in 1955, declined slightly until 1964, and then began a definite downward curve. The drop in crime reached its low point in 1973 and has remained roughly horizontal since then. The national average crime rate in 1975 was 1,103 per 100,000 population, up a mere 8 points from 1,095 in 1973.[4] The crime rate in Okayama prefecture in 1975 was 1,101 per 100,000, the closest prefecture to the national average.[5]

Within this overall dropping or horizontal crime rate, however, several trends are evident that merit our attention. The first is the increasing concentration of crime in the vicinity of large metropolitan areas. For example, in 1975 there were 348,720 reported crimes within a radius of thirty-one miles (50 kilometers) from Tokyo, which was 28.3 percent of the national total of reported crimes. The same year, about 24,070,000 people lived in that same area (21.5% of the national population), indicating an increasing concentration of crime in the greater Tokyo metropolitan area when compared with 1970, as is seen in table 4. The figures in parentheses are the percentage of the national total. Although the crime rate has gone down since 1970 in the Tokyo metropolitan area, the percentage of all crime has increased, showing a greater residual propensity for crime in this highly dense urban center than in other parts of Japan.

When trends in crime within the thirty-one mile radius are further broken down into different distances from central Tokyo and compared with 1970, a "doughnut effect" is observed. From zero to six miles (10 kilometers), crime totals have accompanied a decline in population and are down 14.9 percent, but each increasingly distant outlying area shows rises

---

4. National Police Agency, ed., *Keisatsu hakusho, 1976* [Police white paper] (Tokyo: Okurasho Insatsukyoku, 1976), p. 64.

5. Ibid.

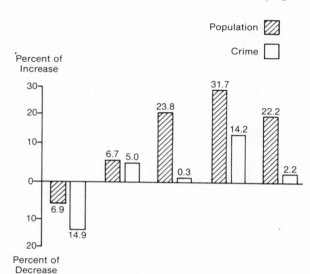

FIGURE 5.   Crime and Population Changes within 31 Miles (50 Kilometers) of
Tokyo, 1970 and 1975

SOURCE: National Police Agency, ed., *Keisatsu hakusho, 1976* [Police white pa-
per], (Tokyo: Okurasho Insatsukyoku, 1976), p. 95.

in crime, especially the belt nineteen to twenty-five miles (30 to 40 kilometers) from central Tokyo (see figure 5; the reason for the rise in these
suburbs is explained below). Although crime is down in the central portions of Tokyo, the concentration of crime occurring in that area is much
higher than in the outlying areas relative to the concentration of population. That is, 28.7 percent of all crimes occurring within a thirty-one-mile
radius of central Tokyo in 1975 occurred in the area up to six miles from
the center, whereas only 16.3 percent of the population lived in that area.
The crime rate was 2,562 per 100,000, whereas the crime rate in the outlying areas was less than half, at 1,233.[6] This is not to imply that downtown Tokyo is crime ridden; the important point for this discussion is the
probable reasons for the higher concentration of crime related to population in the central city areas. As in many cities, the higher concentration
of crime stems not only from the wide variation between daytime and
nighttime populations but also from increased anonymity and a general

6. Ibid., p. 97.

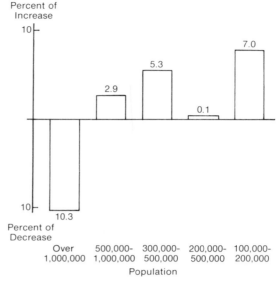

FIGURE 6.   Changes in Crime according to the Population of Cities, 1966 to 1975
SOURCE: *Police White Paper, 1976,* p. 98.

weakening of mechanisms for social control among the population resid-
ing downtown.

Another indication of social changes accompanying the spread of urbanization and modernization is the remarkable rise in crimes occurring in
medium- and smaller-sized cities. In 1975 the crimes in 168 cities with
populations of more than 100,000, or 53.8 percent of Japan's total population, amounted to 70.2 percent of all reported crimes.[7] This is up from
their proportion, 56 percent of all crimes, in 1966. As can be seen in
figure 6, the largest rise is in cities with populations of 100,000 to 200,-
000, which includes many "bedtowns" surrounding Tokyo and Osaka and
accounts for the doughnut effect mentioned above. These residential areas
for commuters have grown in size recently, and their newness, along with
the fact that many of the residents are gone most days, inhibits the development of a sense of community. Cities with populations of 300,000 to
500,000, mostly regional cities, including Okayama and Kurashiki, also
showed noticeable increases. Cities with over a million inhabitants

7. Ibid.

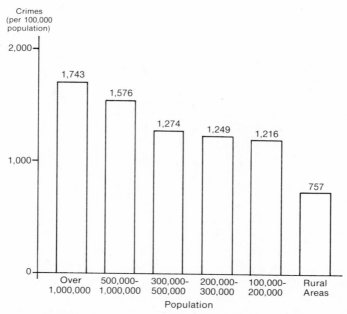

FIGURE 7. Crime Rate according to the Population of Cities, 1975
SOURCE: *Police White Paper, 1976*, p. 99.

showed a major drop in crime. These figures indicate that crime is now spreading not only to the suburbs of Tokyo and Osaka, but also to medium- and smaller-size cities as social change and modernization permeate Japan. They also point out that Japan's overall drop in crime is most evident in the largest urban centers, yet these metropolises still bear the brunt of crime (see figure 7). The larger the city, the higher the crime rate, and cities with over 500,000 people have more than twice the crime rate of rural areas.

A final phenomenon that merits attention is the fact that crimes involving total strangers are markedly higher in urban than in rural areas. Figure 8 compares arrests for "atrocious crimes" (*kyōaku hanzai*: murder, robbery, arson, and rape) and the crime of "violence" (*sobōhan*: assault, battery, intimidation, extortion, and possession of a dangerous weapon) committed by total strangers to the victim in cities of over 100,000 and in towns and rural areas of under 100,000. Violence directed toward

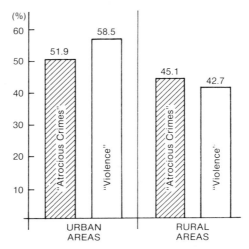

FIGURE 8.   Percentage of Strangers in the Arrests for "Atrocious Crimes" and "Violence," 1975

SOURCE: *Police White Paper, 1976*, p. 100.

strangers shows the greatest variation and is probably the most indicative of the effects of differing degrees of impersonality between urban and rural areas. A more floating or fluid population and increased anonymity in urban areas is at the root of this disparity. Expanding urbanization has also increased the difficulty of police investigation of crimes, which we shall now examine.

THE EFFECT OF URBANIZATION
ON THE INVESTIGATION OF CRIMES

The comparison of several neighborhoods in Kurashiki and Mizushima in the previous chapter showed a degree of variation in the willingness of citizens to cooperate with the police in investigations, and the social and historical characteristics of the neighborhoods were given as a partial explanation of these differences. Police investigations in Japan are generally encountering less citizen cooperation than in the past, and this is probably the most direct evidence of the changes in Japanese social structure caused by rapid urbanization. The rate of arrest is declining, investigations are taking longer, the rate of recovery of stolen goods is going down, and tips from citizens about crimes are harder to obtain.

The rate of arrest for all crimes has declined slightly nationally since

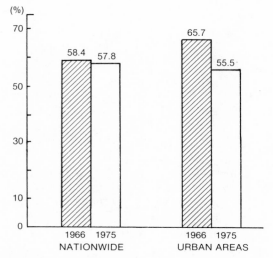

FIGURE 9. Geographic Comparison of Rates of Criminal Arrests, 1966 and 1975
SOURCE: *Police White Paper, 1976*, p. 101.

1966, but the sharpest drop has been in urban areas. Figure 9 shows a decline in the arrest rate in cities from 65.7 percent in 1966 to 55.5 percent in 1975. Urban crime often involves complete strangers, with few leads for the police to follow. The sharp rise in the percentage of criminals who use automobiles in the commission of crimes facilitates their getaway and allows many to commit crimes in several prefectures. The use of automobiles is highest in the "atrocious crimes" of robbery and rape, and in breaking and entering. The growing motorization of crime is alarming to police because it promises to grow as automobile ownership rises. Privately owned automobiles have increased nearly 1,000 percent to over 17 million vehicles since 1964.[8]

A trend that is causing great apprehension among the police is the increasing difficulty of making arrests at an early stage of investigation. As figure 10 illustrates, the percentage of same-day arrests for "atrocious crimes" shows a general decline for each of the four crimes, but the drop for murders is particularly sharp. This illustrates the increase in crime among people who do not know each other, the ease with which criminals can flee with improved transportation, and the degree to which criminals

8. Ibid., p. 215.

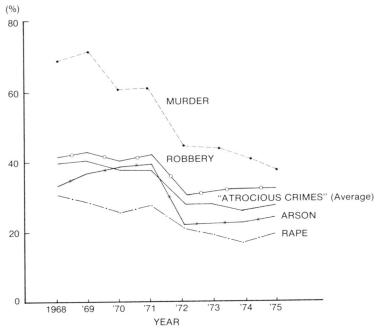

FIGURE 10.   Changes in the Rate of Same-Day Arrests for "Atrocious Crimes,"
1968 to 1975
SOURCE: *Police White Paper, 1976*, p. 101.

are able to blend more easily into anonymous urban surroundings. Once a
criminal slips away, police are hampered because the tying-up of detectives in lengthy investigations delays the initial investigation of new
crimes. Another factor that affects the length of time for solution of crimes
is the type of persons that are committing crimes in the area. Mizushima,
for example, has a much higher ratio of day laborers in its many factories
than does Kurashiki, and these workers can more easily flee from the locality and find work elsewhere than can the more settled residents of Kurashiki. Accordingly, Mizushima's rate of solution of crimes (49.2% in
1973) is lower than Kurashiki's (60.1%).[9]

As same-day arrests decline and investigations lengthen, the rate of recovery of stolen goods has shown a worsening trend. Figure 11 shows that

9. Okayama Prefectural Police Headquarters, ed., *Hanzai tōkeisho, 1973* [Criminal statis-
tics] (Okayama: Okayama Prefectural Police Headquarters, 1973), pp. 96–99.

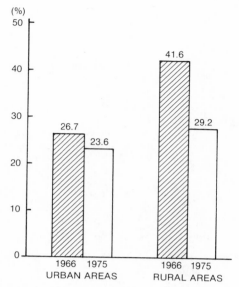

FIGURE 11. Rate of Recovery of Theft Items, according to Geographic Area, 1966 and 1975
SOURCE: *Police White Paper, 1976*, p. 103.

the recovery rate from thefts is down to 23.6 percent in urban areas and 29.2 percent in rural areas. The most interesting feature is the sharp drop in rural areas, with a recovery rate now only slightly higher than in cities. This is clear evidence of the effect of encroaching urbanization on Japan's countryside. Goods stolen during a breaking and entering were recovered at even lower rates: 17.1 percent in cities and 20.3 percent in rural areas in 1975.[10]

One of the primary methods of investigation traditionally relied on by Japanese detectives for solving crimes is to gather tips from local residents about what they saw or heard before, during, or after the occurrence. This is termed *kikikomi* (a tip; literally, "to reach one's ears") investigation and has been extremely effective, especially when the crime was committed by an outsider to rural villages and long-established and stable urban neighborhoods. However, *kikikomi* investigation is becoming much more difficult in both urban and rural areas, which dramatically illustrates the effect of social change on police work in Japan. Figures 12 and 13 com-

10. *Police White Paper*, 1976, p. 103.

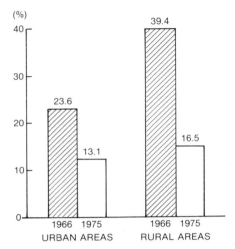

FIGURE 12.   Percentage of Arrests for "Atrocious Crimes" Stemming from *Kiki-komi*, 1966 and 1975
SOURCE: *Police White Paper, 1976*, p. 102.

pare the percentages of arrests for "atrocious crimes" and thefts that initially resulted from *kikikomi* in 1966 and 1975. For instance, arrests that
began with a tip were only 4.5 percent of all arrests for theft in urban areas
in 1975. Similar to the declining rate of recovery of theft items discussed
above, the most precipitous drop is in rural areas, though the percentage
of *kikikomi*-based arrests is lowest in urban areas. The decline in *kikikomi*
makes police investigations infinitely more troublesome.

Behind the falling rate of *kikikomi* are various components of societal
change in Japan. Urbanization has led to a decline in the extended family,
and ties in the nuclear family are less binding than in the past. Thus, if
both parents are working, the grandparents are less likely to be home
watching the house (*rusuban*) than in the past. Changes are also occurring
in the traditional notions of neighborliness. The current phrase *mai homu
shugi* ("my home-ism") connotes a passionate desire among many modern
Japanese for their own homes and, more significantly, an increasing longing for a meaningful life free from the pressures of traditional neighborhood and other groups. Accompanying this phenomenon is a growing concern for the individual and his rights. Individual public spiritedness and
casual involvement in the problems of others has always been rare in Japan, except for a few outgoing local "leaders," and this tendency is mag-

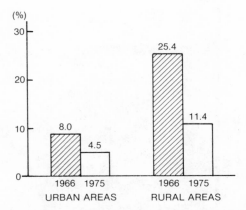

FIGURE 13. Percentage of Arrests for Theft Stemming from *Kikikomi,* 1966 and 1975

SOURCE: *Police White Paper, 1976,* p. 102.

nified through the anonymity arising from urbanization. Thus, when detectives go out on an investigation, they often find no one at home; if someone is home, an attitude of not wanting to get involved is frequently encountered; or if a person wants to cooperate, he very likely will not even know his neighbors' names, especially in apartment complexes.

POLICE ADAPTATION TO SOCIAL CHANGES

Police adaptation to increased urbanization and changing patterns of crime and arrest is characterized by a rising reliance on modern technology, such as the patrol car. Patrol cars are used to back up foot and bicycle patrol officers in *kōban* and *chūzaisho* and provide the primary rapid response to increasingly motorized crime. Patrol cars (*pato kā*, an abbreviation for *patororu kā*, taken from the English words) are the symbol of police mobility in Japan. They are manned by two police officers on shifts, and operate either out of local police stations or out of patrol-car centers established by the prefectural police headquarters. They patrol their assigned jurisdictions and respond to emergency calls from the station or the prefectural headquarters.

The number of patrol cars assigned to police stations is not large. For example, the Kurashiki police station had only three patrol cars in 1974, divided functionally into two patrol-section patrol cars and one traffic-section patrol car. Mizushima had only two patrol cars, one for the patrol

A police officer doing *kikikomi* investigation, after a suspected murder in the neighborhood. As Japanese society changes, people are becoming less willing to talk to police officers about incidents.

section and one for the traffic section. (For other specialized vehicles in use by the Kurashiki and Mizushima police stations in 1974, see table 5.) The traffic-section patrol cars are used essentially for making traffic arrests and for purposes of traffic safety. However, since the gasoline shortage that began in the latter half of 1973, patrol cars in Kurashiki and Mizushima have cut down their time on the road each day, with the result that traffic-section patrol cars operate mainly during the day to catch violators and go out at night only if there is a traffic accident or other traffic-related occurrence. Patrol-section patrol cars go out in the day if there is an errand or an emergency call, and they patrol the jurisdiction mainly at night.

The small number of patrol cars in the Kurashiki and Mizushima police stations is deceptive. Their scarcity is compensated for by the fact that the prefectural police headquarters maintains a mobile police force (*kidō keisatsutai*) in Kurashiki with thirty-seven men and eight marked and unmarked patrol cars. They also have nine motorcycles for making traffic arrests. These patrol cars cover a wide area of the southern portion of the prefecture from slightly west of Okayama City to the Hiroshima prefectural border. They spend most of their time in the jurisdictions of the Ku-

TABLE 5. *Specialized Vehicles in Use by the Kurashiki and Mizushima Police Stations in 1974*

	Kurashiki	Mizushima
Limousine for police chief	1	1
Criminal investigation car (unmarked, with radio)	1	1
Criminal investigation car (unmarked, no radio)	4	2
Large truck for transporting police officers	1	1
Small truck for transporting equipment	2	1
Traffic accident vehicle (station wagon, unmarked)	3	2
Mobile police-box (*idō kōban*)	1	1

SOURCE: Okayama Prefectural Police Headquarters, ed., *Okayama ken keisatsu nenkan, 1972* [Okayama prefectural police yearbook] (Okayama: Okayama Prefectural Police Headquarters, 1972), pp. 64–65.

rashiki and Mizushima police stations, however. Their main function is to respond to emergency calls from the prefectural police headquarters, thus adding additional mobility to the police in the area. The *kidō keisatsutai* is considered an elite group, and only the best seasoned veterans are allowed to serve in the unit. They work grueling shifts of twenty-four hours on duty and twenty-four hours off. Patrol cars from the mobile force are frequently the first at the scene of an incident, and they make a large number of arrests for the small size of the unit. They usually leave after police from the local police station arrive.

One factor in evaluating the effectiveness of patrol cars is their response time, which is the time it takes a patrol car to arrive at the scene of an incident after receiving an emergency call. The response time has become longer in Japan in recent years, increasing from an average of four minutes and thirty-seven seconds in 1969 to five minutes and twenty-one seconds in 1973. Okayama followed a similar trend of increased response time until 1973, when it began to drop. In 1975, it was five minutes and thirty seconds, down from seven minutes and four seconds in 1973.

The increased response time was due mainly to heavier congestion in cities from increased traffic and parking. Okayama prefecture alleviated the problem by banning parking on most streets in Okayama City and Kurashiki. The response time is faster in Mizushima than Kurashiki because the Mizushima police jurisdiction is narrower and has numerous wide and straight roads on its reclaimed land. Kurashiki roads are crowded and narrow, especially in the center of the city, often wide enough for only one car to squeeze through.

Despite the crowded and narrow streets, patrol cars almost always beat a police officer on foot, bicycle, or motorbike from a *kōban* or *chūzaisho* to the scene of emergencies in Kurashiki and Mizushima, partly because of the large jurisdictions of police-boxes following amalgamations. Patrol cars will have to be relied on even more for quick response as the trend toward amalgamation continues. However, heavier use of patrol cars probably has detrimental effects on police relations with the community because of the decreased contacts which local residents can have with police officers patrolling their neighborhoods in automobiles. Policemen on foot or on bicycles, or sitting in a neighborhood *kōban* or *chūzaisho*, are much more readily accessible for a friendly greeting or a chat and, as we have noted, citizens are more likely to cooperate with police officers with whom they are familiar than with those with whom they are not.

Larger jurisdictional areas make it more difficult for citizens to run to the local *kōban* to report incidents when they occur. Residents may also be less willing to do so if they do not know the police officers who man the *kōban*. As a remedy, the police have again relied on technology as an aid and have set up an emergency system whereby citizens dial 110 (*hyakutō ban*) on their telephones. The calls are received in the prefectural police headquarters, which then broadcasts the alert over the police radio. Each police station monitors the prefectural police radio, and when an incident occurs in its jurisdiction, it radios its patrol cars or telephones its police-boxes with orders to dispatch officers to the scene. All police officers in *kōban* and *chūzaisho* carry small pocket radio receivers with ear plugs which allow them to hear emergency 110 dispatches and to respond to those in their jurisdiction. In Okayama, about 95 percent of all emergency incidents are reported to the police by means of citizens dialing *hyakutō ban*.[11]

The rate of emergency 110 calls partially reflects how busy the police are. There seem to be three slight peaks of police activity during the year, as reflected in *hyakutō ban* frequency, each four months apart. Two of the three occur in festival months, and festivals in Japan always involve drinking. The first is April, which coincides with cherry blossom (*sakura*) viewing and the traditional drunkenness that this entails; the second is

11. From an interview with the patrol section chief of the Okayama Prefectural Police Headquarters, 1975.

Emergency 110 Calls

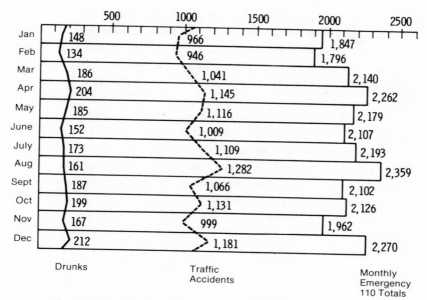

FIGURE 14.   Emergency 110 Calls in Okayama during 1973
SOURCE: Document from the Okayama Prefectural Police Headquarters, 1974.

August, the hottest month of the year, a time when people stay out late at night on weekends and go on trips to seek relief from the heat; the third, December, is marked by a large number of year-end parties (*bōnenkai*) and accompanying drinking. The highest number of drunks are reported in April and December, and the highest number of traffic accidents are in August (see figure 14). *Hyakutō ban* calls during a typical twenty-four-hour period follow the pattern of activity of police officers in *kōban*: they increase in late afternoon, peak between 10:00 P.M. and midnight, fall off abruptly after 2:00 A.M., and reach their lowest point between 4:00 and 6:00 A.M.

Perhaps the most interesting response which the Japanese police have made to changes in society detrimental to police effectiveness does not involve technology, but places an increasing emphasis on community-relations techniques, referred to simply by the English letters CR. CR is a concept borrowed from the American police, which is significant because, in adopting it, the Japanese have recognized an increase in the social distance between police and the community similar to that which community-relations efforts in the United States have attempted to reduce. The Japanese police, of course, have adapted CR methods to their own situation.

Community-relations activities take two forms: efforts to publicize the police and improve their public image (involving essentially one-way communication); and attempts to establish a dialogue with the community regarding police operations, or to help elicit assistance from the community in solving crimes (two-way communication). The former is probably better termed public relations and is accomplished in numerous ways. For example, Okayama maintains a prefectural police band that marches in parades and performs at schools. The prefectural police headquarters publishes a monthly information bulletin and has police-related items broadcast on television during programs sponsored by the prefecture. Many *kōban* and police stations have mimeographed handbills drawn up by the police officers, which contain cartoons and tips on crime prevention and traffic safety, and which are distributed by police officers when they visit homes in their *kōban* jurisdiction.

The attempt to create a dialogue with the community takes place at different levels. For example, a community relations committee—composed of two Okayama University professors (a psychologist and a law professor), officials from the prefectural office, a member of the editorial staff of the main Okayama newspaper and another from the major broadcasting company in the prefecture, and the manager of a marketing research company—meets with the prefectural police at least four times a year to discuss methods of effectively improving police relations with the public. The effort at dialogue is taken to the neighborhood level in most police stations. For instance, I attended a meeting in a neighborhood hall in Kurashiki at which the police chief, the assistant chief, and all the section chiefs, as well as the policemen from the local *kōban*, met with citizens of the neighborhood to give short presentations on matters of public concern in their areas of specialization, and also to hear ideas and complaints from the people. The exchange was frank, although because of natural reticence the head of the neighborhood association sometimes had to prompt questions from the citizens.

The police make effective use of the media both in improving their image and in eliciting cooperation from the community. The media, in general, are supportive of the police, especially in the regional press like that in Okayama. The main Okayama newspaper-television-radio conglomerate, the San'yō Press, seldom criticizes the police. The media cover police-related matters and incidents by way of writers' clubs located in the prefectural police headquarters and in the city offices of the larger cities such as Kurashiki. Press conferences are held every morning in the prefectural police headquarters; the assistant chief of each police station is in charge of press relations, and comments on small incidents, and the police chief makes statements on major ones. The relations between the reporters and the police seem to vary according to the personalities of the reporters, the newspapers' sense of responsibility in reporting, and also the police station. I heard a particularly overworked assistant chief of a police station once grumble that "some bothersome (*urusai*) people are here" when he announced to the chief that several reporters had come for an interview about a recent large incident.

The media gives heavy coverage to the semiannual traffic-safety campaigns, broadcasts descriptions of stolen cars, and even broadcasts daily the photographs and descriptions of criminals most wanted by the police. This is part of the extensive effort exerted by the police in enlisting community involvement in the prevention of crime and traffic accidents. The police do not rely solely on the media in publicizing wanted criminals, however. The National Police Agency periodically issues posters of wanted criminals which the local police post in conspicuous locations. They are always seen in front of *kōban* and *chūzaisho*, in train stations, public bath houses (*sentō*), and other places where people gather. I found some posted on the gates of a Shinto shrine in the hills above Kurashiki. The wide use of "wanted" posters has long historical precedent in Japan. In the Edo period, charcoal drawings on white paper of the faces of wanted criminals (called *ninsōgaki*) were posted on small wooden signboards in various parts of Edo by feudal policemen, *okappiki* and *dōshin*.[12]

The media can be a particularly powerful tool in the hands of the police because one of the strongest factors in social control in Japan is the fear that if one is arrested one's name will appear in the newspaper. Violators often plead with the police to keep their names from the newspapers to avoid loss of face. The police have used the press to create social pressure to eliminate certain offenses. For instance, in rural Kochi prefecture the

12. Supervisory Committee for Commemorative Activities for the Hundred Year Anniversary of the Founding of the Metropolitan Police Department, ed., *Keishichō hyakunen no ayumi* [Hundred-year progress of the Metropolitan Police Department] (Tokyo: Keishicho Soritsu Hyakunen Kinen Gyoji Un'ei Iinkai, 1974), p. 4.

police were faced with a mounting drunk-driving problem, so they began publishing in the morning papers the names, addresses, and companies of the people apprehended the night before. The problem of drunk driving is said to have disappeared rapidly. This method raises serious issues concerning the violation of personal privacy, and the police admit that not all newspapers are willing to cooperate. It has also limited effectiveness in large metropolitan centers because of the widespread anonymity.

A discussion of community relations would not be complete without mention of the broad range of service activities performed by police officers. Service activities are actively encouraged by comn.anding officers in efforts to improve police image, and they find precedent in the ideal of the close and cooperative relation that is traditional between the *chūzai san* and the village community in which he is a resident. The police assist elderly people, especially those living alone, by visiting them occasionally and giving them small presents, or by going to homes for the elderly to entertain them.[13] The police collect money for children whose parents have been killed in traffic accidents and buy them gifts at Christmas to be presented by the policemen in the local *kōban*. In Kurashiki, members of the traffic section frequently visit people who have been hospitalized by traffic accidents to cheer them up and, incidentally, to check on their recovery for purposes of accident reports. Several *kōban* in Kurashiki have their own unique service activities, such as the one that loans bicycles to elderly people visiting the jurisdiction so that they will not have to walk to their destination. The *kōban* in front of the train station regularly loans up to about $1.50 (¥500) to travelers who are stranded without money for train fare, of which more than 70 percent is returned by the borrowers. One police officer who worked there helped a visiting college student during school holiday get a job for three days at a local store in order to earn money to return to Tokyo. *Kōban* also seem to be havens for drunks because the police officers will talk to them and because they are safe locations to sober up before attempting to return home. The recipients of these favors show their gratitude in various ways, and the local newspaper frequently has letters from people thanking the police for assistance or some kind deed.

One of the most interesting service functions performed by the police is that of counseling people about their problems. Police officers, Buddhist

13. In 1974 I went with the Kurashiki police to a home for the elderly where many police officers sang, read poetry, performed skits, and provided other entertainment.

Police officers and meter maids (*junshiin*) entertaining at an old folks home, Kurashiki. They are singing about the riot police.

priests, and schoolteachers have traditionally served as counselors in Japanese society. People with problems come to *kōban* or *chūzaisho* to talk to the police officers, or if the problem is more serious, they go to the police station and talk to policemen in the crime-prevention section. The problems vary: the Kurashiki crime-prevention section, for instance, recorded twenty-four cases of formal counseling in 1974, ranging from marital to money management and apartment rental problems.[14] The solutions suggested by the police are not binding, and the police sometimes act as intermediaries between the parties in disputes. Instances of formal counseling with police officers in *kōban* and *chūzaisho* are much more frequent, though seldom recorded. For example, I was in a *kōban* in Kurashiki when a woman brought in a chain letter that threatened death to the receiver should he or she break the chain by not sending out a large num-

14. From records of the crime-prevention section, Kurashiki police station, 1975.

ber of similar letters to acquaintances. The woman said she would feel better if she gave it to the old police sergeant; he told her to destroy any more that might come and to sprinkle salt around her house for good luck (a practice traditionally thought to drive out evil influences). The woman went away relieved and apparently confident in the advice given her by the police officer. The officer said that a number of people come to him with similar letters every year and he usually gives the same counsel.

The emphasis placed on service activities has great significance to the police reaction to accelerating change in Japanese society. Rapid shifts in the social milieu have created challenges for the police through changing patterns of crime and arrest and in the general decrease in community cooperation. Like police organizations in other countries, the Japanese police have responded through increased reliance on technology, such as patrol cars and emergency telephone systems. But they also have addressed the human aspects of the problem, through public-relations efforts to improve their image and, even more effectively, by institutionalizing and actively encouraging in cities the kind of individualized service functions that are often spontaneously performed in traditional rural settings by *chūzai san*.

Societal change merely alters the types and degrees of challenges faced by the police; they become problems only when the police are unable or unwilling to adapt to them. The Japanese police show flexibility and resiliency in the face of new dilemmas. Despite changes, the police-box system will undoubtedly remain the basic form of police deployment, helping to insure the comparatively close relations that the police still enjoy with the majority of the community. On the whole, the Japanese police system seems to fit Japanese society and to harmonize with its evolving characteristics. The next three chapters will examine the police relationship with several specific types of citizen-clientele, each more or less nonconforming. We shall look first at youth.

four

CONFRONTING YOUTH

Youths present special problems for the police in Japan, as they do in most countries. Young people in general tend to be antagonistic toward police authority, but the challenges for the police arise from more than this. Crimes and delinquent acts committed by youths are of particular concern because of the future consequences to society if the young offenders grow to be hardened adult criminals.[1] Special efforts are thus made to rehabilitate youngsters who commit crimes or acts approaching crimes so that they can become productive members of society when they reach adulthood. The police place great emphasis on the prevention of juvenile crime and delinquency, and they employ a variety of techniques, ranging from counseling of youths by police officers to encouraging the extensive involvement of families, schools, companies, and neighborhoods in preventive efforts. These approaches meet varying degrees of success.

Juvenile crime and delinquency is not the only problem police face with youth. College-age youngsters present a different sort of challenge in the form of radical student groups that constantly confront and do battle with the police. It is not uncommon for Japanese youths to espouse Marxist

---

1. Japanese law defines the categories of youngsters handled by the police as follows: "juvenile criminals" (*hanzai shōnen*), youths fourteen through nineteen who have committed crimes [Juvenile Law, Art. 3, Par. 1, no. 1]; "juvenile offenders" (*shokuhō shōnen*), youths under fourteen who have committed acts that violate criminal statutes [Juvenile Law, Art. 3, Par. 1, no. 2]; and "crime-prone juveniles" (*guhan shōnen*), youths under twenty who, it is feared, will commit crimes in the future, to judge by their personality and actions [Juvenile Law, Art. 3, Par. 1, no. 3]. In addition, "unwholesome-activity juveniles" (*furyō kōi shōnen*) are youths under twenty who engage in acts "injurious to the moral character of themselves and others," such as smoking, drinking, and fighting [Juvenile Police Activity Regulations, Art. 2].

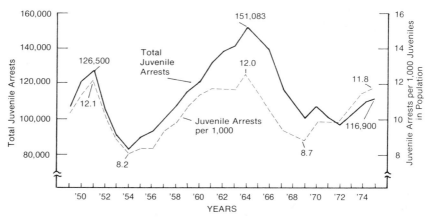

FIGURE 15.   Juvenile Arrests, 1949–1975 (Total number, and per 1,000 Juveniles
in the Population)

NOTE: Juveniles include youths between fourteen and nineteen years of age. Arrests are for criminal offenses.

SOURCES: National Police Agency, ed., *Keisatsu hakusho, 1974* [Police white
paper] (Tokyo: Okurasho Insatsukyoku, 1974), p. 18, and *Police White
Paper, 1976*, pp. 77 and 132.

philosophies and to affiliate with leftist student organizations while in college, and then to become stable members of society after obtaining employment in a reputable company. These groups engage in frequent demonstrations and occasionally in more violent disorders, and are checked by
Japan's highly disciplined and efficient riot police.

This chapter will examine the adaptation of the police to youth problems
in Japan. First it will look at trends in juvenile crime and delinquency,
including the alarming rise in violence by automobile gangs, and how the
police attempt to deal with these dilemmas; then it will examine radical
student movements and the famous riot police.

TRENDS IN JUVENILE CRIME AND DELINQUENCY

Although the overall crime rate in Japan has been generally dropping in
recent years, crimes by juveniles (ages 14 to 19) have not followed the
same pattern. Juvenile crime has had two peaks since World War II, the
first in 1951 during the period of economic and social unrest following the
war, and the second in 1964 as children born during the postwar baby

boom were reaching their late teens.[2] Crimes committed by juveniles dropped until 1972 and then began to rise (see figure 15). Of particular significance is the fact that the ratio of juveniles among the general juvenile population involved in crime has risen in the postwar period, whereas the ratio of adults among the adult population committing crimes has dropped sharply. For example, in 1954, 8.2 juveniles for every 1,000 in the population were arrested for committing a crime, and 6.8 adults for every 1,000 were involved in crime. In 1975, there were 11.8 juveniles arrested for major crimes for every 1,000 in the population, and only 3.2 adults.[3] As figure 15 illustrates, this 1975 figure is exceeded only by the juvenile crime peaks in 1964 and 1951. Of all arrests for crimes in 1975, 32.1 percent were juveniles between the ages of fourteen and nineteen.[4] The vast majority of crimes committed by juveniles in 1975 were various forms of theft (73.5%, compared with 45.5% of all crimes committed by adults), with shoplifting the largest type (27.2%), followed by motorcycle theft (10.1%), bicycle theft (9.9%), and auto theft (3.9%).[5]

Within the overall crime statistics for juveniles, several trends are significant. First, more crimes are being committed by younger juveniles in recent years, as can be seen when we examine the number of young criminals per 1,000 of their age group in the general population. As figure 16 illustrates, the number of fourteen- and fifteen-year-olds arrested for crimes has increased sharply since 1969, arrests of sixteen- and seventeen-year-olds have increased only a bit more slowly, while arrests of eighteen- and nineteen-year-olds decreased during the seven-year period. The second trend, which is probably correlated with the first, shows that the percentage of juveniles arrested for crimes who were students increased rapidly during the period, from 48.9 percent in 1969 to 70.8 percent in 1975. Of these, middle school students (ages 12 to 14) rose from 26.9 percent to 29.8 percent, high school students (ages 15 to 17) shot up dramatically

2. National Police Agency, ed. *Keisatsu hakusho, 1976* [Police white paper] (Tokyo: Okurasho Insatsukyoku, 1976), p. 132.

3. Ibid., pp. 131–132. See also National Police Agency, ed. *Keisatsu hakusho, 1974* [Police white paper] (Tokyo: Okurasho Insatsukyoku, 1974), pp. 17 and 185.

4. *Police White Paper, 1976*, p. 77. Criminal arrests for other age groupings in 1975 were as follows: 20–24 (14.7%); 25–29 (13.9%); 30–39 (19.7%); 40 and over (19.6%).

5. Ibid., p. 133. The next largest type of crime committed by both juveniles and adults were crimes of violence, excluding murder and rape (16.9% for juveniles and 26.4% for adults).

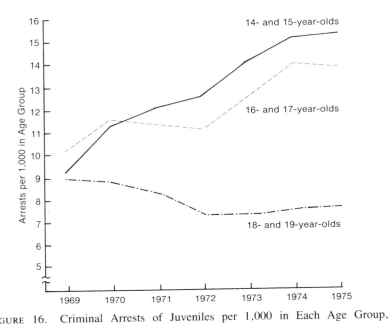

FIGURE 16. Criminal Arrests of Juveniles per 1,000 in Each Age Group, 1969–1975

SOURCES: *Police White Paper, 1974*, pp. 187–188, and *Police White Paper, 1976*, p. 134.

from 18.1 percent to 36.3 percent, and college and other students increased moderately from 3.9 percent to 4.7 percent.[6]

The third trend is that the number of "atrocious crimes"[7] by juveniles has dropped sharply, whereas the number of crimes committed merely for enjoyment has risen. As was noted above, most crimes committed by youths involved some kind of theft, in which they shoplifted on an impulse or stole a motorcycle or a bicycle for a thrill. The tendency toward these "crimes for enjoyment" seems to be most prevalent among high school students, which may explain the sharp rise in arrests of juveniles aged fourteen to seventeen. Police investigations have shown that the majority of these crimes are not necessarily committed by youths from poor families or families with criminal backgrounds. Most of these youths seem to

6. *Police White Paper, 1974*, p. 191, and *Police White Paper, 1976*, p. 135.
7. *Kyōaku hanzai* (murder, robbery, arson, and rape).

have normal personalities, and many come from homes that are average or above average financially. For example, in Kurashiki in the first five months of 1975, the second largest number of youths (by neighborhood) handled by the police for committing crimes or for delinquency were from one of the wealthy new neighborhoods composed mostly of families whose heads work at the managerial level in the large Mizushima industrial plants.[8] This tendency of increasing crimes for enjoyment among youths is certain evidence of social change in Japan and of a decline in traditional societal control mechanisms.

The number of sexual offenses by youths has been steadily dropping, but the types of offenses have become more alarming to the police. For example, cases of prostitution and sex orgies by high school and even middle school girls have increased in recent years, and authorities link this to a relaxing of sexual mores in Japan. Glue-sniffing and the inhaling of paint thinner by youths (hard drugs and marihuana are rigidly controlled and very difficult to obtain in Japan) has also been a problem, which was hard for police to deal with until a law was passed in 1972 outlawing their abuse and making it a criminal offense to knowingly sell paint thinner, glue, or other such items to youths who might abuse them. The abuse of these substances has exhibited rapid fluctuations in recent years. The number of youths handled by police for this problem dropped off sharply in 1972 and 1973 after several years of large rises, then increased in 1974, and shot up almost 75 percent in 1975. Police investigated 1,788 persons for selling these substances to youths in 1975, of whom 262 were arrested.[9]

The number of girls apprehended for criminal offenses has been growing. In the five-year period from 1971 to 1975, of all juveniles apprehended for criminal offenses, those who were girls rose from 10.9 percent to 16.3 percent. There were 19,027 girls apprehended for crimes in 1975, up 10.2 percent from the year before, and 97,755 boys apprehended, down 0.4 percent. The overwhelming majority of girls were involved in theft (90.9%), whereas 70.1 percent of the boys were apprehended for this offense.[10]

8. Data provided by the Kurashiki police station, 1975. Eighteen youths were from Hama no Chaya. The largest number (nineteen) were from the relatively poor, nearby neighborhood of Kita Hama Cho.
9. *Police White Paper, 1976,* p. 147.
10. Ibid., pp. 136–137.

POLICE RESPONSE TO JUVENILE
CRIME AND DELINQUENCY

Youth problems are the responsibility of the juvenile unit in each police station. In Kurashiki, for example, the juvenile unit (*shōnen gakari*) is a part of the crime-prevention section and is staffed by three male police officers and two female civilian employees of the police who serve as juvenile-guidance officers (*fujin hodōin*, commonly called "mama police"). None of the juvenile-unit police officers or employees are uniformed. Their function is to nip delinquency in the bud by discovering youths with these tendencies at an early stage and help them return to wholesome activities.

The main method employed by members of the juvenile unit to find delinquent youths or those on their way to delinquency is "street guidance" (*gaitō hodō*). Juvenile officers and "mama police" patrol shopping malls, parks, train stations, and other places where youths tend to gather, looking for young runaways, juveniles smoking, entering pachinko parlors or pornographic movie theaters, or engaging in other undesirable activities. They approach the youths and warn them to stop the particular behavior, or they initiate other appropriate action. The youths invariably stand sheepishly with bowed head and do what the juvenile-unit members instruct them. Street guidance is increased in times of particular danger of delinquency, such as at New Year's, in the spring and summer, and during school vacations or festivals.

The juvenile unit of a police station devotes considerable energy to counseling young people and their parents on a variety of youth-related concerns. There were 77,000 recorded cases of counseling on juvenile problems nationally in 1975, a small fraction of the actual number of times police officers provided counseling if informal counseling is included. Of these official cases, about 60 percent were with adults and 40 percent were with juveniles; among the youths, middle and high school students were the overwhelming majority, and girls outnumbered boys. The content of the counseling was not limited to delinquency, but included worries about sex, school and jobs, future plans, health, friends, and family matters. Youths were most concerned about relations with the opposite sex (22.4%), followed by worries about friends (12.7%), and adults came to consult most often about children's running away from home (22.0%) and their delinquency (20.0%).[11]

The juvenile unit is aided by "youth assistants" (*shōnen kyōjoin*), adult volunteers who help in street-guidance activities of the police. The system began in 1962, and there were 150,000 commissioned by the prefectural governors and the heads of the prefectural police headquarters across Japan in 1975. In Kurashiki, for example, there were 60 such assistants recommended by the police officers of the local police-boxes and organized into squads for each middle school district. Their average age was forty-nine, 85 percent were men, and nearly 50 percent were shopkeepers.[12] Like juvenile-unit members, they do most of their guidance work when students are out of school, during holidays or festivals. They talk to youths found smoking, loitering in undesirable locations, or doing other things they should not be doing. Youth assistants wear a badge and carry a card to identify themselves. The effectiveness of the volunteers varies from individual to individual and depends on the time they spend.

The police enlist the support of schools, workplaces, and families in their efforts to combat youth crime and delinquency. The police meet periodically with the principals of all schools in their jurisdiction to share information on offenses and other problems under the auspices of the police school liaison council (*gakkō keisatsu renraku kyōgikai*). A similar police workplace liaison council (*shokuba keisatsu renraku kyōgikai*) helps prevent delinquency among working youths. In actuality the police work closely with elementary and middle schools, but their relationship with high schools is often strained (the *honne* in police school relations). For example, if juvenile-unit officers notice a youth smoking, they take his cigarettes and counsel him not to smoke. They find out where he obtained the cigarettes and inform his parents of his behavior. If the student is in elementary or middle school, the police also call the student-guidance counselor of the school (*seito shidō shuji*) so that the school can also help prevent further delinquent behavior. If a high school student is caught committing an offense, however, the police seldom notify the school. The police say that high schools automatically punish students who commit offenses, and the punishments are frequently severe (such as a one-week suspension from school for minor offenses or expulsion for major ones).

11. *Police White Paper, 1976*, pp. 149–150.
12. Statistics provided by the Kurashiki police station, 1975.

Elementary and middle schools do not automatically punish students apprehended by the police for offenses. Thus, when a high school student is caught, the police prefer to handle the offense with the youth's family without involving the school. Student deans in high schools have privately expressed frustration when commenting on the lack of cooperation they have from the police.

A remarkable example of the use of schools for social control purposes occurred during the annual national high school baseball tournament in 1975. This tournament is the most popular sports event in Japan, except perhaps for the periodic sumo wrestling tournaments. One of the teams competing in the finals was disqualified because two students of the high school (not members of the team) were arrested for kidnapping a child and assaulting its mother.[13] The school bond is very strong in Japan, resembling that of the traditional village, and the peer and teacher pressure on students not to commit acts that would bring disgrace on the school harks back to the Edo period *gonin gumi* notion of collective responsibility for crimes.

WORSENING PROBLEM OF AUTO GANGS

A recent problem for the police in Japan is the rapid rise of youthful automobile gangs (*bōsōzoku*, "reckless driving tribes") since the early 1970s, coinciding with the general increase in automobile ownership. There were an estimated eight-hundred gangs with 25,000 members in 1975.[14] Most members are young company employees (over 60%) or high school students (over 30%), and besides racing on public roads, they have increasingly been committing robberies, rapes, and other crimes, as well as engaging in pitched battles with rival gangs. The biggest incidents occur during the spring and summer months, and the gangs have attacked police officers, patrol cars, and *chūzaisho* that have attempted to control them. For example, in one night in May 1975, forty-four police officers in the city of Kobe were injured trying to apprehend speeding gang members.[15] Several weeks later, 600 members of two rival gangs had a battle on a national highway near Kamakura, in which four autos were burned and another twenty-eight demolished and twenty-two people were injured,

13. *San'yō shimbun* (Okayama), 28 March 1975, p. 19.
14. *Japan Times* (Tokyo), 25 May 1975, p. 12.
15. *Asahi shimbun* (Tokyo), 19 May 1975, p. 23.

including five police officers.[16] In another incident in Niigata, gang members drove to a *chūzaisho* late one night and smashed all the windows as revenge because the *chūzai san* had ticketed them earlier. In Okayama, groups race their automobiles in front of the Okayama train station during the summer, spurred on by crowds of cheering young onlookers. Youths also race their automobiles at night on the broad Skyline Drive in the hills overlooking the Mizushima industrial complex, and they frequently stone police cars patrolling this highway.

The police made a survey of 741 members of young auto gangs in the summer of 1975 and inquired about their motives for joining. Forty-one percent said that they joined because "it was fun to be with large crowds" of other youths. When this response is added to those who said they did so because "everyone else was joining" (14%) or because they "wanted comrades" (11%), it is apparent that about 66 percent associated with gangs to find companionship in the increasing anonymity of urban society in Japan.[17] The same survey investigated the attitudes of the parents of gang members and found that 10 percent approved of their children's membership, 17 percent had simply resigned themselves to their activities, 28 percent were unaware of their membership, and 43 percent were opposed.[18]

The police have devised several strategies to suppress these unruly groups. They have increased their street-guidance efforts in places where the members congregate and have used the riot police to help stop the racing. Even more potentially effective, however, are the attempts to use informal social and family pressure to discourage youth participation and membership. The police have begun a "letter strategy" (*retā sakusen*) of sending letters to the families of youths identified as gang members, hoping to enlist pressure from the large percentage of parents who oppose these activities. They have also given the names of gang members and leaders to their schools and places of employment to increase social pressure. The police have called gang leaders into police stations for severe rebukes and have stepped up their information gathering on gang members and activities. Despite these efforts, however, auto gangs show no sign of abating in the near future.

16. Ibid., 9 June 1975, p. 23.
17. *Police White Paper, 1976*, p. 144.
18. Ibid.

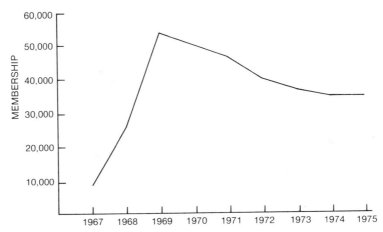

FIGURE 17.   Membership Strength of Radical Student Groups, 1967–1975
SOURCE: *Police White Paper, 1976*, p. 268.

STUDENT RADICALS AND THE RIOT POLICE

Groups of youths that present the strongest challenge to the police are the various factions of student radicals. Unlike auto gangs, they form groups based on ideology, and their core members are fanatical in their antipathy for the ruling political and economic establishment of Japan and the police who try to check them. The police must therefore use a different method to control radicals than they use with youthful delinquents or auto gangs: they adapt by employing overwhelming but well-focused and re-strained force through the renowned riot police.

As figure 17 shows, membership in radical student groups peaked in 1969 and has leveled out at about 35,000.[19] The apex of student violence was in 1970, and since then the scale and ferocity of student riots and school occupations has declined steadily. Although dropping in numbers, radical groups have tended to become more tightly closed and militaristic in their organization, and their tactics have exhibited terrorist and guerrilla characteristics. Student groups have carried out bombing campaigns against industrial targets and police facilities, and have rioted and thrown "Molotov cocktails" to oppose such events as the emperor's visit to the United States and a tour of Okinawa by the crown prince.

19. These figures, like most police statistics in Japan, are probably reliable owing to the wide network of informers available to police and the obviousness of radical-group member-ship because of helmets worn and frequent demonstrations.

The effectiveness of police crackdowns in the late 1960s caused many of Japan's hard-core radicals to flee the country, which then led to the international atrocities and incidents committed by the terrorist Japanese Red Army. In recent years, radical students in fiercely rival organizations have directed much of their violence to one another into bloody internecine clashes, destroying property and frequently injuring and sometimes claiming the lives of innocent bystanders. There were 229 such incidents in 1975, resulting in 20 fatalities and 543 people injured.[20] One leftist student of Okayama University was killed by rival radicals in 1975.[21] One of the largest internecine clashes occurred in July 1975, in which the two main rival student groups (Chūkaku and Kakumaru) accidentally met and fought in the Shinbashi train station in Tokyo, destroying train cars, killing 1 student, and injuring 45 people, including 9 innocent train passengers.[22] Police have intensified their efforts to stop these incidents because of their unsettling effect on the populace.

As was noted, the response of the police to radical student violence and other civil disorders was the formation of the famous riot-police units, known as the *kidōtai* ("mobile force"). This crack force was organized in 1952 to fill the peacekeeping gap left by the departing occupation troops and filled before the war by the Japanese army. The ten-thousand nationwide riot policemen, including three-thousand in ten units organized within the Tokyo Metropolitan Police Department, constitute a superbly trained body of police officers organized like military units, who can respond quickly and effectively to large-scale violence or other incidents. Riot policemen are mobilized most often to control riots and demonstrations, but they are also used, especially in the districts, to back up regular police officers in situations calling for their specialized training and ability to function as a coordinated group, such as in lifesaving activities, bomb disposal, traffic law enforcement, and patrolling en masse in entertainment and bar districts on Saturday evenings. In addition, the riot police in Tokyo provide guards for the national Diet building, the prime minister's residence, airports, and other locations subject to violent attack by radicals. They served as bodyguards for important government figures and visiting foreign dignitaries until a specialized police unit (know as SP, Special Police) was formed in late 1975 for this purpose.

20. Ibid., pp. 272–273.
21. *Asahi shimbun* (Tokyo), 14 June 1975, p. 23.
22. *Yomiuri shimbun* (Tokyo), 18 July 1975, p. 23.

Armored water cannon at a riot police headquarters, Tokyo. This vehicle was used in the seige on the Asama Sansō, during which a riot police commander was shot to death.

The full-time riot police in every prefecture are augmented by the regional riot police (*kanku kidōtai*), which is composed of select patrolmen, traffic policemen, detectives, and others from police stations who train regularly for riot police activities. In addition, many prefectures, including Okayama, have a reserve force called the second riot police (*dai ni kidōtai*), which is made up of other regular police officers who train only twice a month for riot duty. Complete riot-police uniforms and equipment for their use are stored in each police station. These reserve forces, composed of virtually all but the oldest police officers, account for the vast numbers of riot policemen often reported in the press as responding to large-scale incidents, such as the total of 160,000 riot policemen who mobilized to guard President Ford when he visited Japan in 1974.[23]

23. *Japan Times* (Tokyo), 16 November 1974, p. 2. Mobilization figures are often deceptive because each time a police officer is mobilized counts as another officer responding (e.g., 20 riot policemen mobilized three times for a particular incident is reported as 60 riot policemen mobilizing).

Riot policemen and "demonstrators" (other riot policemen in white helmets) in training exercise at the corps headquarters.

Regular riot policemen, who are mostly young men, live a highly regimented life and go through rigorous physical, mental, and tactical training daily. In Tokyo, the riot police begin a normal day in their walled compounds at 8:30 A.M., when they line up outside the headquarters for the flag raising and the national anthem.[24] They hear the plan of the day's activities over a loudspeaker, and about once a week undergo an inspection in this formation. If they have no assignments away from the headquarters, they spend the next two hours in the classroom for instruction on aspects of police work and law. An hour is used before lunch for activities such as uniform repair and cleanup. After lunch, they have two hours of riot training, which the police try to make as realistic as possible. Half of the men play the role of riot policemen wearing complete protective gear, and half play the role of student radicals by wearing helmets emblazoned with the symbols of radical groups, carrying bamboo poles with red flags attached, and throwing gasoline-filled "Molotov cocktails" and chunks of wood to simulate rocks. This training usually ends with all the officers and

24. This recounts the schedule of a day I spent with the Seventh Riot Police, Tokyo, 1975.

men (in complete armor) running several laps (about a mile total) around the open area inside the compound. The men then participate in judo and kendo practice in the martial arts hall until about 4:30 P.M. After soaking in the hot bath, they again line up in front of the headquarters building at 5:15 P.M., sing a police or other song to build morale, hear the plan of the next day's activities, and participate in the flag-lowering ceremony. The bachelors (the large majority of the men) live in a dormitory within the compound and are available for mobilization at any time. The commander lives in a house near the headquarters compound. A number of men are assigned to night duty each evening.

An actual student demonstration by the Kakumaru faction that I witnessed in Tokyo in 1975 will illustrate the techniques used by the riot police to control student radicals. The demonstration seemed formalized, almost as if it had been entirely rehearsed by both students and police. This was because the students, like the police, had practiced their tactics, and the same route had been used numerous times by the demonstrators. Both parties seemed to have an implicit understanding of what the other would do at each point along the demonstration route. It started with a three-hour rally in a park in one part of Tokyo, where student leaders whipped up the helmeted students with impassioned speeches and led them in practice "snake dances" through the park. Plainclothes security police stood beside a truck that carried a large sign listing the student demands, took notes on the speeches, and were completely ignored by radical students standing next to them holding the sign; there was no open animosity.

The students had to obtain advance police clearance on the demonstration time and route of march. The police allow demonstrators only along this one well-prepared route. At the specified time of departure from the park, the police announced to the demonstrators over loudspeakers that it was time to begin. The demonstrators (about 600 students) formed a long line, five abreast, led by a group holding bamboo poles from which red flags fluttered. A student sound-car blaring their grievances led the entire procession. The police separated the pole-carrying group from the rest of the column to prevent the marchers' massing behind the poles and using them as weapons. They also divided the column into two groups of about three-hundred each by inserting a body of police officers between them. A riot-police command vehicle, on top of which the riot police commander

The author participating in training exercise in full riot gear at the headquarters of the Seventh Riot Police, Tokyo.

stood in a small enclosure, moved in front of the pole-carrying group, and another drove at the end of the column.

A student leader, using a whistle to call cadence, walked backwards in front of the column of students, directing the movements of the column by grasping a thick bamboo pole, which the front five students held onto to keep in formation. The students behind them held onto the students ahead of them to keep a tightly massed and thus more powerful unit. The riot policemen also grasped the thick pole to pull the students up when they tried to sit down, and to pull them forward when they tried to stop. A riot policeman linked arms with each outside student on the right edge of the column, forcing the column against the curb guardrail on the left for better control.[25] (The guardrail is there obstensibly to protect pedestrians from

25. Riot policemen told me that having to link arms with the students is distasteful because the students hurl epithets at them during the demonstration. Those most often used are *porikō* (formed by combining the katakana syllables *pori*, short for *porisu*, or police, and the character *kō*, also read as *ōyake*, meaning government). They also call police *inu* (dog), *zeikin no inu* (tax dog), or *zeikin dorobō* (tax thief), a disparaging reference to the police as a waste of tax money.

traffic—but an important secondary purpose along this route in particular is to help contain demonstrators.) At each location where the route of march was supposed to change direction, massed riot-police units and armored buses blocked all other possible routes. Two flying squads of riot policemen trotted ahead of the demonstrators and formed barricades with their shields at small cross-streets to prevent any diversion of the march.

The riot-police command vehicles were equipped with loudspeakers, over which the police constantly warned the demonstrators of illegal movements (such as "snake dancing" to block traffic) and apologized to motorists for the traffic congestion caused by the demonstration. Whenever the demonstrators made an illegal move, scores of plainclothes police photographers took pictures for evidence.

When the demonstration reached its terminal point in another park several miles across Tokyo, the riot police created a funnel by lining up armored buses to channel the students into the park. A water cannon was ready in case heavy violence broke out. After the main group of students had entered the park, the pole carriers furled their flags and used the poles as lances with which to charge the police. The police used their metal shields to fend off the thrusts. The main group of students often bombard the police with rocks while the flag bearers charge the police with their poles, but such a fusillade did not occur this time. Other squads of riot policemen ran to seal off the other entrances to the park to prevent the students from leaving en masse. The demonstration ended with speeches, still fiery, by student leaders in the park.

The methods used by the police to control demonstrations and riots by student radicals are quite different from those employed to prevent other forms of youthful antisocial behavior. The police try to check juvenile crimes such as shoplifting or bicycle theft by apprehending the offenders and invoking the juvenile justice system, and also through the informal involvement of families, school, and the workplace and through general social pressure against deviancy. The same combined approach is used by the police in their efforts to control the increasing problem of young auto gangs. Student radicals present the police with a problem of a different nature, however, and they must alter their adaptive response accordingly. Young radicals seem to be motivated more by ideology and less by traditional Japanese values and norms than are the usual juvenile delinquents. Attempts to generate group pressure for reform or to shame them into conformity are usually ineffectual.[26] The police have responded by bringing the vast power of the state to bear on student radicals through rigid and formal law enforcement efforts by the formidable riot police.[27] Yet informal societal mechanisms are operative to an extent even among radicals, as is seen, for example, in the unspoken ground rules followed by both the students and the riot police in the demonstration described above. Radicals are, after all, still Japanese. Police reactions to leftist ideologies will be dealt with in later chapters; here we need only note that the tough riot-police response is prompted by the fact that the police perceive leftists as the greatest threat to themselves and peace and order in Japan.

In the next chapter we shall see how the approach of the police in dealing with two types of social outcastes, Koreans and *burakumin*, differs in ways that parallel the contrasting approaches by the police in controlling student radicals and other "regular" youthful offenders.

26. The police do attempt to involve the families of individual radicals in attempts to "rehabilitate" them, with limited success.

27. The rigor of law enforcement efforts by the riot police has been the subject of critical comment in the media and, on occasion, has led to legal problems for the police.

five

DEALING WITH SOCIETY'S OUTCASTES

The cultural and racial homogeneity of the Japanese people is often commented on. Japan's virtual isolation, caused by its geographic separation from the Asian mainland and 250 years of self-imposed seclusion during the Edo period, has allowed the Japanese to mingle and become one of the most thoroughly socially unified and culturally homogeneous large blocs of people in the world.[1]

There are exceptions, however. Some foreigners have been brought into Japan in this century through the creation of the Japanese empire, and the only sizable group of these are Koreans. They are physically almost indistinguishable from the Japanese, and their language is the most closely affiliated of the adjacent Asian languages.[2] Yet the 600,000 Koreans now resident in Japan have not been absorbed either culturally or racially into Japanese society. The ethnocentric Japanese try to keep the Koreans separate, make it extremely difficult for them to become Japanese citizens, and have discriminated against them socially and economically. The Koreans resent this treatment and past injustices suffered during the Japanese occupation of their homeland, as well as their being brought to Japan through force or fraud, and they often cling tenaciously to their cultural identity.[3]

Another exception to Japanese homogeneity is the survival from ancient

---

1. The general introductory remarks to this chapter rely on Edwin O. Reischauer, *The Japanese* (Cambridge: Belknap Press of Harvard University Press, 1977).
2. Joseph K. Yamagiwa, "Language as an Expression of Japanese Culture," in *Twelve Doors to Japan*, ed. John Whitney Hall and Richard K. Beardsley (New York: McGraw-Hill, 1965), p. 198.
3. Many, in fact, do not want to become naturalized Japanese citizens, even though they were born in Japan and speak only Japanese, because of the degree of their resentment.

94

times of a sort of outcaste group, which may amount to about 2 percent of the population, known usually as *burakumin* ("hamlet people").[4] This group probably had various origins, such as the defeated in wars and those who engaged in occupations considered particularly demeaning—for example, butchers and leather workers, because of Buddhist prohibitions on taking the lives of animals. They are not foreigners like Koreans, and are indistinguishable from other Japanese physically, culturally, and linguistically. Although no longer legally of outcaste status, they have been the object of extreme prejudice of all sorts. People are reluctant to have contact with them and carefully check family records before weddings to avoid intermarriage.

Koreans and *burakumin* are both, in effect, "outcastes" in Japanese society and subject to prejudice and discrimination, though the origins of their status are quite different.[5] The police must deal with both as segments of the community, but the nature and degree of their interaction differs, as one might expect. To state the conclusion first, there seems to be considerable social distance and little cooperation between police and the "foreign" Korean community, while there is much more interaction and understanding between the police and *burakumin*, though definite tension exists. This chapter will not explore in a general way the extremely complex Korean or *burakumin* problems in Japan, but will merely examine briefly how the police adapt to the special problems of police interaction with these two groups of people, especially as I observed it in Okayama.[6] It will shed some light on police relations with minorities in a society that is otherwise homogeneous and without sharp cleavages between classes.

POLICE AND THE KOREAN COMMUNITY

Koreans were brought to Japan in large numbers during World War II to replace the many Japanese workers fighting in the war. They worked as

4. For further information on *burakumin*, see George De Vos and Hiroshi Wagatsuma, *Japan's Invisible Race* (Berkeley and Los Angeles: University of California Press, 1972). I do not discuss the *ainu*, a proto-Caucasoid people now concentrated in the northern island of Hokkaido, who once populated all of Japan before the coming of the present Japanese. They too have been subject to discrimination in Japan.

5. I use the terms "outcaste" and "caste" in a loose sense and not as they are applied to the Indian caste system. There are some similarities, however, between the Indian system and the status of *burakumin*.

6. Discrimination against *burakumin*, and possibly also Koreans, is most overt and severe in western Japan (Kansai, including Okayama) owing to the high concentration of these groups in this region. Discrimination is probably more latent in the Tokyo area.

forced laborers in factories and in other unskilled jobs. For example, in the Mizushima industrial area that I studied, Korean laborers in 1941 were used to reclaim land from the Inland Sea and then to build on that land a huge Mitsubishi plant that produced aircraft for the war. There were fifteen-thousand Koreans in Mizushima during the wartime peak.[7] When the factory was destroyed in an air raid at the close of the war and its employees left the area, the Koreans moved into the nearby company housing as squatters and remain there today. There are now about four-thousand Koreans in Mizushima, divided almost equally between two mutually antagonistic neighborhoods of those whose families came from the northern or the southern part of the Korean peninsula. Their passionate allegiance to one or the other of the two rival Korean governments injects a disruptive element into Japanese society and politics and is a matter of police concern. Mizushima is said to have the largest concentration of Koreans in Okayama prefecture.

Koreans find it difficult to get desirable jobs even today in Japan because of lingering prejudice. Many are common laborers, scrap-metal collectors, shopkeepers, or run small Korean-style restaurants or bars. Most pachinko parlors in Okayama are said to be owned by Koreans, many of whom accumulated the wealth to buy them by running restaurants. Although income from these establishments can be high, their ownership is not considered socially respectable. Koreans have often been unsuccessful when applying for employment in large companies, essentially because of discrimination against them.[8] Japanese who live near Korean neighborhoods show their prejudice by often commenting disparagingly on foul odors or the run-down condition of many of the houses. Perhaps the most tragic example of the depth of Japanese prejudice was the massacre of many Koreans by rampaging crowds of Japanese after the great 1923 Tokyo earthquake, merely on the basis of wild rumors. Social and economic

---

7. Figures provided by police officers in the Mizushima police station, 1974.

8. The Yokohama District Court ruled in 1974 that a subsidiary of Hitachi, Ltd., had based its dismissal of a Korean employee, hired when he used his Japanese name on the application, on the invalid ground of "racial discrimination." It ordered the payment of a solatium and back pay to the Korean. The case caused wide sensation in the press. *Japan Times* (Tokyo), 23 June 1974, pp. 1–2. Article 3 of the Labor Standards Act prohibits employers from treating "workers differently in terms of their wages, working hours, or other conditions because of their nationality, creed, or social status." It is difficult to apply to the de facto discrimination usually encountered by Koreans, however.

discrimination results today in a higher than average number of families in Korean neighborhoods receiving public welfare payments.[9]

The Korean community is tightly knit, though there are no neighborhood associations like those found in most Japanese neighborhoods. Instead, community solidarity seems to focus on local chapters of the two rival Korean residents' associations (Mindan for South Koreans and Sōren for northerners). Korean schools also play a crucial role in maintaining ethnic identity and solidarity. In Mizushima, the North Korean neighborhood has a combined elementary and middle school, but the South Koreans have only a school that teaches children Korean at night. This probably indicates that the southerners are slightly less alienated from Japanese society because their children attend regular Japanese schools. Family ties among Korean residents are said to remain stronger than among most Japanese, and extend into their business ventures. Neighborhood leaders, or bosses, who also serve as the local heads of the Korean residents' associations, come from the more wealthy families. They often intervene when deviant behavior occurs in the community, and handle most problems internally. This is perhaps reflected in the fact that reported crimes in the neighborhoods I studied were below average.[10]

Instances of police interaction with the local Korean community can probably be best described as considerably less frequent than the average. On the whole, Koreans are not cooperative with the police, owing mainly to the Korean perception of them as agents of the Japanese establishment that has abused and oppressed them. They may also remember the brutality and excesses of the police during the Japanese occupation of their homeland.[11] In the South Korean neighborhood that I studied, there was an average number of houses designated by the police as crime-prevention checkpoints (*bōhan renrakusho*), but they were almost all the homes of Japanese shopkeepers. The police sometimes tend to aggravate the problem of social distance between themselves and the Korean community by occasionally betraying the prejudices they share with other Japanese, or through subtle harassment of the Koreans. I heard officers on more than one occasion comment on what they considered to be offensive smells or

9. From figures provided by the Kurashiki City Office, 1975.
10. Figures on crimes provided by the Mizushima police station, 1975.
11. I heard a young Korean professor tell of his grandmother's asking him when he was a child what was the most horrible and frightening thing on earth. When he answered, "a monster," she corrected him—"the Japanese police."

filth in the neighborhood and make remarks about Koreans they spotted driving expensive-looking automobiles. Some officers are unusually verbally abusive toward Koreans who are caught without their alien registration booklets or who commit other petty offenses. Most officers, however, try to be very proper with the Koreans and, in fact, sometimes complain of the extreme amount of tact they feel they must use when dealing with them. The police, in short, have few intermeshing ties with Korean neighborhoods like those that are so important to the police in most Japanese neighborhoods. The police are essentially outsiders, and their insular situation is disconcerting.

Despite discrimination, Koreans in recent years have not committed an inordinate number of crimes or caused excessive problems for the police. For instance, Koreans in Mizushima composed about 4.3 percent of the population in 1975 and committed 6.3 percent of the crimes.[12] There are also few Koreans in Mizushima who are young toughs (*chinpira*, as hooligans of any ethnic background are called) or members of gangster groups, and this was apparently true even immediately after the war when Koreans resident in Japan felt an explosive sense of liberation. However, Koreans as a whole in Mizushima were very troublesome to the police in the early postwar years, mainly because they operated in the black market and brewed bootleg sake to sell. In 1947, police officers from all over the prefecture were brought to Mizushima in rented trucks (the police did not have many of their own at the time) to clamp down on the bootlegging. Older police officers told me that they fought pitched battles with the Koreans and that the Koreans hurled rocks and even human excrement and urine at the attacking officers before they were finally overpowered.[13]

Probably the most delicate aspect of police concern about Koreans now is public security and the political overtones of the activities of organizations of Korean residents in Japan and overseas. People accused of being North Korean spies are apprehended periodically in North Korean neighborhoods, and the kidnapping of the South Korean opposition leader Kim Dae Jung from a Tokyo hotel by what was probably the South Korean KCIA caused great embarrassment for the Japanese police and the government. An even more disastrous incident for the police occurred in August

12. Based on statistics provided by the Mizushima police station, 1975.
13. Throwing heated excrement over the walls onto attackers was a traditional tactic used by defenders of castles in feudal Japan. Perhaps the same method was used in ancient Korea.

1974, when a young Korean resident in Japan stole a pistol from a *kōban* while the officers were sleeping and used it to try to assassinate the South Korean president, but killed the president's wife instead. To help in gathering information on the Koreans, several of the security police officers in Mizushima are fluent in Korean, and they can be seen visiting the neighborhoods regularly. Patrol policemen also report to the local security officers any tips they may glean while on their rounds.

Police relations with Koreans are difficult because they are, in effect, foreigners and do not share the norms and values of the wider Japanese society. Like student radicals, who are distinguished by ideology rather than ethnicity, they do not follow the unspoken cultural rules and do not submit to police authority in situations where most Japanese usually would. Thus, the police must employ different techniques in dealing with them as in dealing with the radicals. For instance, detectives have confided that Koreans arrested for crimes often obstinately refuse to confess,—like leftist radicals but unlike most other Japanese criminals— and that they must sometimes resort to the use of lie detectors in interrogations, devices that are infrequently used by the police in criminal investigations. As will be seen later, the criminal justice system in Japan is premised on the expectation that most suspects will confess early on in the investigative process, and indeed most actually do. The resistence of Koreans is galling and an affront to the police. But it is a reaction probably to be expected from an alienated ethnic minority.

POLICE AND *BURAKUMIN*

Burakumin differ from Koreans in that they are not a distinct ethnic group but are indistinguishable from the majority of Japanese in almost all respects. They thus share to a great extent the wider Japanese cultural and normative framework that colors their interaction with the police. Their dealings with policemen have a different flavor and are more extensive than the police contacts with Koreans. Yet similarities exist because the *burakumin*, too, have developed a strong sense of group identity and solidarity through subjection to extreme prejudice and discrimination over the years, which makes the police outsiders and cooperation with them suspect. Yet many do cooperate to one degree or another. With *burakumin*, at least, there may be the beginning of trends that might portend change in their economic, if not social, position and their sense of separateness and isolation from the rest of society. These may have profound effects on their relationship with the police and the authority structure that they represent, to the extent that these changes are ever realized.

The origins of *burakumin* are obscured in the distant past. In the Edo period, Japanese society consisted of four principal classes: warriors (*shi*), farmers (*nō*), artisans (*kō*), and merchants (*shō*). Below these came the outcastes (*senmin*), which were essentially of two types: *eta* and *hinin*. One explanation of the derivation of the word *eta* is that it came from *etori*, or a "feed catcher," because these people were engaged in obtaining meat and intestines as feed for the falcons and dogs of the feudal nobility (the character for *eta* means "filthy").[14] They also worked animal hides into leather products, which was associated with filth and uncleanliness because of Buddhist precepts against killing and eating animals, as was noted earlier. *Eta*, whose status was hereditary, were forced to live together in isolated areas and were forbidden to intermarry with other Japanese. *Eta* villages became refuges for outlaws, runaway samurai, or the destitute fleeing oppressive taxes, because the authorities would never attempt to follow them there. *Hinin*, on the other hand, included itinerant hunters and entertainers, bearers of the palanquins of feudal lords, executioners, and gravediggers. They also handled prisoners and served the feudal police as *okappiki*, or *meakashi*, in the often dangerous job of apprehending miscreant samurai. Like *eta*, they were not considered human and were classified as large four-legged animals by the Edo government. But *hinin* were not isolated in their own villages, and their status was not inherited or necessarily permanent: one fell into *hinin* status through misfortune, and it was conceivable that it could be overcome after proper purification.

The "castes" of *eta* and *hinin* were abolished by decree in 1871 after the Meiji Restoration, which ended their legal outcaste status but did not alter their economic or social conditions. They had no choice but to follow the same types of occupations as in the feudal period, to fill undesirable roles such as unskilled construction workers, stevedores, road sweepers, leather workers, or rag pickers. Because *hinin* did not congregate in one locality, owing to the diversity of their pursuits, and because their status was not inherited, they were better able to mix with the general population after the Meiji period. *Eta* (now better referred to as *burakumin*), however,

14. *Japan Times* (Tokyo), 1 January 1975, p. 6. I rely on this excellent article in several places in my general discussion of *burakumin*.

continued to be identified primarily by their village or neighborhood of origin, as well as occupation. Family registers kept in the city office noted their formerly outcaste status by the word *shinheimin* ("new commoner"), to distinguish them from the "old" commoners of the feudal period—farmers, artisans, and merchants. Discovery of such a reference would become an impenetrable barrier to marriage with an ordinary Japanese or to employment in a respectable company. In fact, it is still a barrier today. Although notation of formerly outcaste status is now prohibited on family registers, private investigation agencies are frequently employed to trace families to their villages of origin and thereby identify people of *burakumin* background.

Most identifiable *burakumin* are found today in western Japan, particularly along the Inland Sea. This reflects the fact that their status originated while this region was the social and political center of Japan. Accordingly, there are many of them in Okayama prefecture. In 1975 there were nearly five-thousand in Kurashiki City living in *burakumin* villages or neighborhoods, constituting about 1.2 percent of the population.[15] This does not include, however, an unknown but substantial number living in mixed neighborhoods and whose *burakumin* origins are undoubtedly known to their neighbors. Thus, the real proportion of *burakumin* in the Kurashiki population is probably much larger. I studied in some detail the largest *burakumin* village in Kurashiki, with about fifteen hundred inhabitants, as well as one smaller village, and these served as the basis of many of my observations.

The larger village is now actually two villages that were a single one a number of years ago. They adjoin each other, separated by an irrigation ditch. The land surrounding them is farmland, and many families farm part time while holding another job. One of the villages is much wealthier than the other, with nicer houses and more land. There is a sizable number of people receiving welfare in the poorer one. The village from which the two sprang has been in existence for several hundred years, though many newcomers moved into the wealthier village when Kurashiki began to mushroom in the mid-1960s. The village is divided into thirteen associations, which base membership on religious sect (ten are Shingon, one is Nichiren, and two are Soka Gakkai—all are Buddhist) and there is no single village association that unifies it. There are, however, many active

15. From documents supplied by the Kurashiki City Office, 1975.

groups for old folks, women, and children, organized on the basis of religion or by the Buraku Liberation League (Buraku Kaihō Dōmei), a national movement active in most such villages.

The police are particularly interested in the political infighting between the Socialists and Communists as they attempt to win allegiance of the *burakumin*. Most villagers in these two villages, especially the one that is better off economically, are conservative and support candidates from the ruling Liberal Democratic party. These villagers probably correspond to those affiliated with the traditional Buddhist sects of Shingon and Nichiren. A certain vociferous element, however, is loyal to the Japan Communist party and are the bitter enemies of those in the other, smaller *burakumin* village that I studied who align with the Socialists. The security police from the local police station spend a good deal of their time approaching informers within the villages, or those with ties to the villages who live elsewhere, to gather information on the machinations of these leftists.

Other branches of the local police also seem to have frequent contact with the *burakumin*. Police officers and other sources confirmed that the great majority of juvenile delinquents (said to be up to 80%) who are dealt with by the police in Kurashiki, as well as over half of the adults whom the police must handle for drunkenness, fighting, or similar conduct, are *burakumin*. In addition, the poorer half of the large village that I studied is reputed to be a gangster stronghold. Thus, juvenile officers and detectives frequently come to the village, and a sizable percentage of the *burakumin* report that they have opportunities to talk to police officers periodically concerning some sort of investigation.[16]

Yet, there is little overt cooperation in the village with the police. There is no crime-prevention association and few crime-prevention checkpoints (this may be due in part to the low incidence of crime in the village—outsiders seldom venture in because they would be conspicuous, and any *burakumin* committing crimes go to other neighborhoods to do so). Few residents participate in volunteer police-support functions, such as juvenile assistants (*shōnen kyōjoin*), and one *burakumin* who very actively participated reported being ostracized by his fellow villagers. Many *bur-*

16. This fact was discovered in the survey that I administered in this village as well as ten other neighborhoods in Kurashiki and Mizushima. Although only 38.3% said they had talked to a policeman in the last year (lower than the 48.9% average for all neighborhoods), roughly 40 percent of those were during an investigation (16% was the average for investigations in all eleven neighborhoods).

akumin actually tend to badger the police: I have seen drunks from the village stop while passing a nearby *kōban* on their way home from drinking in town to deride the police officers or simply rattle the windows and doors to taunt them. Some village leaders demand that the highest local police officials personally come to the village to inspect problems that they want the police to handle and which are normally taken care of by low-ranking officers, such as roads that need no-parking signs. Rather than stir up trouble, the police show great circumspection and usually comply tactfully. It is significant that, unlike Koreans, *burakumin* who are arrested for crimes usually confess readily. As Japanese, they share with the wider society values that the police skillfully play upon during interrogations. Thus, informal societal and cultural mechanisms can be effectively employed by the police in their dealings with *burakumin*.

Local and national government began to take active measures in the late 1960s to improve the lot of *burakumin*. For instance, in 1974 alone Kurashiki City spent about $3,500,000 to raise the standards of housing, education, and employment of *burakumin* up to those of the rest of society. Only about $150,000 came from the national government.[17] There has apparently been some progress, for many have noted that the mental frame of consciousness of young *burakumin* is changing and that they are trying to identify less with other *burakumin* and are said to feel less alienated or isolated from the wider society than do their elders, who are the most active in the leftist organizations and "liberation" movements. If this trend is, indeed, a reality and if it should intensify, it could have a profound effect on the Japanese police. With greater social and economic opportunities and less psychological barriers to advancement, this minority will probably be less involved in juvenile delinquency and other incidents that now consume such a large percentage of the efforts of the local police.

Perhaps such a projection is too sanguine. Prejudice against any minority, either ethnic, as against the Koreans, or more complex in origin, as against the *burakumin*, is likely to occur and be extremely deep-rooted in a homogeneous and vertically structured society like Japan. In the Edo Period and before, there was little loyalty to the nation, but a personal bond was felt to the feudal lord or to one's superior. Even in modern times until the end of World War II, the primary element of allegiance was a personal bond to the emperor rather than to the nation as an abstract en-

17. Figures provided by the Kurashiki City Office, 1975. (¥300 = $1.)

tity.[18] Indeed, the two characters used today for the word "nation" (*kokka*) mean literally "country" and "household." The pervasive and enduring familial and personal sort of relations that characterize Japan inevitably tend to aggravate prejudice against people seen as somehow different. We shall turn now to another type of nonconforming clientele of the police who are also treated as outsiders—that is, gangsters.

18. In the Meiji era, the emperor himself was thought of as a living state through the mysterious notion of *kokutai* ("national body").

six

POLICE AND ORGANIZED CRIME

During my fieldwork on the police, I had numerous opportunities to observe police interaction with *yakuza* (gangsters).[1] I was struck by the remarkable cordiality between gangsters and the police and the general openness of Japanese gangs. I shall give a few examples.

Police officials in Okayama prefecture told me that a large, gangster funeral would soon be held and said they could arrange for me to attend. On the appointed day, I went to a large Buddhist temple in Okayama City with a detective from one of the nearby police stations. Five or six American luxury cars with license plates from various prefectures in western Japan were parked directly in front. Black-and-white-striped funeral bunting was draped on the wall surrounding the temple courtyard, and the diamond-shaped symbol of Japan's largest gangster syndicate, the Yamaguchi *gumi* (gang), to which the local gang belonged, hung over the gate into the courtyard. Thousands of rings of artificial flowers lined the courtyard and were donated by small businesses, bars and cabarets, city assemblymen, and citizens. The courtyard was filled with hundreds of gangsters from all over western Japan, in dark suits, with closely cropped hair, all wearing black armbands and lapel pins declaring the names of their gangs. Dozens of gangsters were still arriving and were met with loud shouts of greeting (*osu!*) from the others in the courtyard.

1. Two of the few sources in English dealing with Japanese gangsters are Donald Kirk, "Crime, Politics and Finger Chopping," *New York Times Magazine*, 12 December 1976, pp. 60 ff., and George A. DeVos with Keiichi Mizushima, "Organization and Social Function of Japanese Gangs: Historical Development and Modern Parallels," in *Socialization for Achievement*, ed. George A. DeVos (Berkeley and Los Angeles: University of California Press, 1973), pp. 280–310.

Gangsters lining the temple courtyard during a gang funeral. Note the gang lapel pins and the flower rings donated as condolences.

A number of police officers stood across the street from the temple entrance watching the gangsters arrive, most of whom said hello to the police. Several of the gangsters from local gangs walked up to the police officers I was with and jokingly commented that they had carefully parked their cars in parking lots so they would not get parking tickets.[2] The police knew the gangsters by name and bantered with them. One of the policemen asked the gang leaders standing by the gate if I might go inside to watch the funeral, explaining I was a student from America. I was then ushered into the courtyard and led to the main temple building where I watched the ceremony, surrounded by the top gangster bosses from western Japan. After the ceremony, gangsters with armbands stood in the intersections near the temple and directed traffic as the other gangsters left, while the police continued to watch from nearby.

2. The police in some prefectures, including Tokyo, have resorted to towing away illegally parked gangster cars during funerals and other large ceremonies in an effort to harass the gangsters. See *Japan Times* (Tokyo), 28 November 1974, p. 2.

The openness of gangsters and their cordiality with police was manifest on other occasions. I went with police officers for casual visits to gangster offices (storefront headquarters of local gangs with signs in front bearing the name of the gang and its syndicate affiliation). I accompanied the police official responsible for gangster affairs in Okayama prefecture to the opulent homes of several gang bosses, and while I interviewed the bosses he chatted amiably with their underlings in another room. Interrogations of arrested gangsters which I sometimes overheard in the police station invariably involved constant joking. I witnessed a brawl in a restaurant between members of the same local gang, and the police merely tried to restrain the two fighting factions until the gang boss arrived to settle the dispute. The police officers called many of the gangsters by name while trying to restrain the combatants.

The police have extensive records on gangsters. Every police box and police station is equipped with a book that lists all of the gangs in the area, their members, organization charts indicating who is linked to whom through fictive kinship bonds, histories of the gangs, their major sources of income, and sometimes even photos of the gang members. Police officers say that they must have this kind of detailed information on gangs or they will be "ridiculed" by the gangsters during interrogations.

The openness of Japanese gangs and their relationship to the police are often baffling to Western observers and can only be understood when notions of American Mafia are dismissed from the mind and Japanese gangsters and police are seen in their own historical, cultural, and ideological contexts. Their cordiality does not necessarily imply corruption, as it might between American gangsters and police, and should not be confused with friendship, because definite tension exists between police and gangsters. Japanese relationships that are characterized by incessant joking, as is the relationship between gangsters and police, are usually marked by potential hostility. The relationship is mutually beneficial: police and gangsters each find it advantageous to maintain rapport and to enhance it with a façade of cordiality. This nucleus of goodwill and understanding seems to remain even when the police must severely crack down on a gang after a major incident. A complete rupture in the relationship would be counterproductive for both parties.

Police and politicians have used gangsters throughout Japan's modern history to help maintain social order, especially to counterbalance the burgeoning strength of leftists. Only since about 1960 have Japan's ruling circles begun to worry about the increasing power of gangs, especially large nationwide syndicates, and taken steps to suppress them. Yet, the continuing overlap of the traditional conservative ideals of gangsterism with the ideology of police officers, ruling conservative politicians, and large segments of Japanese society still fosters a degree of sympathy and attraction toward the world of gangsters.

WHAT ARE GANGSTERS?

Gangs per se are not illegal in Japan and have operated openly for centuries. Gangsters have traditionally been called *yakuza*, a word that is synonymous with gambling and takes its meaning from the worst possible hand in the Japanese card game *hanafuda*. The worst score is 20, which is the sum of 8 (*ya*), 9 (*ku*) and 3 (*za*). The term connotes the sympathetic notion that gangsters are losers in society, and affiliate with gangs because of their unfortunate circumstances. *Yakuza* are also referred to as *bakuto*, which means literally a gambler. A *yakuza* is not just any gambler or rough, but one who has formed a fictive parent-child (*oyabun-kobun*) or brother-brother (*kyōdaibun*) bond through a formal ritual closely paralleling the Japanese marriage ceremony. The core of gangs is the intense and binding patron-client relations that tie the members together in formal bonds of obligation and indebtedness.

The ritual for forming the fictive bonds is very formal.[3] It is usually performed at a Japanese-style restaurant on tatami mats, with participants dressed in ceremonial robes (*haori hakama*) and a go-between (*nakōdo*) to help perform and witness the rite. Printed invitations are sent out. An offering is first made to the Shinto god enshrined in an altar, which is set up for the occasion and before which the ritual is performed. The two men who will form the relationship are seated on the tatami with the go-between near them. If a brother-brother relationship is to be created, two wine cups are brought and sake, likened to blood, is poured into them. Each drinks one-half of the sake in his cup, and the remainder is poured into a deep rice (*domburi*) bowl and mixed by the go-between. If the participants are to be brothers of equal status, equal amounts are poured back into each cup, and they drink it, thus forming the bond. If the relationship is to be one of elder brother–younger brother, six-tenths of the

---

3. Details of gangster ceremonies and organization were related during an extensive interview with the boss of a gang of street-stall vendors (*tekiya*) in his home in 1975; he frequently serves as the go-between in fictive kinship ceremonies for *yakuza* throughout western Japan.

sake from the bowl is poured into the cup of the elder brother and four-tenths into the cup of the younger brother. In a parent-child bond, only one wine cup is used, and after the sake is poured in, the *oyabun* drinks one-half of it and either passes the remainder to the *kobun* to drink or has it refilled and passes the cup to the *kobun*, if he holds him in particularly high regard. After some brother-brother ceremonies, a third party of higher status than either of the participants and with no relation to them is asked to take the two wine cups and keep them. He then has the responsibility, along with the go-between, to mediate any disputes that might arise between the two fictive brothers. When two gang bosses form brother-brother relations, they usually keep their own cups and settle any problems between themselves by relying on the strength of their gangs.

Terms of address deriving from Japanese kinship relations are used within gangs. As was noted above, a gang boss is referred to as the *oyabun* ("parent role") of the gang, and is called *oyaji* ("father") when addressed by his underlings, or *ojiisan* ("grandfather") after he retires. The boss refers to his followers as *kobun* ("child role") or *wakaimono* ("youngsters"), whose chief is the *wakagashira* ("head youngster"). When a gangster collects his own followers within the larger gang of the *oyabun*, an *ikka*, or "a large household with several families," is formed. If he gathers enough followers, he forms a *bunke* ("branch household"), which is outside the gang of the original gang boss yet closely affiliated and subordinate to it. The gangster then becomes the *oyabun* of his own subgang. When a *bunke* is formed, the name sign in front of the gang office usually declares the gang's *bunke* status and the name of the main gang, or *honke* ("main household"). The *honke-bunke* terminology used by gangs is borrowed from kinship terms traditionally used to designate household relationships in farm villages and in certain urban commercial settings, as when a shop opened up a branch to be run by a former apprentice.

Edo-period firemen (*machi hikeshi*) are usually thought of as the spiritual predecessors of today's *yakuza*. There were forty-eight *machi hikeshi* gangs located in Edo in the early eighteenth century, with a headman leading each group. Under the headman were various followers linked in patron-client relationships and ranked in a manner similar to modern gangsters. *Machi hikeshi* worked as carpenters and plasterers on high-scaffolding construction jobs (*tobishoku*), a common occupation among modern *yakuza* as well, and mobilized as fire fighters only when fires occurred. When there was a fire, the *machi hikeshi* gang boss quickly

Gangster cleaning the car of the gang boss, in front of the gang office, Kurashiki.

decided the main goal for their fire-fighting, and the gang's standard-bearer (*matoi mochi*; each gang had its own distinctive standard and *happi* coats)[4] would climb to the roof of the target building and wave the standard furiously as a focal point while the gang members tore down the surrounding buildings and pumped water on the fire. For the sake of the gang's honor, he was never to descend, even if the fire began to consume the building.[5] If several gangs arrived at the scene at the same time, they would usually fight each other to determine which would have the glory of raising its standard. The open display of gang symbols by modern gangsters on their armbands, lapel pins, funeral bunting, office signs, and even gang flags probably has its origin in the *machi hikeshi* gangs of Edo. The honor and fame of the gang is the most important consideration.

A fascinating aspect of gangster lore that receives frequent attention, especially in movies, is *jingi*, or the code of morality and highly formal-

4. The *happi* worn by the *machi hikeshi* gave rise to the tradition whereby present-day volunteer fire brigades have their own *happi* with the brigade's symbol emblazoned on the back.
5. Ino Kenji, *Yakuza to Nihonjin* [Gangsters and Japanese] (Tokyo: Mikasa Shobo, 1974), p. 57.

ized words and actions of greeting peculiar to gangsters.[6] *Jingi* entails care and protection by the *oyabun* for his gang members and absolute loyalty by the *kobun* to their boss. If a gangster is disloyal to his *oyabun* or causes trouble for his gang, it has traditionally been considered proper according to *jingi* for him to cut off a joint of his finger to show repentance. Gangsters also have their bodies tattooed, sometimes the entire body from the neck down and from the elbows and knees up, to demonstrate manliness by stoically enduring the pain of application.[7] Because of the social stigma accompanying tattoos in Japan, they also signify a resolve never to abandon gangster life. The code of loyalty and the extremely honorific greetings of gangster *jingi* are said to closely resemble the morality and conduct of samurai on the battlefield. This is of significance because the Japanese police trace their spiritual ancestry to the feudal samurai.

Other groups besides *yakuza*, or gamblers, are lumped under the term "gangs" in Japan. Perhaps the most interesting are *tekiya*, or street-stall vendors.[8] *Tekiya* operate small, sidewalk stands serving simple foods late in the evenings in the center of cities and also stalls that sell usually shoddy and overpriced items at shrine festivals. *Tekiya* were more numerous during the desperate years following World War II, and now are frequently ex-convicts having trouble securing regular employment. The *tekiya* boss determines stall locations, which is crucial to the amount of sales. A new *tekiya* used to sell goods in the boss's stall for several years as an apprentice after forming the *kobun* tie, but this practice is now declining. *Tekiya* groups have their own formal turf (*nawabari*) and employ *yakuza* to protect it. *Tekiya* bosses in the Tokyo region are reputed to control *yakuza* bosses, but in western Japan there is a sharp distinction between *tekiya* and *yakuza*. Even though they are separate, *tekiya* bosses in western Japan serve as go-betweens and also sometimes hold the ceremon-

6. For a full discussion of the traditional words and actions of *jingi*, see Iwai Hiroaki, *Byōri shūdan no kōzō* [The structure of pathological groups] (Tokyo: Seishin Shobo, 1969), pp. 261–262.

7. A study by social scientists working for the police indicated that 42 percent of *yakusa* had cut off part of a finger and 10 percent had done so at least twice. Nearly 80 percent had been tattooed, and the motivation was usually cosmetic (53%). See Mugishima Fumio, Hoshino Kanehiro, and Kiyonaga Kenji, *Bōryokudanin no danshi to shisei* [Tattooing and cutting off of finger joints by members of criminal gangs], a pamphlet published by the National Institute of Police Science, n.d. Survey conducted in 1971.

8. Details about *tekiya* were supplied by a *tekiya* boss in Okayama, 1975. He gave me a *tekiya* handbook and several issues of the *tekiya* newspaper. He also suggested that much of the fictive-kinship ceremony employed by *yakuza* was originated by *tekiya*.

ial wine cups of *yakuza* bosses who have cemented fictive brother-brother relations, and hence can call on the *yakuza* for assistance if muscle is necessary to insure good selling locations for their followers. Traditional *tekiya* gangs were given a "democratic" window-dressing under pressure from the American occupation. They are now organized into "cooperative associations" (*kyōdō kumiai*), which require "association fees" instead of the kickbacks (*kasuri*) formerly exacted from outside *tekiya* who wanted to sell at a festival in a boss's area. The boss is termed the "managing director" (*rijichō*) of the association. *Tekiya* newspapers and handbooks advertise festival dates and wholesale outlets for goods, and even provide detailed instructions concerning the performance of *oyabun-kobun* ceremonies.

In addition to *tekiya*, juvenile-delinquent street gangs (*gurentai*, or more recently, *seishōnen furyōdan*), longshoremen, coal miners, and other unskilled laborers often utilize patron-client relations to cement gang or group membership. A recent survey indicated that up to 80 percent of Japanese construction workers still obtain employment through ties to labor bosses, especially those workers in the less economically developed regions of Tohoku and Kyushu.[9] Patron-client relations offer a degree of stability in these often insecure occupations. Juvenile gangs and groups of unskilled workers are usually not highly organized, nor do they have the deep historical traditions and ritual that are associated with *yakuza* and *tekiya*. Many *gurentai* groups have loose affiliation with *yakuza* gangs, and young *gurentai* who are particularly tough or intelligent are often inducted into a *yakuza* gang through formal patron-client bonds.

SOCIAL ORIGINS

Gangsters are drawn almost exclusively from the lowest levels of Japanese society, strata that are subject to severe prejudice and social and economic discrimination.[10] I was told by reliable sources that up to 70 percent of the gangsters in western Japan are of *burakumin* origin. Ethnic Koreans and Chinese, also subject to prejudice, join gangs in lesser numbers. Gangsters were not always heavily of outcaste origin, however. During the Edo period, most *yakuza* came from among lower-class samurai, farm-

9. *Japan Times* (Tokyo), 17 September 1974, p. 2.
10. Mugishima Fumio, "Sōshiki hanzai [Organized crime]," in *Hanzai shinrigaku: hanzai kōdō no gendaiteki rikai* [Criminal psychology: a modern understanding of criminal behavior], ed. Ako Hiroshi, and Mugishima Fumio (Tokyo: Yuhikaku, 1975), p. 301.

ers, artisans, and petty merchants fallen on hard times. In the Meiji period, new gangsters were usually members of the fallen samurai class and desperately poor farmers, fishermen, miners, stevedores, and other laborers. *Burakumin*, Koreans, and Chinese began to join gangs in increasing numbers only after World War II.[11]

Gangsters today tend to come from poor or single-parent families, are rejected by society when they are young because of criminal activities, and find it difficult to secure employment when they get older. Police surveys of gangsters indicate that 43 percent of the boys who become gangsters come from families with only one parent, a higher rate of broken families than for ordinary delinquents. They tend to have more brothers and sisters than the average. The occupations of the parents are of particularly low status: 58 percent hold some sort of blue-collar jobs or are unemployed, and only 13 percent are in white-collar jobs.[12] More gangsters tend to come from families in which the father or the mother is an invalid than do other delinquents. Those with records as juvenile delinquents are in the majority, and 43 percent of the gangsters surveyed had run away from home. Sixty-five percent have had less than the compulsory level of education, and this percentage rises to 80 percent with the inclusion of those who dropped out of secondary school.[13] Over half of all gangsters are unemployed when they join gangs, and those with economically insecure blue-collar or small-shop jobs amount to about 40 percent. They also characteristically become financially independent from their families very early. As a gang leader said in an interview with a journalist, "Who in this society is willing to give a fair chance to a teenager who has no education, no money, no family background? Nobody but us."[14] Gangs offer an income and a feeling of security and solidarity within the group for those who are isolated and lonely.

One of the gang bosses I interviewed in Okayama told me that he was born in a small industrial and fishing town along the Inland Sea. His father was very poor right after the war, and made his living trying to sell fuel to fishing boats coming to port. He said they had little food and ragged clothes. He dropped out of school and could not find a good job because

11. *Gangsters and Japanese*, pp. 13 and 262–263.
12. Mugishima, "Organized Crime," p. 301. These figures, and those that follow, are probably reliable. Police have extensive statistical data on gangsters, both those arrested and those not arrested, adding to the credibility of the information.
13. Ibid.
14. *Ann Arbor News*, 18 February 1976, p. 35.

of his lack of education. He liked to fight as a youth, was arrested several times, and was sent to a juvenile detention center twice. His older brother was a gangster on the island of Shikoku, and he decided to become a *yakuza* when he was about fifteen years old. He said he was attracted to gangster life because it was "beautiful." His father opposed his becoming a gangster because of his fear that his son would kill someone or be killed. He said his father still did not approve even after he became a successful gang boss. His wife had a similarly difficult childhood. Her parents and brothers and sisters all died when she was an infant, hence she never knew them. He said that his wife would like him to quit gangsterism and that he does not want his son to become a gangster. He said gangsters always end up causing problems for society, and he wants his son to get a stable job and not be "shiftless like a gangster."

Certain aspects of gangster subculture probably stem from attempts to compensate for their low social status. The manners of gangsters are usually impeccable when they are dealing with people they respect. For instance, when I visited the home of a gangster boss in Okayama, the boss and his immediate *kobun* came out to my car to greet me when I arrived (a favor usually reserved for only the most honored guests in Japan), and then formally escorted me to my car after the interview. Several of the gangsters stopped traffic so I could leave easily. While I was at his home, one of his underlings shined my shoes, which I had doffed while chatting with the boss in another room.

Gangsters are very concerned with "face" (*kao* or *mentsu*), and a gangster's power is directly related to his reputation. One of the bosses I interviewed bragged that he is nationally known, and said that when he goes to the national Diet building in Tokyo, the guards recognize him, salute, and allow him to go inside to drink coffee and chat with the Dietmen. Although this may be an exaggeration, it shows the longing of gangsters to be recognized and accepted by society. The surprising openness of Japanese gangsters, in sharp contrast with the secretive nature of the American Mafia, is probably a result of their desire for fame. The Japanese saying that "face is more powerful than money" (*okane yori kao ga kiku*) is taken to heart by *yakuza*.[15]

---

15. As an example of the function of money in the social status mechanism, the young men who operate pumping trucks that regularly empty excrement from the cesspools of homes, and who are invariably *burakumin*, have high incomes but are at the nadir of the social ladder. Many have new homes and drive expensive foreign automobiles.

Sign in front of pachinko hall, indicating that intimidation from gangsters will not be tolerated. The character depicted is stereotypic of gangster attire.

Another manifestation that probably arises as a compensation for social inferiority is the tendency of gangsters toward ostentatious display. Gang bosses have a penchant for expensive foreign automobiles, and one gang boss estimated that up to 70 percent of the *oyabun* drive such cars. A Lincoln Continental, a favorite gangster car, had a base price of $26,500 in Okayama in early 1975. Gangsters also prefer flashy styles of dress, and often wear colorful Hawaiian shirts, dark glasses, black shirts with white ties, or other unusual clothing.[16] Interestingly, a few lower-ranking

16. A cabaret in Kurashiki had a large sign in front proclaiming in detail the types of attire not allowed inside, almost all indicative of the local *yakuza* mode of dress (e.g., "no one who

young police officers dress in somewhat *yakuza* style of clothing on their days off.

SOURCES OF INCOME

Gangs engage in both legitimate and illegitimate activities to earn money. Police surveys indicate that only about a quarter of all gangsters make their living solely through illegal means. Members of one of the smaller gangs in Okayama prefecture entertain at bars in the city by singing and playing guitars, and several of the gangsters are said to be so good at it that the police once asked them to give a musical performance while they were incarcerated in the police station jail. Other local gangs specialize in loan-sharking or construction subcontracting. Some gangsters sell items such as picture frames or hand towels (*oshibori*) to restaurants and bars or work as common day laborers to earn additional income. The wives, parents, or other relatives of many gangsters, and sometimes the gangsters themselves, often run small restaurants or bars.

The police know a good deal about the personal lives of gangsters and how they obtain and spend their money. The average gangster uses from 70 to 80 percent of his income for pocket money and food.[17] About half live in their own homes with their families, but there are many among the lower-level younger gangsters who have no fixed place of residence. Forty percent live with a lawful wife, and 30 percent with a common-law wife; 10 percent have a specific girlfriend, and a number have a relation with several women.[18] Many of these women work as hostesses in bars or cabarets to provide the financial support for the gangster. Thirty percent of the lower-level gang members said that they support themselves financially, whereas 60 to 70 percent at the leadership level said that they did so.[19] The rest rely on others, including wives or mistresses, parents or siblings, or the gang itself. For instance, when gangsters must raise money for bail after arrest, 30 percent provide it themselves, and about 25 percent look to wives or girlfriends, 30 percent to parents or other relatives, and 15 percent to the gang.[20] Thus, many gangsters appear to continue significant

---

is tattooed, no one wearing *geta* [wooden clogs], no one wearing *zōri* [straw sandals], no one wearing short pants or knickers, no one wearing three-quarter-length sleeves, no one wearing white shoes, no one wearing dark glasses").

17. Mugishima, "Organized Crime," p. 303. As in the figures on the personal backgrounds of gangsters, I have no reason to doubt the reliability of these data.

18. Ibid.   19. Ibid.   20. Ibid.

interaction and contact with parents and other relatives even after forming
fictive parent-child bonds with a gang boss.

Gangs collect money from a wide variety of illegal activities. Most
gangs have income from skimming money from bars, restaurants, and
pachinko halls as payments for not disrupting business or for handling any
problems that occur at the establishments. Gangs also use threats in collecting debts for a fee (serving as *jidanya*, or "makers of compromise"),
deal in stimulant drugs and pornography, and engage in gambling. There
are no Okayama gangs that specialize in prostitution, as many gangs in
Osaka are said to do.

Officials note that gangs are changing their methods of illegal operations as Japanese society and economy changes. They are relying more on
sophisticated "crimes of intellect" (*chinōhan*), which are harder to detect
than extortion or threats, and are thus becoming more like the American
Mafia. Large syndicates are said to have connections with the world of
entertainment, including some movie companies, and are involved in ca-
sino and cabaret management in Korea, Taiwan, Hong Kong, the Philip-
pines, Singapore, and Thailand. They are also dealing in the importation
into Japan from these countries of such legal commodities as bananas and
folk art items and such contraband as drugs and firearms.[21] A Tokyo-based
syndicate is said to be operating in Hawaii a prostitution hotel and massage
parlors catering to Japanese tourists.

Gangsters are also beginning to operate as *sōkaiya* ("stockholders'
meeting specialists"), by buying a few shares in a number of corporations
and extorting money from the companies by threatening to disrupt their
stockholders' meetings, or offering to smooth the proceedings by intimidating dissident stockholders in exchange for a sizable payoff from the
management. This is in keeping with the practice of corporations before
the war to hire gangsters to help solve labor disputes by intimidating stri-
kers. Consumer groups complain that companies are hesitant to call police
when *sōkaiya* disrupt meetings, and that police are often slow to respond
once they are called. The power of *sōkaiya* is seen by a party held at a
large Tokyo hotel in 1975 in honor of the head of a famous so-called
economic research institute that was attended by officers of 450 leading
corporations and which netted for the *sōkaiya* boss about $100,000 in
"gifts" from those attending.[22]

21. *Yomiuri Shimbun* (Tokyo), 8 June 1975, p. 19.
22. *Japan Times* (Tokyo), 14 May 1975, p. 2.

A gathering of the main gang bosses of the Yamaguchi *gumi*. The head of the syndicate, Taoka Kazuo, is seated in a light-colored robe at the center.

Gangster income and strength have been enhanced by the nature of the national syndicates, which resemble large corporations to an extent. In the Yamaguchi *gumi*, for instance, the direct *kobun* of the boss (who are *oyabun* of their own gangs) meet on the fifth day of each month in the syndicate headquarters in Kobe in a sort of directors' meeting. They meet to plan syndicate strategy and solve problems, as well as to increase brotherly solidarity between the gang leaders. The local affiliates and the syndicate each issue a financial report once a year. The local gangs are expected to help support the syndicate through monthly levies averaging $1,500 per month per gang in 1976, in addition to a New Year's contribution of $150, a payment of $300 for each gangster released from prison, and money to help pay for the syndicate boss's inspection trips.[23] Huge increases in the expected contributions in the last few years have led to difficulty for some of the gang leaders in meeting their quotas.

The scale and organization of the Yamaguchi *gumi* is seen in the syndicate magazine (called the *Yamaguchi gumi jihō*), which is sent to all member gangsters. The 1973 New Year's issue pictured the brown syndicate flag in front of a display of *machi hikeshi* standards on the cover, and the syndicate creed was printed on the inside of the cover (the same creed is prominently displayed in every gang office). Two pages of New Year's greetings from the syndicate boss (with his picture) were followed by greetings from several of the top leaders of the syndicate and a few of the local gang leaders. A two-page article with photos described the third

23. Ibid., 16 April 1977, p. 12.

The New Year issue of the Yamaguchi *gumi* magazine.

gathering of the "National Narcotics Banishment and Purification of the Homeland League" composed of uniformed Yamaguchi gangsters from various parts of western Japan who gathered at a Shinto shrine in Nagoya. The article complained of police harassment during the function because the riot police had repeatedly warned them by megaphone, but it said that they answered back to the police by megaphone and had a successful gathering anyway. This article, like many of the earlier ones by various gang leaders, complained of being misunderstood by the police and the public, which is curious considering that gangsters are the ones usually selling drugs in Japan. A four-page legal section (called the "law classroom," *hōritsu kyōshitsu*) explained certain parts of the Code of Criminal Procedure and featured a photo of the Osaka Bar Association building. There was even a two-page poetry section with poems written by gangsters in the syndicate. Several pages of photos and announcements of fictive-kinship ceremonies, celebrations for gangsters released from prison, gang funerals, and the names of gangsters who had been imprisoned were located at the end of the magazine. There is a resemblance between this magazine and the periodicals published for their employees by large corporations and other organizations (including the prefectural police) in Japan. The gangster magazine, like the other house organs, serves as a socialization tool to inculcate the values of the organization into the members.

SHARED VALUES

A certain folklore has grown up around gangsters, and many Japanese identify positively with the values expressed in gangsterism. Gangsters represent the traditional Japanese core values of *giri* ("obligation and loyalty") and *ninjō* ("humanity and compassion"). They describe their world as that of *ninkyōdō*, or the "way of chivalry." Famous gangsters of the Edo period, such as Kunisada Chuji (1810–1850) and Shimizu no Jirocho (1820–1893), are the subjects of popular stories and movies extolling their Robin Hood–like images of protecting the weak of society against powerful tyrants and unjust government officials. Gangsters traditionally shared the tenet of not bothering "citizens under the sun" (*katagi no shu*, respectable people in normal society), isolating themselves in the shadows of society, and dealing only with people who sought out what the gangs had to offer. Gangs have long been tolerated by citizens and police because they were not perceived as a threat; they were seldom involved in street crime. Attraction to gangster ideals and the glamorous, masculine, physical gangster image is not limited to any particular segments of society, but seems to be most pronounced among the lower working classes, such as truckers.[24] This attraction can also be seen in the strong emotional appeal

24. Dump-truck drivers and drivers for small trucking companies, who, like gangsters, are often of low-class or *burakumin* origin, frequently embellish their vehicles with gangster slogans, such as *Tōkaidō hitoritabi* ("a lonely journey on the Tokaido"), signifying the loneliness or isolation felt by gangsters. Truckers also tend to attract attention by ostentation, not necessarily in their dress as do gangsters, but in the way they decorate their trucks with colored lights and hang chains and trinkets inside the cab. It is said that trucker subculture stems from the Edo-period palanquin bearers (*kumosuke*), who carried on their shoulders small basket-like chambers suspended from poles in which the wealthy would ride, and who sometimes robbed their passengers on remote stretches of highway.

to many Japanese of *naniwa bushi*, long ballads that often have gangster protagonists and themes stressing sadness, isolation, frustration, or loyalty and obligation.

Gangsters have long had a special relationship with conservative politicians because of their right-wing ideals. The creed of the Yamaguchi *gumi* illustrates their high-minded and traditional ideology:

The Yamaguchi *gumi* pledges to contribute to the prosperity of the national polity based on the spirit of chivalry.

Therefore, gang members are required to embody each clause below:

— Value highly friendship and unity in order to strengthen the group.

— Esteem fidelity and possess love when in contact with outsiders.

— Understand that elders come first and always show courtesy.

— When dealing with the world, remember who you are and do not invite censure.

— Learn from the experiences of your predecessors and strive to improve your character.

The gangsters, of course, do not always live up to their exemplary creed.

The Yamaguchi *gumi* creed of *giri-ninjō*, published in the inside front cover of their magazine.

Gangsters honor the emperor and are vehemently patriotic, as can be seen in the ceremonies to cement patron-client relations, which are almost always conducted before a Shinto altar dedicated to Amaterasu-omikami, the Sun Goddess and mythical ancestress of the imperial line. A large Japanese flag often is hung above the altar. Right-wing activists such as the Patriotic party (Aikokutō) have strong ties to gangs. Gangsters complain that they are misunderstood when they are reproached for their misdeeds, insisting that they are in fact protecting those aspects of Japanese society of the greatest worth.

Many police officers are attracted to gangsters because of their conservative orientation and emphasis on the traditional ideals of *giri* and *ninjō*. Before the war, gangsters supported themselves through legal means much more than gangsters do now, such as running inns or brothels, or acting as bosses of gangs of stevedores or miners. Local police chiefs and conservative politicians sent flower rings to gangster funerals and visited gangsters when they were sick, and gangsters would bring gifts to police officers who were to be transferred.

Rapport between police and gangsters has not been based solely on shared ideology—they have consciously cooperated with each other for their mutual benefit. Gangsters would get help from the police by having them ignore some of their less serious illegal activities, or by informing the police about the crimes of rivals in order to have them arrested. The government, in turn, has relied on gangsters as disciplined fighting forces since at least the beginning of the Meiji period. In the civil war that led to the end of the Tokugawa government and reestablished the emperor as the supreme authority, the armies of the Tokugawa and of the Meiji emperor both tried to enlist the assistance of such famous gangsters as Shimizu no Jirocho.[25]

A remarkable example of the degree to which police and conservative politicians have relied on gangsters for social control occurred in 1960 during the violent disorder surrounding the renewal of Japan's security

25. DeVos, "Organization and Social Function of Japanese Gangs," p. 291. *Yakuza* organization is said to have originated toward the end of the Edo era (*bakumatsu*). People who were taken out of their family register, or who were never listed there (*mushukunin*, "a person without a house"), gathered together and formed gangster groups and supported themselves by managing gambling houses. They were found particularly in the shogun's private lands around Edo (Kanhasshu) and in the Tokai region, where governmental authority was looser than in the fiefs of *daimyō*. In these areas, they often served as the officially authorized *okappiki*, keeping public order in the locality.

treaty with the United States and the scheduled visit to Japan by President Eisenhower. According to one account, the plan for the visit called for President Eisenhower and Emperor Hirohito to ride in an open car in a parade from Haneda Airport to the Imperial Palace, a distance of about eleven miles.[26] It was estimated that eighteen thousand police officers would have to be stationed along the route to provide adequate protection, but judging from the masses of demonstrators surging around the Diet building for weeks in opposition to the treaty renewal, the police were convinced they did not have enough men to insure the security of the visit.

Leaders of the Liberal Democratic party approached Kodama Yoshio,[27] a right-wing boss with extensive ties to gangsters, and asked him to enlist the aid of the underworld in controlling the anticipated violence of the leftists.[28] He met with several of the strongest gang bosses in the Tokyo area, and they agreed to assist. In subsequent secret meetings between Liberal Democratic leaders and the gangster bosses, it was decided that it would be possible to secure the help of roughly twenty-eight thousand gangsters, about four thousand members of right-wing political groups, and several thousand people affiliated with other organizations.[29] The plan involved a full-scale mobilization: the gangsters prepared banners, arm-bands, and lapel pins; arranged for a helicopter and a Cessna to drop handbills; prepared food, sound trucks, and trucks and cars to transport gangsters; set up a command post in an inn near the parade route; and organized a squad of women to distribute rice to the gangsters. This preparation was all completed in about ten days.[30] The gang bosses agreed to absorb all costs of the operation.

The plan called for the gangsters to divide into a number of smaller units of about three thousand each, distributed at various strategic spots along the route to be ready for trouble, and for the rest to mingle with onlookers in order to intimidate the demonstrators. This massive mobilization was never fully implemented, however, because President Eisenhower canceled his visit. But it dramatically demonstrates the degree of

26. *Gangsters and Japanese*, pp. 254–258.

27. Kodama Yoshio is known most recently because of the central role he played in the Lockheed bribery scandal of 1975–76, when he demonstrated his pervasive influence in conservative politics in the postwar period.

28. Some observers say that the gang bosses volunteered their services to the Liberal Democratic party without being solicited, because of their revulsion toward the disruption caused by leftist demonstrators at the time. See *Gangsters and Japanese*, p. 255.

29. Ibid., pp. 255–256.

30. Ibid., p. 256.

cooperation between police, politicians, and gangsters at the high point of their cordiality.[31]

EFFORTS TO FIGHT GANGSTERS

Even while the police and politicians were relying on the underworld to help suppress leftists, they began to be alarmed at the increase in the number of gangs and gangsters. In the early 1960s they came to the belated conclusion that changes in Japan's economic, social, and political structure after the war had caused gangsters also to change, and that, in reality, they were now merely criminals (the *honne*) with a glamorous façade of *giri* and *ninjo* (the *tatemae*). The police stopped using the term *yakuza* with its appealing *ninkyōdō* overtones and began calling gangs *bōryokudan* ("violence groups"). The police also started to compile information on gangs and to circulate the data throughout the land. Nationally coordinated crackdowns were started, destroying many small gangs and forcing the surviving ones to join large syndicates to better withstand the police pressure. This had the unforeseen consequence, however, of increasing *nawabari* ("turf") wars between small independent gangs and those affiliated with the large syndicates that were attempting to invade their territory. This violence, in turn, led to demands for harsher police crackdowns on gangs.

The police, for the first time, initiated a citizens' movement to drive out gangsters, in about 1960, coinciding with the rapid growth of national syndicates. The movement has been based mainly on voluntary neighborhood and small-business crime-prevention associations. Signs have been posted on business establishments and in neighborhoods declaring that violence by gangsters would not be tolerated, handbills have been distributed, and city and town assemblies have been urged to pass periodic resolutions condemning violence by gangsters. The police have organized meetings for citizens in neighborhoods and have held seminars at police stations for owners of bars, cabarets, pachinko halls, and other establishments especially prone to gangster intimidation to encourage them to report to the police any violence or threats from gangsters. Editorials in

---

31. The police also used gangsters immediately after World War II to help suppress the Koreans, who were organizing and causing problems in the general chaos following defeat. Police and politicians are said to have secretly encouraged the growth of the fledgling Yamaguchi *gumi* in Kobe after the war for that purpose.

newspapers and on radio and television have urged citizens to cooperate with the police.

A fascinating example of how a crime-prevention association fought efforts of gangsters to infiltrate a bar district in Mizushima was related by the leaders of the association. Particularly interesting is the degree to which the police allowed and even encouraged bar owners to handle the problem themselves through mutual help. The restaurants and bars in the area are comparatively new, and a branch (*bunke*) of a Mizushima gang decided to open up an office in the neighborhood to extort money from them. The gangsters went around to all of the bars and restaurants, introducing themselves, saying they would soon open up a local gang office, and inviting the owners to provide them with congratulatory gifts of money and festive flower rings to place in front of their office. Instead of accommodating them, the owners decided to unite and fight the gangsters, so they formed a crime-prevention association. The association placed signs near the entrances of most of the establishments declaring that gangsters and violence would not be tolerated, and they set up a system of bells, to be rung in times of emergency, linking all of the bars. The head of the association is a bar owner who holds a black belt in *shōrinji kempō* (related to karate), with enough physical strength to give pause to most gangsters.

The gangsters tried to destroy the association through various stratagems. They first tried to intimidate the bars one by one into paying protection and thus break the association's unity. Several gangsters would enter a bar and sit on either side of a customer and stare at him until he became nervous and left. Soon the bar would be empty. The owner would ring the bell when this happened, and the owners of the neighboring bars and restaurants would run to the bar and force the gangsters to leave. The gang boss alternated threats of violence with flattery to try to convince the head to disband his association. He once came into the association head's bar, ordered a drink for himself and the owner, then proposed that since both were bosses of organizations, they should work together instead of against each other. The gangsters attempted another ploy by recording the closing times of the bars and reporting to the police when the bars were late; the gang boss told the association head that they would stop informing the police if the association would cooperate with the gangsters (the police said they ignored the gangsters' tips). The gang even tried pleading on one

Two bar owners, leaders of a Mizushima crime-prevention association that confronted gangsters. They are in front of the "snack" (a bar serving light snacks) belonging to the leader on the left. The sign to their rear, near the entrance, was posted by the association in front of all member establishments; it declares gang violence will not be tolerated.

occasion: the boss came to the association head and asked him to take down the anti-gangster signs from the bars for just one day because the boss of the largest gang in Okayama was soon going to visit the local gangster office. He said he did not want to be embarrassed by his gang's lack of strength that was manifested by the numerous signs. The signs stayed up. The gang eventually made some inroads with a few bars owned by people with gangster leanings, but the situation was still a standoff between the gang and the association when I left Kurashiki.

The police have intensified their anti-gangster campaigns since 1975 because of sharp increases in intergang warfare caused by the continued expansion of large-scale syndicates and, more recently, a power struggle growing out of the declining health of the boss of the Yamaguchi *gumi*. Shoot-outs between gangs have occurred on city streets, and innocent bystanders and police officers have been wounded, in gross violation of the old *yakuza* tenet never to bother citizens in normal society. The police have reacted by trying to embarrass and isolate gangsters, both powerful weapons in closely knit Japanese society. Landlords have been encouraged not to renew the leases for gang offices. Citizens have been urged to ostracize gangster families by not allowing their children to play with the children of gangsters and not offering the customary greetings to the wives of gangsters when they go shopping.[32] The police are also trying to harass gangsters by requiring permits before gangs can stage elaborate funerals or celebrations for the installation of new bosses.[33] Gang bosses have even been summoned to police stations for humiliating tongue-lashings and denunciations by police officers.

The police make periodic raids on gangster headquarters throughout Japan, rounding up hundreds of gangsters and seizing drugs, illegal firearms, and swords. However, these raids assume an almost ritual air because most of the gangsters are released in a few days through lack of evidence of criminal acts or because their offenses were minor. It has been remarked by observers, including police officers, that many of the gangs usually receive warning before these massive raids and that most of the weapons and evidence of wrongdoing are concealed and the highest bosses go into hiding. A police officer confided that they are usually allowed by the gangsters to confiscate a few guns during these raids to save face.

The police turn over to tax officials figures of estimated illegal income obtained from statements made by gangsters during interrogation, and after allowances are made for "business expenses," the tax agency tries to collect. For example, in 83 cases investigated by police between 1973 and 1975, $6,331,000 in income from illegal means was documented, but only $2,532,000, or 40 percent of the reported total, was considered taxable because $3,799,000 was recognized by the National Tax Agency as necessary expenses. Included in the deductible expenses were rental of facilities for gambling, per diem allowances for gangsters sent out for intimidation purposes, payments for lookouts during illegal gambling sessions, and reported expenses of pimps.[34] Tax authorities said that they obtained more than 8 million dollars in taxes from gangs in 139 separate cases in

32. See *New York Times*, 17 March 1977, p. A-8, and *Time*, 17 October 1977, for recent developments in public attempts to harass gangsters.
33. *Japan Times* (Tokyo), 30 June 1977, p. 12.
34. *Pacific Stars and Stripes* (Tokyo), 9 July 1975, p. 23 (from an Associated Press wire dispatch). The article continues, "The officials said that the income of organized crime is considered taxable and that those who pay the tax can make deductions for business expenses in the same way legitimate businesses do. Under relevant tax laws, all incomes, regardless of whether they have been obtained by illegal means, are considered taxable."

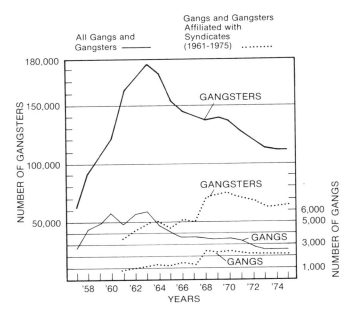

FIGURE 18. Changes in the Number of Gangs and Gangsters, 1957–1975
SOURCE: National Police Agency, ed., *Keisatsu hakusho, 1978* [Police white paper] (Tokyo: Okurasho Insatsukyoku, 1978), p. 22.

1974 alone.[35] The combined efforts by citizens, police, and other governmental agencies have been generally successful. The postwar peak in 1963 of 6,000 gangs and 180,000 gangsters has declined by almost half since then. (See figure 18) However, the strength of nationwide syndicates has increased correspondingly, and these syndicates, with their greater resources and stronger organization, are much more difficult to root out than the small independent gangs of the past.[36]

Despite postwar changes in gangsters and despite increased police crackdowns, rapport still exists between police and *yakuza*. Many police officers remain attracted to gangsters, and gangsters often identify with certain aspects of the police image. For instance, the gangsters in a gang

35. *Ann Arbor News*, 18 February 1976, p. 35.
36. Between 1964 and 1973, the total number of gangs declined from 4,573 to 2,723 (a decline of 41%), and the total number of gangsters dropped from 177,035 to 114,506 (down 35%). During the same period, however, the number of syndicates rose from 1,242 to 2,032 (up 61%) and the number of gangsters affiliated with large syndicates climbed from 49,609 to 64,506 (a rise of 77%). *Police White Paper, 1974*, p. 170.

office that I visited in Okayama were all wearing blue fatigues that looked exactly like those worn by the paramilitary riot police. This is noteworthy because the riot police are the chief postwar repository of the ideals of patriotism and absolute loyalty of the prewar police and army. As police efforts to control gangsters become more strict, general cooperation between gangsters and the police appears to be declining. Cooperation now tends to be based almost solely on personal bonds formed between individual police officers and gangsters in the course of prolonged contact during investigations.

Older gangsters express frustration because politicians encouraged gangs to grow in order to counterbalance the power of leftists and then abruptly changed their attitude in about 1960 and urged the police to crack down on them. They feel that they have been used by those in power and then discarded when they were no longer useful. Japan's gangster underworld is unlikely to disappear in the near future. Gangsters come from those strata of society that feel isolated, unwanted, and like outsiders. The essential issue in controlling gangsters is how to integrate social outcastes into the normal world, which is a problem that must be faced by Japanese society and not just the police.

seven

HANDLING SPECIAL PROBLEMS

Policemen in *kōban* and *chūzaisho* are the first to react to almost any incident that occurs in their jurisdictions. Many matters can be resolved by patrolmen alone, but the more specialized and complex ones must be handled differently. The police adapt to specialized problems and crimes by rapidly referring them to police specialists. The police are divided according to function into different specialized branches, all of which operate at the local level out of the central police station.

Most citizens have much less contact with police specialists than they have with the patrolmen in the neighborhood *kōban*. Yet these specialists are a part of a unified police organization, and the way in which they perform their jobs reflects on the citizen perception of the entire organization. They, in turn, must rely on the community—even more than patrolmen must—if they are to operate effectively. Because they are not regularly deployed throughout the jurisdiction, they must rely on a network of informants and citizens willing to assist them. This is particularly true of detectives, crime-prevention police, and security police. This chapter will focus on these three specializations and how they adapt to community and societal norms and values.

DETECTIVES

Whenever a crime occurs, the criminal investigation section of the police station becomes involved. In Kurashiki and many other police stations in Japan, criminal investigation is divided into three main branches: gangster-related crimes and "crimes of intellect" (*chinōhan*, or white-collar crime), handled by section two; all other crimes, by section one; and

130

criminal identification (*kanshiki*). The stationhouse jail (*ryūchijo*, or *buta bako*, "pig box," the slang term) is also under the jurisdiction of criminal investigation.

One of the most important aspects of the job of detectives (*keiji*) of both sections one and two is "cultivating the field" (*hatake wo tagayasu*), that is, nurturing their informants or tipsters. Young *keiji* are exhorted to enlarge their "field," because "if the field is large, then the harvest is large."[1] Detectives spend a large part of their time visiting with their tipsters (called *kyōryokusha*, "cooperators") to deepen their personal bonds of friendship and obligation (*giri*). Whenever there is a death in the family of a tipster, a marriage, or any other event, the *keiji* always comes with an appropriate gift to symbolize the relationship. Cultivating the field involves spending a large amount of off-duty time with many *kyōryokusha*, usually at night, drinking, playing Mah-Jongg, and the like. The *keiji* work hard to build relationships of mutual confidence so that the tipster will provide information should he or she become aware of a crime. The *keiji* continue the agricultural analogy by stating that this investment is similar to the long hours spent by a farmer weeding and fertilizing his fields.

The "field" of a *keiji* consists of various types of collaborators or tipsters: people who run bars, bar hostesses, managers of rooming houses, pachinko hall operators, volunteer probation officers (*hogoshi*) and welfare workers (*minseiiin*), or pawnshop proprietors. They frequently start the relationships by chance, when the tipster is a witness to or victim of a crime. The relationship is carefully nurtured by the *keiji* until the tipster is indebted and willingly assists him. The police are not insincere in their relationships of friendliness with collaborators; if they were insincere the relationship would not develop. The relationships of *keiji* with their informants typify the ideals of *ninjō*, especially in terms of the kindness, sympathy, or tenderness that is implied in the concept. The police emphasis on *giri* and *ninjō* appeals to Japanese with a traditional or conservative orientation, especially gangsters (*yakuza*) and their ilk.

The *keiji* recruit a high proportion of their tipsters from people they themselves have arrested, interrogated, and created affective bonds with. The method of interrogation used by *keiji* creates emotional ties, which are strengthened in those instances when the *keiji* look out for the family

1. Interview with criminal investigator, Kurashiki police station, 1974.

232 / POLICE AND COMMUNITY IN JAPAN

of the criminal while he is imprisoned. For instance, the *keiji* of the Kojima police station in Kurashiki City gathered over a hundred items of
clothing and school supplies at Christmas in 1973 for families of imprisoned criminals whom they had arrested.[2] Such convicts are deeply grateful
to the *keiji* for helping their families, and many willingly assist the police
after they are released from prison. I read several letters written by convicts from prison to the *keiji* who had handled their cases in Kurashiki.
The men thanked the *keiji* for doing their jobs, said they frequently reflected on the *keiji*'s counsel while in prison, and had resolved to change
their lives.[3] The *keiji* help the ex-convicts adjust to society after their re-
lease, a problem compounded by the fact that Japanese companies have a
strong aversion to hiring people with criminal records. Lack of stable employment for ex-convicts is a major factor in Japan's high rate of recidi-
vism.

Cultivating a field of informants takes time, and *keiji* are frequently
assigned to one police station for a longer time than the policemen of other
specializations. In Kurashiki, for instance, six of the twenty-eight *keiji*
have worked in the police station for over fifteen years, three of them for
over twenty-five years. The most senior *keiji* had been in Kurashiki for
thirty-three years in 1975.[4] Many of the police officers of other specializations who have worked in Kurashiki for long periods have spent portions
of their careers in Kurashiki as *keiji*. The lengthy time spent by detectives
in one police station is significant because the norm is to transfer policemen to another location every five or six years, as we shall see later.
Command-level officers are transferred even more frequently. The policemen with the longest time in the police station are never command officers, but are in key positions to employ their extensive contacts and deep
knowledge of the jurisdiction.

The cases to which criminal investigators must turn their attention and
resources cover a wide range. For instance, *keiji* always change into their
fatigues (similar in appearance to the riot police uniform) and go to fires
to sift through the ashes and determine the cause of the blaze. They are
also involved, especially in industrial areas like Mizushima, in establishing the cause and assigning blame in industrial accidents that result in

2. *San'yō shimbun* (Okayama), 10 December 1973, p. 4.
3. Letters from three convicts, copies of which were given to me by criminal investigators
of the Kurashiki police station, 1974.
4. From documents supplied by the Kurashiki police station.

injury or death. This can often be very complex, and outside experts are frequently asked by the police to assist in investigations. These wide-ranging investigative duties have antecedents in the vast powers and extensive areas of responsibility of the prewar police, and find legal basis in the broad concept of the offense of negligence (*kashitsu han*) in the Japanese Penal Code.

When a crime has been committed, the detectives mobilize their network of informants and use other investigative techniques until they have a suspect. If there is not sufficient evidence to make an arrest (*taihō*), they will often request a "voluntary" appearance (*nin'i dōkō*) by the suspect to the police station to answer some questions. Without a warrant, they cannot compel him to appear, but most people readily comply. This chapter will not consider the rights of the accused in Japan, but will focus on the techniques used by detectives during their interrogation of a suspect.[5] This will shed light on how individuals perceive themselves and their position in relation to police officers, and also on the use of traditional norms and values of Japanese society by police officers in the course of their official duties. An actual case investigated by detectives in Kurashiki will serve as an illustration.[6]

In the middle of May 1974, an electronic watch was reported stolen from a chemical-company dormitory in Kurashiki. The police began an investigation by going to pawnshops in the area and notifying them to be on the lookout for the watch.[7] In November, a pawnshop owner was about to sell a watch in pawn from a person who had not repaid the loan. A *keiji* dropped in the pawnshop on one of his periodic visits, looked through the register, and recognized the watch as similar to the one stolen.

5. For further information on the rights of the accused in Japan, see generally George M. Koshi, *The Japanese Legal Advisor: Crimes and Punishments* (Rutland, Vt., and Tokyo: Charles E. Tuttle Company, 1970); B. J. George, Jr., "Impact of the Past upon the Rights of the Accused in Japan," *American Journal of Comparative Law* 14 (1965–66):672; and Shigemitsu Dando, *Criminal Procedure*, trans. B. James George, Jr. (South Hackensack, N.J.: Fred B. Rothman and Company, 1965).

6. Related to me by a criminal investigator, Kurashiki, 1975.

7. *Keiji* always go to pawnshops and check the register of pawned items whenever there is a burglary. Pawnshops are a traditional institution in Japan, lending money at an interest rate set nationally. In Kurashiki, pawnshops do most of their business by buying and selling telephones. When an item is pawned the individual must sign his name, address, and put his fingerprint in the register. The *keiji* make their rounds of pawnshops frequently to check the register. When a stolen item is found in a pawnshop, the pawnshop owner suffers the financial loss. Frequently the person whose item was recovered will pay the pawnshop owner one-third to one-half of the money he lost; also, the friends or relatives of the thief sometimes compensate the pawnshop owner.

The *keiji* investigated the person who pawned the watch and found that he worked next door to the dormitory where it was stolen. The *keiji* checked into his family background, employment, and criminal record (he had no previous record). He was nineteen years old. The *keiji* found that he was not a very serious worker at his company; of the five people in his family, his father was an invalid, and his mother was living with another man. He was the financial provider for the family. The *keiji* discussed the case with the head of criminal investigation at the police station, and they decided he was the kind of person to commit such a crime.

The *keiji* showed the watch to the victim, but since he could not make a positive identification, an arrest warrant could not be issued. The police went to the suspect's house, invited him to come to the police station for questioning, and he complied.

Two *keiji* took the young man into one of the small interrogation rooms of the criminal investigation section (it has a table with a chair on either side of it; the suspect is seated so that he cannot look out the window and thus be distracted) and asked him to tell them all the bad things he had done recently (they did not mention the stolen watch lest he would talk only about the watch, and leave them unaware of any other crimes he may have committed). He denied any wrongdoing.[8]

The *keiji* used two lines of questioning. They would yell at the suspect when he refused to admit he had done wrong, and then would change to a sympathetic *ninjō* approach in order to establish heart-to-heart rapport. When they yelled, they would use very rough language in Okayama dialect. The *ninjō* method was to show they understood his difficult family background and felt sorry for him. They said it was unfortunate that he could not spend his money on an automobile and skiing like other youths. They talked about the consequences of being a thief—he would have difficulty in getting married, and it would affect his children (they could not get married or hold good jobs).[9] They said he was still young and could change his life if he tried.

8. Only when a formal arrest has been made are the police required to advise a person that he does not have to make a confession. The police circumvent this by requesting a "voluntary" appearance for questioning without actually arresting him. They then arrest him after he has admitted the crime.

9. There is a strong social stigma against people with criminal records, which extends to the entire family. The Japanese have a saying that "a thief influences the third generation" (*nusutō wa sandai tataru*), i.e., even the grandchildren of a thief feel the consequences. In the Edo period, two black stripes were tattooed on a thief's forearm to identify his misdeeds publicly.

After half a day, they convinced the young man that they indeed knew of his misdeeds. The fellow faintly said, "I'm sorry to have caused you problems; I'll talk" (*meiwaku wo kakete, sumimasen*; *o hanashi wo shimasu*). He then confessed to nine different burglaries in Kasaoka (west of Kurashiki) and in Kurashiki. The police then arrested him. They investigated the burglaries to substantiate the confession, wrote up voluminous documents, and eventually sent him and the amassed evidence to the procurator's office on four counts of burglary (they could only substantiate four of the confessed cases).

A number of things stand out as distinctive in the interaction of detectives with suspects. The first is the apparent cordiality frequently seen between them. For instance, I once saw two *keiji* bring a criminal to Kurashiki from Osaka by train. He was in handcuffs, and they had a rope around his waist which one *keiji* was holding. The man was smiling and chatting with the Osaka *keiji*, and even discussed with them which super-express they should board to return to Osaka. The same friendliness and lack of tension is often seen in the police station when a man is being interrogated. I have seen criminal investigators hold the rope around their suspect's waist between two fingers, confident that he will not attempt to flee. They tie it to his chair or to a bar on the window when they are actually interrogating him.[10]

This lack of tension stems from the basic tenet of detectives in Japan, that is, "hate the sin and not the sinner" (*tsumi wo nikunde hito wo nikumazu*). This is an old Japanese proverb that every *keiji* recites when he is asked why his kind seems on such good relations with suspects.[11] The police actually seem to play the role of a social worker or a clergyman in their approach. They investigate the suspect's personal background and try to determine why he went wrong. They convince the suspect that he is essentially a good person, but that he made a mistake. If they yell at him in the interrogation, their anger is not because they hate him, but because he is a good person who did wrong and will not admit it. It is similar to the tongue-lashings given to students by teachers in Japanese schools.[12]

10. Tying a rope around the waist of a suspect to restrain him is a tradition that goes back to the Edo period. *Okappiki* used ropes to restrain captives exactly the way *keiji* use them today.

11. This proverb is based on an ancient Buddhist precept.

12. I saw a male teacher give a male high school student a tongue-lashing at a high school in Kurashiki that was far more verbally violent than any I have witnessed given by a *keiji* during an interrogation in a police station. The student stood at rigid attention with his hands at his sides and his head bowed during the scolding.

The suspect usually buckles under and confesses if the police can convince him that he is a good person who has simply made a mistake. The confession also comes because most Japanese find it difficult to confront someone in a position of authority, such as teachers or the police. The police are *okami* ("one who is above"), a word used in reference to the emperor, one's lord, or the authorities. Confessing one's errors is an important part of the Japanese cultural tradition.[13]

The police obtain confessions at the astounding rate of about 95 percent of the persons they interrogate.[14] Many lawyers and young judges are convinced that the police use physical violence or other illegal methods of overbearing to obtain such a high rate of confessions. Violence was sometimes used before the war, but it seems practically unheard of now.[15] The police use psychological methods to create rapport and to convince the suspect that they are truly interested in helping him. However, police are sometimes accused of "forcing" a confession by putting the suspect in their debt (that is, bound by *giri*). For instance, in 1974, the Osaka District Court tried a case in which the police admitted inducing a confession from a suspect by taking him first to a restaurant for dinner and then bowling. The man claimed he made a false confession "so that 'the kind detectives' would get credit for solving his alleged theft."[16] *Keiji* can show kindness to a suspect as long as it is "sincere" and not an attempt to induce a confession. For instance, a *keiji* in Okayama City told me that he brought *o zoni* (a traditional New Year's food treat) from his home to a man in jail during the New Year's holiday to show he respected him as a person. He maintained that this was merely a kind gesture, but in a society in which obligation plays such a key part, the line between inducing a confession through indebtedness and "sincere" tokens of esteem is, indeed, a fine one.

13. For example, many Japanese children's stories end with the villain begging forgiveness and then being forgiven because of his sincere contrition. In the Japanese adaptation of *Little Red Riding Hood*, the wolf falls on his knees before the irate woodsman, confesses his crime of eating grandmother, and begs forgiveness. Instead of meeting immediate retributive justice through a blow of the woodsman's axe, the wolf is then forgiven because of his sincerity, and the story ends. This is in keeping with the Japanese criminal-justice system in general, which seems to try to preserve the social fabric through forgiveness rather than disrupt relations by always insisting on "justice being done."

14. Interview with criminal-investigation section chief, Okayama Prefectural Police Headquarters, 1975.

15. A young man claimed he was kicked in the abdomen and had his arm broken during an interrogation in Tokyo in 1974, but the police denied it. See *Asahi Evening News* (Tokyo), 4 April 1974, p. 3. This sort of report is rare.

16. *Japan Times* (Tokyo), 22 November 1974, p. 2.

Personal bonds of indebtedness to particular *keiji* are relied upon by ex-convicts who later commit crimes again. A man may commit a crime in another police station's jurisdiction, and then telephone the *keiji* who interrogated him before and say he wants to surrender. The *keiji* will then arrange to meet the criminal, who will surrender to his friend. Some *keiji* develop a mystique or a reputation for being sympathetic (*ninjōteki*) and fair, and criminals who do not know them will offer, through an intermediary, to surrender if they can be interrogated by a certain *keiji*.

Not all criminals readily confess. If a confession is not forthcoming, the police try to wear the suspect down. In the past, interrogation occurred in tatami rooms, and the interrogator and suspect would kneel in formal fashion on the floor. One's legs soon become numb when one sits in this manner, yet if the suspect tried to stretch his legs out, the detectives could effectively humble him by snarling that they are sitting in that manner also.[17] I have seen a *keiji* interrogate a suspect while grating stones together in his hand in an irritating way in order to induce the person to cease his resistance. Interrogation often lasts for hours on end to wear the suspect down. Lie detector tests are used only occasionally in Okayama on suspects who refuse to admit their crimes.

The police have the greatest difficulty in obtaining confessions from foreigners, especially Koreans, and radicals, as was noted earlier. I was told by a seasoned *keiji* that Koreans will seldom admit a crime when confronted with the evidence. Leftist radical students also stubbornly resist police efforts to befriend them in order to prompt a confession. The traditional approach of *giri* and *ninjō* does not seem to work with these two types of suspects. A high criminal-investigation official in Okayama told me that "ultra-leftists may speak Japanese, but they are not Japanese; their hearts are different."[18] Radicals feel that their actions are correct even when they violate the law; a thief knows he was wrong and is more susceptible to the interrogation of the *keiji*. The visceral reaction of the police to ideological leftists stems partly from the fact that they do not respond like other criminals. They and foreigners frustrate the criminal justice system, which assumes that criminals will confess their crimes before appearing in court.

Criminal investigators forward information on the criminal's personal

17. An interview in the criminal investigation section, Okayama Prefectural Police Headquarters, 1975. Tatami rooms are now seldom used for interrogation.
18. Interview in the Okayama Prefectural Police Headquarters, 1975.

circumstances to the procurator, including the man's family conditions, his character, his past criminal record, and the *keiji*'s opinion of whether he is likely to commit a crime again. The *keiji* also recommends the punishment for the criminal, which the procurator often follows. In a few simple cases (such as a brawl in a bar), the *keiji* are authorized by the Code of Criminal Procedure to have the person write an apology (*tenmatsusho*) and to let him go with a warning that he will be sent to the procurator if they apprehend him again.

CRIME-PREVENTION POLICE

The responsibilities of police officers in the crime-prevention section of a local police station are much broader than the name implies. Although there is some variation between prefectures, the crime-prevention police (*bōhan keisatsu*) in Okayama handle three basic functions: the investigation of violations of "special laws" (*tokubetsu hō*), the licensing of firearms and of businesses that affect the public morals (*fūzoku eigyō*), and, of course, the coordination of neighborhood crime-prevention associations. The juvenile unit is also located within the crime-prevention section. The crime-prevention police in their first two functions are the successors to the prewar economic police to the extent to which they supervise and interact with business establishments, though the scope of their responsibilities is now much narrower. Their investigative techniques are similar to those used by detectives, and many officers who serve in this section have worked previously in criminal investigation, and vice versa. We shall focus here on the enforcement of "special laws" and the licensing functions of crime-prevention police.

In Kurashiki, officers in the crime-prevention section estimate that they spend about 60 percent of their time investigating violations of the special laws. These include any violations that are not covered by the criminal code and thus investigated by detectives, such as narcotics, smuggling, illegal possession of firearms or other weapons, pornography, prostitution, hunting violations, and industrial pollution. Like detectives, these specialists obtain information on most of these violations through tips, and they must cultivate their tipsters. When they apprehend violators, they interrogate them and elicit confessions in a manner very similar to that of detectives. Industrial pollution is a different and a perplexing matter for the police, however, because of its technical complexity and the nontraditional methods essential for investigation. Pollution cases illustrate the adaptation of the police to problems that grow out of radically new responsibilities.

The primary responsibility for investigating cases of industrial pollution falls on the police. Cities with high concentrations of industry, like Kurashiki, share in the pollution-control function and have sophisticated measurement equipment. The police are mainly responsible for establishing criminal negligence in pollution cases and sending paperwork to the procurators so they can levy fines.

The police are relatively new at actively investigating pollution, and their equipment and level of expertise are still primitive. A pollution section was first set up in the Okayama Prefectural Police Headquarters in 1970. By 1974 it was staffed by five police officers, one of whom was a college graduate in agricultural chemistry and was the key technical expert in the unit. The crime-prevention section of each police station is responsible for the investigation of cases of industrial pollution within their own jurisdictions. The police officers in charge of pollution cases received their first training in 1974 at a special training session taught by the staff of the pollution section in the prefectural police headquarters. Before then, police officers bought their own books on pollution and studied them to learn how to investigate cases. The Okayama Prefecture Pollution Prevention Center, and even the research laboratories of industries, have been called on in the past for technical assistance in investigations of pollution, raising questions, in the latter case, about how well industry can investigate itself. Patrol policemen are now issued handbooks to assist them in recognizing cases of industrial pollution, but it is doubtful that many have ever read them. The police are severely hampered in pollution cases not only by their lack of equipment and technical expertise but also by the maze of complex and confusing laws on pollution. This undoubtedly accounts for the small number of pollution cases handled by the police, as is seen by the fact that the eighty-seven cases investigated in 1974 in Okayama prefecture represent an increase of 321 percent over the year before.[19]

When the police investigate pollution cases, they frequently take the explanation offered by the company, have a free meal, and then write up their reports. An example of this occurred in Mizushima in 1973 when the fish in a pond next to a former fishing hamlet that is now surrounded by

19. Okayama Prefectural Police Headquarters, *Bōhan-hoan keisatsu no ayumi, 1974* [Activities of the crime-prevention and safety police] (Okayama: Okayama Prefectural Police Headquarters, 1974), p. 53.

petrochemical plants suddenly died one evening. The villagers insisted that a chemical discharge from one of the bordering plants killed the fish, and they called the police to investigate. Two police officers from the crime-prevention section of the Mizushima police station came, as well as the local *chūzai san*, took a water sample and a few of the dead fish, and then, after hearing the residents' allegations and the company's explanation, they left. I was told by a police officer involved in the investigation that they did not know how to determine whether the fish were poisoned, and that they simply accepted the company explanation that a rain that night had stirred up sludge in the pond, which killed the fish by taking the oxygen from the water.

Even if the local police had the technical know-how, many Japanese feel it is doubtful whether they would clamp down severely on the polluting large industries whose head offices are in Tokyo (the *honne* of police enforcement of pollution laws). Large industries and politicians have close ties because of corporate donations for election campaigns, and the prime minister and cabinet members are said to influence the police in their degree of investigations.[20] The relation of the local police to large industry also raises questions in the minds of some as to who controls whom. In the pollution incident described above, the *chūzai san* who came to investigate the dead fish lives in a *chūzaisho* in front of an apartment complex for workers of one of the chemical companies. The land and the *chūzaisho* building are provided by the company, and the *chūzai san* attends an annual year-end party (*bōnenkai*) thrown by the company to show its appreciation for the maintenance of order in the company housing area. It can be argued that the strong Japanese sense of obligation for benefits and kindness received might influence the *chūzai san*'s perceptions in one way or another.

Licensing of firearms is another important function of officers in the crime-prevention section. Guns are rigorously controlled in Japan, and this is undoubtedly an important factor in Japan's low crime rate. Cutting and stabbing weapons are most frequently used in murders and other crimes in Japan, not firearms. It is impossible to own a handgun legally in

20. A pollution incident of national scale occurred in Mizushima in December 1974, when an oil tank of the Mitsubishi Oil Company refinery emptied over 11 million gallons of heavy oil into the Inland Sea. An incident of this scale was, of course, no longer solely in the hands of the local or prefectural police, because numerous national agencies and technical experts became involved. This was the largest oil pollution incident in history in Japan and it was beyond the range of political influence.

Japan, unless one is a member of an international shooting team. Shot-guns, rifles, and air rifles may be purchased for hunting if the buyer has a permit from the prefectural public-safety commission. The person's back-ground is investigated by the crime-prevention section before a permit is issued, and if he has a criminal record, he cannot receive a permit. The weapon must be brought to the crime-prevention section in the local police station every five years for inspection for the permit to be renewed, and the gun owner must hear a lecture on gun safety from the police officers. There were 20,989 registered firearms in Okayama prefecture in 1974.[21] Gangsters use guns occasionally in crimes (usually in shoot-outs with rival gangs), and these are usually either smuggled into Japan or converted from realistic, metal toy guns. The National Police Agency recently forced model-gun manufacturers to modify the toys so that they cannot be easily converted.[22] Criminals occasionally attack policemen in an attempt to steal their revolvers.[23] The Japanese, for historical reasons, revere swords to an equal or greater extent than Americans revere firearms, and the Japanese police experience problems in controlling swords similar to those encoun-tered by Americans concerning guns.

Licenses for businesses that affect the public morals (*fūzoku eigyō*), are issued by the prefectural public-safety commission through the local crime-prevention section. The police are charged with the supervision of these businesses. Some of these facilities engage in some sort of gam-bling, such as pachinko halls and Mah-Jongg parlors, and police licensing and supervision is aimed essentially at countering gangster influence. Other establishments under crime-prevention police control include bars, cabarets, turkish baths, pornographic movie theaters, strip shows, and mo-tels, the last being used almost exclusively for furtive sex in Japan. Con-trol of these facilities is aimed not only at thwarting inroads by gangsters, but at prostitution, which was finally outlawed in 1956. Crime-prevention police in Okayama estimate that they spend about 20 percent of their time handling violations by *fūzoku eigyō*.

The basic method of control over *fūzoku eigyō* is through crime-preven-tion associations organized by the police according to the type of business. These associations not only educate their member establishments in crime-

21. *Crime-Prevention and Safety Police*, p. 78
22. "Toy Gun Peril Halted," *Ann Arbor News*, 20 October 1975, p. 5.
23. An older police sergeant in the Kurashiki police station was attacked by a youth and stabbed five times in an attempt to steal his revolver. The officer survived, and the youth was caught immediately. This was the only incident of its kind in Kurashiki in recent years.

prevention methods, they also serve to develop collaborators for the police within these businesses to keep the police informed. Like neighborhood crime-prevention associations, the leaders of these associations are usually the ones most likely to be cooperative with the police.

It can be argued that strict police enforcement of regulations governing *fūzoku eigyō* may be compromised by the fact that police officers frequent these establishments on their days off and often accept gratuities from them. Officers in the crime-prevention section and also in *kōban* that have movie theaters or other *fūzoku eigyō* within their jurisdiction constantly receive free items such as tickets to pornographic movies. Many policemen have a passion for pachinko and Mah-Jongg and go to such parlors for recreation whenever possible when off duty. The police chief is usually careful to avoid bars within his station's area lest he be seen in a compromising condition, but high prefectural police officials in Okayama often use a particular bar located on a quiet back street near the headquarters.[24] I have been told that police chiefs are said to receive sums of money from *fūzoku eigyō*, especially Mah-Jongg parlors and pachinko halls, as farewell gifts (*o sembetsu*) when they are transferred. High police officials, like other bureaucrats or company officials in Japan, take several days to go around to all of their main contacts when they are transferred, to say good-bye and to receive gifts of money.[25]

SECURITY POLICE

The duty of the security police (*keibi keisatsu*)[26] is to monitor groups that are perceived as threats to the public security and political status quo in Japan. Public security is probably the most sensitive responsibility of the police today, because of their vast authority in this area before and

24. When the head of the Okayama Prefectural Police Headquarters was transferred to Tokyo, numerous headquarters and prefectural officials and other notables gathered at the train station to see him off. Many were accompanied by their wives, and the wives all gathered in a group in the background, and only the female proprietor (*mama san*) of the well-patronized Okayama bar stood among the men waving him off. Most of the high police officials there seemed to be well acquainted with her.

25. Gifts of money in moderate amounts to one leaving is an acceptable tradition in Japan. However, I suspect and have been told that farewell gifts to police officials sometimes shade into the unacceptable.

26. At the police-station level in Okayama, security police are actually called "guard" police (the literal meaning of *keibi*). At the prefectural police headquarters and national levels, they are more correctly called *kōan keisatsu* ("public order police"). The use of the word "guard" may be euphemistic.

during the war. Critics of the police assert that the security police, including the riot police, are the modern equivalent of the feared prewar Special Higher Police, or *tokkō*.[27] Structurally, at least, there may be a certain amount of validity to that claim. For instance, the security section in the police station has frequent direct contact with the security division (*keibibu*) of the prefectural police headquarters, without going through the police chief in many instances, as other sections must do. The security division of the prefectural police headquarters then has a direct link to Tokyo, through the regional police bureau. This is due to the national nature of many of the incidents with which it deals, yet it is reminiscent of the *tokkō* that had direct links to the prewar Home Ministry.

The sensitivity of the public-security activities of the police is augmented by the potentially explosive role played by ideology in Japanese society. The police display an almost visceral reaction to leftists, and this is probably based to a greater extent on the Japanese reaction to ideology than on the adamant refusal of leftists to confess their crimes, as was noted earlier. The Japanese are particularly intolerant of ideological differences, often a product of conflicting group allegiances, which are powerful in Japan, combined with the struggle between the group that is "in" (controlling the political and economic power structure) and the group that is "out." The "ins" are mostly conservative and are bolstered by the police, whose job is to maintain social order (the status quo), and the "outs" are, by and large, leftists. The tight-knit and closed nature of Japanese groups impedes a sustained dialogue between the establishment and those on the outside, so the interaction degenerates into a confrontation. The usual forums for their shouting matches are the streets, the Diet, the universities, and the media.

The police try to maintain neutrality in the ideological struggle (the *tatemae*), but they do not succeed very well (the *honne*). Many citizens perceive the police as tilted toward the right and against the left.[28] Their bias is evident in the many posters for student radicals wanted for terror-

27. See Hironaka Toshio, *Sengō Nihon no keisatsu* [Postwar Japanese police] (Tokyo: Iwanami Shoten, 1968), p. 143. See also Hironaka Toshio, *Nihon no keisatsu* [Japanese police], rev. ed. (Tokyo: Tokyo Daigaku Shuppankai, 1958), pp. 204–236. The Public Security Intelligence Agency (Kōan Chōsachō) also performs some former *tokkō* duties.
28. In a survey conducted by a national newspaper in 1974, 38 percent of the respondents felt the police were biased towards the right, 30 percent felt they were neutral, and 32 percent did not have an opinion. *Sankei shimbun* (Tokyo), 1 August 1974, page unknown.

ism that are distributed perhaps even more widely than those for ordinary criminals.[29] The police seem to be galvanized when discussing Communists or leftist labor unions, and they told me on numerous occasions that they consider them a threat to Japanese society and to the police establishment. While I was in Kurashiki the police had to mobilize on several occasions to guard visiting leftist politicians from potential attack by right-wing extremist groups. When the head of the Japan Communist party visited Kurashiki in 1974, several police officers who were waiting in riot gear to be called in case of violence commented that they felt it was an irony for them to be "protecting the head of a party that wants to abolish the police," or at least the security police. Indeed, leaders of the Communist party in Okayama told me that patrol, traffic, crime prevention, and criminal investigation are important police functions that protect the life and property of citizens. But they strongly objected to the security police who gathered information and spied on them in what they feel is a violation of the right to freedom of political activity guaranteed by the constitution.

Radical unionists in Okayama related an incident to me that they felt reveals the political bias of the police. They said that members of the often violent right-wing Patriotic party (Aikokutō) invaded a meeting of the Okayama branch of the extremely activist Japan Teachers Union (Nik-kyōsō) being held in the center of Okayama City and began assaulting the unionists. The police were called, but they took more than twenty-five minutes to arrive on the scene, during which time the invaders fled, so no arrests were made. The government of former Prime Minister Tanaka used the police for a politically inspired vendetta against the teachers union in 1974. Twenty top union leaders were arrested after urging teachers to strike, which is illegal for teachers and other government workers in Japan.[30] The arrests provoked wide media coverage and critical comment throughout Japan and even overseas.

29. I have never seen a "wanted" poster for a right-wing extremist; perhaps this is because there are fewer activist right-wingers than leftists, and their organizations and whereabouts are more commonly known and less secretive than are the leftist radicals.

30. The relevant statutory provision is Article 98, Paragraph 2, of the National Public Employees Act (*kokka kōmuin hō*). The Japanese Supreme Court decision in *Tsuruzono vs. Japan*, 27 Keishu 547 (April 25, 1973) states that the right of public workers to strike is guaranteed by the constitution for the purpose of advancing economic and working conditions, but is "not absolute and [is] subject to restrictions imposed for the common interest of the people as a whole, including workers." Police, prison guards, and Marine Safety Agency (Kaijō Hoanchō) personnel are prohibited from forming unions by the National Public Employees Act (Article 108.2 (5)).

The groups monitored by the security police vary from police station to police station according to the characteristics of the jurisdictions. In Kurashiki, owing to the high concentration of facilities run by the national, prefectural, and city governments, such as a large post office, a train station, a telephone company, the city office, and a branch of the prefectural office, many highly political and leftist government employee labor unions of the Sōhyō confederation are active. The outcaste (*burakumin*) political organization Kaihō Dōmei, associated with the Japan Socialist party, is also active because of the large number of *burakumin* in the area. Communists are making inroads in some outcaste areas of Kurashiki, and have a small office in the center of the city.

The groups that are monitored most heavily in Mizushima are the large Korean population, especially the North Korean neighborhoods, and a Communist-run hospital in the area (Kyōdō Byōin). The hospital always arises as a topic of conversation with security police in Mizushima, for its staff helps organize citizen movements against pollution from the large factories in Mizushima, its director is one of two Communist members of the prefectural assembly, and a member of its staff is one of three Communists in the city assembly. Labor unions at the factories are mostly of the more moderate Dōmei confederation and are not a major concern of the police. The security police also handle relations and incidents concerning the forty thousand foreign seamen who visit the Mizushima harbor aboard an average of eighteen hundred foreign vessels each year.[31]

The security police use several different techniques for gathering information on groups and individuals. One is the use of electronic, photographic, and other technical means. The security police insist that they do not use eavesdropping devices (which would be a violation of Article 21 and Article 35 of the constitution). Informed observers, such as members of the police oversight committee of the prefectural assembly and older police officers who once worked in security, assert without direct proof that they must be using them (the *honne*?). They do use telephoto equipment to photograph people surreptitiously (they are the only section in the police station with their own darkroom), and they use transmitters hidden under their clothing to broadcast messages to the police station when they are trailing a person. Other police, such as those in *kōban*, assist the security police whenever possible, such as having them come to the *kōban*

31. Figures supplied by the Mizushima Police Station, 1974.

to get the fingerprints of a person under observation, from a teacup he used while visiting the *kōban*.[32]

One of the most successful and effective methods of the security police is to cultivate tipsters within the target organizations.[33] This is similar to the technique of "cultivating the field" employed by detectives. They meet a Communist, for instance, through a trusted third party and build up "human relations" (*ningen kankei*) by helping him with his marriage, assisting him in purchasing an automobile cheaply, or going drinking with him. After a period of time, when the person comes to feel thoroughly indebted to them, they reveal their identity as police officers, if they had not done so before. They ask the person to supply information on the organization, secure documents, or take photographs. They often meet with the informant secretly at night, in a location where they cannot be detected (such as a hotel), and get the information and other items.[34] A minor furor arose in the Okayama Prefectural Assembly in 1974 when the Communists discovered that a young member of their local organization had been supplying information to the police after they befriended him and helped him buy a washing machine cheaply. The police response was that they only recommended him to a store and did not buy it for him. The issue was not actively pursued by the conservative-controlled prefectural assembly.[35]

The security police "field" also includes normal citizens in the community, especially officers of the local neighborhood associations (*chōnaikai*). These form the core of the security as well as the criminal police's body of informants. As was noted, officers of these organizations are usually

32. An incident reported to me in an interview with a police officer, Kurashiki, 1975.

33. The security police and the national Public Safety Investigation Agency (Kōan Chōsachō) are said to be antagonistic in their relationships. The security police insist that they are more subtle in their efforts to obtain information by painstakingly cultivating "human relations" with their potential informants, and do not simply bribe them with large amounts of money, as they say the Kōan Chōsachō does. They also claim that the Kōan Chōsachō, unlike their own branch, does make use of electronic bugging devices. There is only one office of the Kōan Chōsachō in the prefecture—in Okayama City—and apparently it does not have the manpower of the police for slowly winning over informants. Several police officers told me that the security police frequently do not fully cooperate with the Kōan Chōsachō in their investigations; they are proud of their position as heirs of the tradition of the prewar intelligence arm of the police and do not wish to share this status with the newly formed agency.

34. These methods were described to me by security police officers in Kurashiki and Okayama, 1974 and 1975.

35. Interviews with prefectural assemblymen, Okayama, 1975.

older people who are stable, longtime residents of the area and who are mostly conservative in their political orientation. They usually cooperate willingly with the police—security police or any other specialization—in providing information on the movements of suspicious people or other matters.

Several aspects of the relation of security police officers to other police officers in the same police station are worthy of note. First, the security police are very secretive about their work, even toward other police officers. Security police are hardly ever seen in a *kōban* chatting with the patrol police, as criminal investigators frequently are. They have difficulty in mixing with fellow police officers in the bachelor police officers' dormitory because of the secret nature of their work, which is at odds with the propensity of off-duty police officers to chat about their police experiences.[36] Second, the security police are considered to be somewhat of an elite in the police station. It is rumored among police officers that the men with the best intellects are chosen for security work. It should be pointed out that the prewar *tokkō* were also an elite group, and perhaps more pronouncedly so than the present security police.

A final aspect of the relation of security police to other officers is the marked rivalry between the security and the criminal police that extends from the top of the National Police Agency down to the police station level. For instance, the rivalry is seen in the usual custom of rotating the position of director general of the National Police Agency between veterans of these two specializations. A clear example of this rivalry involved a series of eleven bombings of large businesses in 1974 and 1975 by a student anarchist group. The anarchists eventually were arrested by a team of 150 investigators of the security division of the Metropolitan Police Department who worked on the case so secretly that police officers in other divisions did not even know of their progress. At the moment of the criminals' arrest, the criminal investigation division was still meticulously investigating the bombings with its usual approach: tracking down fragments of the bomb containers, picked up with tweezers at the scenes of the explosions, and tracing them to their sources. The surprise and chagrin of the criminal-investigation division officers was so great that the superintendent general of the Metropolitan Police Department had to apologize

36. Interview with young traffic-police officer, Kurashiki, 1974.

personally to them. The head of the criminal investigation division threatened never to work on a case of this type again.[37]

We have examined in this chapter the adaptation of the police organization to specialized crimes and problems through the use of police specialists. The galvanic reaction of the police to ideological leftists can be partially understood by looking at police officers as individuals—their backgrounds, training, and sense of solidarity—and by examining the values and outlook that pervade the police organization. We shall now turn to these topics in the two chapters in Part Two.

37. *Japan Times*, 2 June 1975, p. 14; also "Bakudan jiken omowanu hamon [Unexpected ripples of the bombing incident]," *Shukan bunshun* (Tokyo), 11 June 1975, pp. 144–151.

INCULCATING SOLIDARITY AND LOYALTY

eight

THE MAKING OF POLICE OFFICERS

Joining the police in Japan involves, in most instances, a lifetime commitment to the profession. New recruits must be not only trained in the technical skills of police work, but also completely socialized in the police way of life, "even down to their way of eating."[1] For example, the first goal of the training program for new recruits in Okayama is "complete life guidance," which is further defined as "the development of a just and cheerful character and harmonious good sense."[2] The primary objective is to thoroughly inculcate into nascent police officers the ideas, values, and perceptions of "police society"—the subculture that sets the police somewhat apart from the rest of Japanese society.

One of the most fundamental values impressed upon police officers from their earliest training is the need for absolute loyalty and solidarity within the police institution. The motto of the Okayama police, which is prominently displayed in every police office and on the back cover of the monthly prefectural police journal, emphasizes this point forcefully in its first line. The motto in its entirety is as follows:

> *Chi no kayotta danketsu*
> *Shinsetsu meirō na ōtai*
> *Tsuyoku tadashii shikkōmu*

---

1. Told to me by a high official in the training section, Okayama Prefectural Police Headquarters, 1974.
2. Okayama Prefectural Police Headquarters, *Okayama ken keisatsu nenkan, 1972* [Okayama Prefectural Police yearbook] (Okayama: Okayama Prefectural Police Headquarters, 1972), p. 309, and a document given me by the Okayama Prefectural Police, 1974.

> Warm and human solidarity
> Kind, cheerful reception
> Strong, correct enforcement[3]

The second phrase, about reception, refers to the receiving or meeting of citizens in a kind and cheerful manner. The first line portrays the kind of solidarity that should pervade the police organization as that of a warm and living organism, held together by ties of human relations (*ningen kankei*). The police see themselves as the bastion of justice and order in society, and feel that their strength lies in the loyalty and unity of purpose of police officers.

This chapter deals with the molding of police officers and the building up within them of the values and loyalty demanded in the police profession. First it will analyze the Japanese police subculture as it affects individual police officers and public perception of the police, and then examine the backgrounds, recruitment, and training or socialization of policemen, the latter being accomplished through police schools and other less formal mechanisms. The next chapter will discuss various methods employed in the process of maintaining solidarity and loyalty within the police organization once these values are instilled.

POLICE SUBCULTURE

Police systems approach what are sometimes called "total institutions," such as mental hospitals, prisons, and the military, and they tend to develop their own "subculture." Mental hospitals, prisons, and to a lesser extent the military physically limit the contact between the individuals in them and the surrounding larger society. This limited interaction with the outside, and certain shared characteristics of the individuals who enter the institutions, tend to foster common values and outlook ("world view," as anthropologists say), which are somewhat distinctive from those held by the wider society, and which may be termed the subculture of the institution.[4]

---

3. Japanese businesses and other organizations typically have at least one motto, more often a set. I saw a slogan on the wall of a Toyota service center on the outskirts of Kurashiki exhorting the repairmen to be in correct uniform, have cheerful attitudes, show bravery, work hard, be enthusiastic and sincere, keep the shop clean, and be pure.

4. See Samuel E. Wallace (ed.), *Total Institutions* (Chicago: Aldine, 1971). I am taking some liberty in using the phrase "total institution" in a context in which it was not originally intended. The police does not deprive its members of their liberty by confining them to a building or grounds as do prisons, reformatories, psychiatric hospitals, boarding schools, and

The entrance to the Kurashiki police station. The signs in front urge traffic safety and crime prevention and announce that police officers are being recruited.

Police officers are by no means physically separated from society; the very nature of the police profession demands frequent and intimate contact with the community. Yet the police, like the institutions mentioned above, also tend to develop their own subculture. This subculture develops from the heavy demands of loyalty and solidarity that are an integral factor in the police ideology; from the extended socialization process within the police organization which instills the values of the police establishment in the minds of the young recruits; and also from a certain similarity in the young men (and women) who are attracted to the police. Other factors, some of which will be discussed at greater length in the next chapter, include the long hours of police work, which leave little chance for outside recreation; police apartment houses and dormitories, which keep police officers physically together; and the fact that police officers have the most frequent contact with a rather narrow spectrum of Japanese society. Many of these factors, however, are part of the employment philosophy of most

the like. However, the intensity of the inward stress on loyalty and solidarity, and the all-encompassing nature of Japanese organizations like the police make the use of this phrase apropos, I feel, in this context.

Japanese companies, so the police are not unique in this regard. Yet the uniformity of police values and outlook should not be overstated, because significant age differences and other cleavages seem to exist within the police at present. This disparity will be discussed fully in the next chapter.

The subculture shared by Japanese police officers within "police society" is not radically different from Japanese society in general, but is distinguished mostly by differences in emphasis. Because the locus of the values and norms making up a subculture is in the mind, it is manifest in part in the self-image shared by policemen. This self-image in many ways parallels the image of samurai. It should be recalled that policemen in the early Meiji period were drawn almost exclusively from the samurai class, bringing with them samurai ideals as the official police ideology. However, the samurai who joined the police were, by and large, lower-status samurai from the countryside (gōshi); the higher-level samurai who lived in castle towns (jōka no shi) joined the army and navy in great numbers. Thus, early-Meiji police officers brought with them samurai ideals, but they did not necessarily represent the pinnacle of feudal society. The distinctiveness of the samurai-like image of the police today results from its somewhat anachronistic character in the context of modern Japanese society.

The epitome of police subculture is perhaps best seen in the riot police, the unit of police organization most isolated from normal interaction with the wider community. The riot police as a socialization mechanism will be discussed later in this chapter. The extreme loyalty to the group, the devotion and concern characterizing the relationship between inferiors and superiors, and the overt manifestations of patriotism that mark the riot police are also found, in somewhat different form, in Japanese gangs.[5] Both come close to being totally encompassing institutions.

Police image, like that of the feudal samurai (as well as gangsters), is definitely very masculine, as is probably the case in most countries. This is best typified by two sorts of police specialists, motorcycle-riding traffic policemen and detectives. Recruitment posters place heavy emphasis on these two specializations because of their masculine glamour. The head of the Okayama Police School told me that these two images appeal to two different target groups for recruitment. High school graduates are most attracted to the image of motorcycle police, and college graduates seem to

5. See chapter six for a detailed discussion of police and gangsters in Japan.

identify with the image of the detective.[6] Motorcycle policemen wear sleek uniforms with ascots and ride powerful Honda motorcycles laden with a siren, a speaker, and lights, and they often execute tricky and dangerous maneuvers on the crowded roads to catch offenders. Many Japanese youths like to ride motorcycles and are naturally attracted to the dashing image of the young motorcycle policeman.[7] Detectives usually wear a business suit and are commonly thought of as using their wits to outsmart and trap criminals. Japanese television programs about police dwell almost exclusively on these two types of police officers, especially detectives.

The image of the police is not only strongly masculine, it is almost elitely so. This is consistent with the samurai parallel because the samurai class as a whole formed the apex of feudal Japanese society. The police in Japan have relatively high social status, at least when compared with police in the United States.[8] The social status of the police profession not only influences the quality of people attracted to police work, but is also a key factor in overall community cooperation with the police. The status of individual police officers is enhanced by the authority of the police organization as a whole, which, although prefecturally based, ultimately represents the prestige of the national government. Social status in Japan is heavily influenced by educational level; for example, many large corporations classify high school graduates as blue-collar and college graduates as white-collar, rather than basing the distinction on the type of work they perform. Thus, as the number of college graduates within the police increases, the social status of police officers is likely to rise even further.

6. Interview with the head of the Okayama Police School, 1974.

7. Police officers seem to be fascinated by automobiles and speed—especially young policemen—and the rate of automobile ownership among policemen is slightly higher than in the society at large. In Okayama prefecture in 1974 there was one privately owned automobile for every 1.44 males between the ages of twenty and fifty-nine. (Computed from automobile ownership figures provided by the Okayama Prefectural Police Headquarters and population figures from the Okayama Prefectural Office. This is based on the assumption that very few women own automobiles in Okayama.) For police officers in the Kurashiki police station (also males with approximately the same age span), there was one automobile for every 1.29 policemen. Among young police officers with the rank of policeman (*junsa*), other than the 10 who had joined the police that year, 44 out of 45 (97.7%) owned automobiles. (Computed from information supplied by the Kurashiki police station.)

8. Detailed comparisons of the social status of occupations is risky, partly because of the different character and content of the seemingly same professions in the different societies. An example is the difference between construction laborers in Japan (who are often poorly paid day laborers and similar to gangsters in many respects) and those in the United States (who are often unionized and share common characteristics with the wider spectrum of labor).

However, the social status of a patrolman who works in a *kōban* is vastly different from that of a member of the police administrative elite, most of whom are Tokyo University graduates. We shall consider here only the social status of a patrolman.

In a survey of occupational social status by the Japan Sociological Society in 1955, the police were ranked ninth in thirty-two occupations, just ahead of office workers in a nationwide sample.[9] In another survey, in the city of Kita Kyushu in 1973, the police ranked eighteenth in thirty-six occupations, just after restaurant owners but ahead of office workers.[10] Policemen are located approximately in the middle stratum of occupational social status in both surveys, yet are definitely not considered to be blue-collar, even though the majority of them are only high school graduates.[11] The authority of the police organization undoubtedly lifts police officers above the blue-collar level.

Police self-image in Japan also involves a strong sense of decorum and dignity like that of the proud samurai. This is vividly portrayed in two examples of how the police viewed the role of uniformed officers in controlling certain kinds of public behavior. The first was the annual Naked Festival (*hadaka matsuri*) held in February at the large Buddhist temple at Saidaiji in Okayama prefecture. Four thousand men dressed only in loin cloths mass together in the temple area at midnight in an effort to catch a stick thrown from the building, in order to win a large cash prize. The friction of their naked bodies rubbing together keeps them warm in the freezing night air, actually causing steam to rise when water is thrown on them to cool them. Police from all over southern Okayama in 1974 were assigned to help control the crowd of spectators, estimated at over sixteen

9. Japan Sociological Society, ed., *Nihon shakai no kaisōteki kōzō* [Status structure of Japanese society] (Tokyo: Yuhikaku, 1958), p. 330.

10. Noboru Yamamoto and Kiyoko Nakagawa, "Daitoshi ken ni okeru kaisō kōsei to seikatsu ishiki [Status composition and life consciousness in the area of metropolises]," *Toshi mondai kenkyū* [Research in urban problems], vol. 25, no. 6 (n.d.), p. 8.

11. In a study of the occupational prestige of ninety professions by the National Opinion Research Center in 1947, replicated later in 1963, American police officers were ranked fifty-fifth (1947) and forty-seventh (1963). The results showed a nine percent rise in the fifteen-year-period from approximately the bottom one-third to the middle. As individuals, police officers in the two countries may be beginning to occupy similar positions in social status, but the prestige afforded the police organization per se in the two countries is still vastly different, with the Japanese police in a much higher position. See Robert W. Hodge, Paul M. Siegel, and Peter H. Rossi, "Occupational Prestige in the United States: 1925–1963," in Reinhard Bendix and Seymour Martin Lipset, eds., *Class, Status and Power: Social Stratification in Comparative Perspective*, 2nd ed. (London: Routledge and Kegan Paul, 1967), p. 327.

thousand, yet the police did not directly intervene in the control of the throbbing mass of naked participants, who were often provoked to fighting in the frenzy to grab the stick. The local volunteer fire brigade (*shōbōdan*), composed of local townspeople wearing *happi* coats, performed this function. A police official observed that it would not appear proper for uniformed police officers to be seen grappling with naked men in front of thousands of spectators and a nationwide television audience.

The other example involves the short-lived fad of "streaking" imported from America in 1974. When the first few "streakers" appeared on the streets of Tokyo in March, the Metropolitan Police Department made immediate plans for countermeasures. The method of handling them, however, did not involve uniformed police officers, because it was feared this would be too degrading to the police. In an article in the *Asahi Evening News*, the following was reported:

Police also feel streakers should not be chased by officers in uniform. So they may have to assign plain-clothesmen to places where many people congregate, such as "pedestrians' paradises" [malls]. Blankets may be readied at some policeboxes for use to cover up streakers taken into custody.[12]

This sense of decorum stems from the positive, dignified image that the police have of themselves. Recall that police dignity is that of anointed agents of the central government, which until World War II was in turn the agent of a divine emperor. It is also connected with the generally high social status afforded police officers by the public.

The police self-image of masculinity does not preclude an interest in many cultural activities that are common in Japan, which is consistent with the traditional samurai ideal that a warrior should also be cultured (*bunbu ryōdō*). For instance, Kurashiki is an art-oriented city because of the famous Ohara Art Museum located in the oldest section of town. This cultural influence is reflected in the police station. Oil paintings and prints of famous pictures from the museum hang in such unlikely locations as the criminal investigation and patrol sections. The police chief has handmade pottery on display in his office and a large ten-volume set of art books on his bookshelf. A large number of police officers, including the police chief and traffic-section chief, make pottery in their spare time. The traffic-section chief even keeps a potter's wheel in a locker near his desk and sometimes throws pots at his desk when he is on duty late at night and

12. *Asahi Evening News* (Tokyo), 15 March 1974, p. 5.

The police chief of an Okayama police station in his office. The decor is typical.

there is no business he must attend to. One can usually see pots drying on the top of the locker near his desk. The assistant police chief in Kurashiki often carves lovely wooden serving trays (*ujō bori*), for which Okayama prefecture is famous, during his lunch break or after hours.

I once saw the tough crime-prevention section chief, who interrogates prostitutes, juvenile delinquents, and other offenders in his regular duties, stop and quickly rearrange an *ikebana* display in the lobby of the police station on his way from the police chief's office to his own office. Flower arrangements (*ikebana*) and miniature trees (*bonsai*) are almost constantly on display in various parts of the police station and are also frequently found in police-boxes, the flowers being provided by local residents. Club activities take place every Friday evening in the police station for an hour or so and include calligraphy (*shodō*), poetry singing (*shigin*), pottery making, and flower arranging. There is also a fashion club for the ladies that meets on Saturdays after work. Perhaps the best example of the samurai tradition is the commander of a riot police unit in Tokyo with whom I am acquainted and who, after a day of strenuous duty preparing to battle leftists, puts on his kimono and does calligraphy in the serenity of the Japanese-style drawing room of his home. The fact that these apparently "feminine" activities (in American eyes) can be engaged in by very masculine and tough-minded police officers points to the culturally relative way in which they are perceived.

A key aspect of police self-image is their attraction to certain traditional core values in Japanese culture that were very important for the samurai (as well as gangsters). As we have seen, police strongly identify with the traditional notions of obligation, loyalty, and human relations that are summed up by the terms *giri-ninjō*. *Giri-ninjō* is instrumental for the police during interrogation of suspects and in their relationships with tipsters and gangsters, yet they not only use these values, they also accept them. The concepts of *giri-ninjō* are often poignantly expressed in songs, such as the old *naniwa bushi* style of narratives (which frequently have gangster or parent-child themes) and in old war songs (*gunka*) from the army or navy. The police are deeply affected by these songs: a large appendix of the Metropolitan Police Department songbook is made up of them, and police officers often sing them while drinking together at parties, such as year-end *bōnenkai* ("forget the old year meetings").

A touching example of the effect on police officers of songs with *giri-ninjō* themes is a *naniwa bushi* style of record that was very popular among police officers and concerned the famous Asama Sansō incident of February 1972.[13] The incident occurred in the snowy mountains of Nagano prefecture. The ballad depicts the mutual and absolute devotion and loyalty of the men of the Metropolitan Police Department's Second Riot Police, who were called to assist the Nagano prefectural police, and their commander, Uchida Naotaka. The commander was shot dead while leading his men in a final assault on the mountain villa held by five heavily armed terrorists of the Japanese Red Army, who were holding the villa keeper's wife as hostage. The police had tried every conceivable stratagem to no avail over a ten-day period to get the young criminals to surrender. Under mounting public pressure to resolve the incident, yet determined to capture all the terrorists alive and save the life of the hostage, the police finally resorted to the tactic of battering down the walls and roof of the villa with a hastily armored wrecking crane while spraying the villa and its occupants in the subfreezing weather with water from water cannons. The gripping drama of the final day of the seige was carried live on Japanese television and the entire nation watched, transfixed. In the final assault, riot-police volunteers led by Commander Uchida advanced room by

13. "Aa kidōtai [O riot police]," Roon Record Company, RD–5007.

room, holding armored shields as their only protection from the fusillade, and finally captured all of the terrorists and freed the hostage. Uchida was killed, according to the ballad, while trying to caution one of his men to retreat from a dangerously exposed position. I sat one evening with a seasoned patrol-car driver in his home in Kurashiki, who openly wept as he played the recording for me. The devotion of the commander for his men and their absolute loyalty to him depicted in the record are not unlike the extremely affective relationship between samurai and their lord, pre-war army troops and their commanders, or gangsters and their gang boss.

A final observation on police image concerns the public perception of them as being frequently arrogant or supercilious in their interactions with citizens, similar to the often haughty samurai. The low-status feudal *okappiki* and *meakashi*, semi-official persons who performed a policing function in the Edo period, were also notoriously contemptuous. Police arrogance was especially common before World War II, when police were referred to as "*oi kora keisatsu*," an extremely offensive phrase in Kagoshima prefecture dialect meaning literally the "'hey you, come here!' police." Many early police officers were former samurai from Kagoshima. Although administrative police officials tried to change this image after the war, with emphasis on the "democratic" and egalitarian nature of the police, it is still evident at times in certain police activities, especially in the way they snarl at traffic offenders and in their cold and sometimes rude manner of handling driver's license applications at police stations. In a national survey conducted by the Prime Minister's Office in 1974, the largest number of respondents reporting offensive language or attitudes of police officers were those who had been apprehended for traffic violations.[14] This irritating feeling of condescension is also seen in the "guidance" (*shidō*) activities that occupy a large portion of the time of traffic police. Traffic policemen ride around blaring warnings about traffic law

14. About 50 percent of the 2,000 respondents said that they had talked to a police officer during the preceding year. Of these, a visit by a police officer to their home constituted the largest percentage (27%), and all other encounters were each less than 10 percent (e.g., asking street directions was 9% and incurring a traffic violation 7%). The language of the police officer and his attitude during these meetings were classified as "good" for over 50 percent of the encounters through visiting the home, asking street directions, reporting a burglary, and reporting a lost or found item, but only 33 percent when reporting a traffic accident, 27 percent when having incurred a traffic offense, and 38 percent during investigation of a crime. Those reporting "bad" language or attitude in highest proportion (30%) were persons in traffic offenses. Prime Minister's Office, *Keisatsu ni kansuru seron chōsa* [Public opinion survey concerning the police], 1974, pp. 3 and 14–23.

violations or instructions on traffic safety principles to pedestrians, bicyclists, or other drivers through loudspeakers mounted on the roofs of their patrol cars. They can also often be seen standing at street corners and using loudspeakers attached to a nearby *kōban* or telephone poles to instruct pedestrians on proper methods of crossing the street.[15] The power and prestige of government authorities in Japan (referred to as *okami*, "one who is above") aggravates this tendency toward haughtiness.

Police image is not entirely unmixed. The samurai image, with its high-minded values and ideals, is the official ideology of the police (the *tatemae*). Police officers, however, deal with many of the lower elements of society on an intimate daily basis. They thus share in certain aspects of the subculture of criminals and gangsters (the *honne*). A fascinating example of this is the use of criminal argot (*ingo*, or "hidden language") by detectives and patrolmen, especially older police officers. Certain of these words are directly borrowed from criminal jargon and are not in common usage. The main groups from which these words come are burglars, pickpockets, street-stall keepers, juvenile delinquent street gangs, red light districts, swindlers, black marketeers, gamblers, gangsters, criminals dealing in narcotics, construction workers, stevedores, and counterfeiters.[16] *Ingo* serves the function of mutual recognition among professional criminals and expresses ideas secretly in such a way that ordinary people cannot understand, and its development testifies to the social isolation of these offenders. Police officers apprehend and interrogate these criminals and must understand the jargon used by each group. The police naturally begin to use these words among themselves when discussing crime-related topics.

"Hidden language" is formed in four ways. First, figurative expressions are used to describe an object or an action. For instance, a word of burglar origin for storehouse is *musume* (a young maiden or woman) because a storehouse, like a maiden, is white in color, replete with clothing, and is well cared for. Second, the syllables of a word may be reversed in order to obscure its meaning—for example, a word of pickpocket origin for a satchel (*kaban*) is *banka*. Third, a word may be simply abbreviated—for

---

15. The wide use of loudspeakers is not unique to the police, but pervades Japanese society: sound-cars ply the streets with booming announcements during election campaigns, and tour leaders shout instructions to their groups through hand-held power megaphones.
16. Metropolitan Police Department, ed., *Keisatsu ingo ruishū* [Collection of police secret language] (Tokyo: Criminal Division, Metropolitan Police Department, 1956), p. 4.

instance, the word for a criminal record (*zenka*) is called by burglars simply *mae* (the *kun yomi*, or familiar reading, of the first character *zen* in the word *zenka*). Fourth, words are used which have conceptual associations with certain objects or actions—for example, burglars call a dog a *shūtome* (mother-in-law) because both are always in the house and are annoying.[17]

BACKGROUNDS OF POLICE OFFICERS AND RECRUITMENT

A large number of all Japanese policemen are of rural origin; police officers with rural backgrounds run 87 percent in Tokyo, about 80 percent in Okayama.[18] As in other occupations, recruitment to police reflects a long-term pattern of drift to urban centers. Until about ten years ago, Okayama men in large numbers joined the police of Osaka and Kobe (Hyogo prefecture), the closest metropolitan centers; in the mid-1950s the highest officers in the Osaka Prefectural Police were said to be heavily of Okayama origin, and many of the highest officers in the Hyogo Prefectural Police still are Okayama men.[19] The slacking of this flow in the last decade reflects not only Okayama's sharp urban growth, but also the "U-turn" phenomenon of people losing their hankering after life in a metropolis and returning home (or nearby). As an example of "U-turn," three police officers in the Kurashiki police station had shifted to Okayama from police work in Tokyo because of disillusionment with the largest metropolis.

The occupations of the fathers of police recruits confirm relatively frequent rural origins. In Tokyo, 30 percent of the fathers of police officers are farmers, 19 percent are company employees, 18 percent work in small factories, 15 percent are civil servants, 1 percent are teachers, and 17 percent have other occupations.[20] For Okayama exact figures are not available, and the rural coloration seems less clear from personnel-officer impressions that paternal occupations of new recruits are almost equally divided between farming, companies, and civil service.[21]

A police recruit's family background is a very sensitive matter, and the police carefully investigate the families of applicants before they join the

---

17. Ibid., pp. 6–7.
18. Figures supplied by the Metropolitan Police Department and the Okayama Prefectural Police Headquarters, 1974.
19. Told to me by officials in the Okayama Prefectural Police Headquarters, 1974.
20. Figures supplied by the Metropolitan Police Department, 1974.
21. From an interview with an official of the personnel section, Okayama Prefectural Police Headquarters, 1974.

police. If one has a criminal record, he is, of course, disqualified from becoming a policeman, but this prohibition also extends to an applicant's parents, grandparents, siblings, aunts, uncles, and cousins. The family of the spouse of a potential recruit is also investigated. The police feel that if any family member or relative has committed a crime, this will undoubtedly affect the recruit because of family bonds and the family environment in which he was raised. Mental illness in the family is also usually a disqualifying factor. If the recruit has any left-wing political leanings, he is considered unfit for police work.[22] I was told that one reason the police investigate backgrounds so thoroughly is to weed out any members of the formerly outcaste strata.[23] This is often difficult in such large metropolitan police organizations as Tokyo and Osaka because the recruits come from all over the country, but it is generally understood in Okayama that there are no people of this background in the Okayama Prefectural Police. Since most police recruits come from rural areas, the *chūzai san* over the jurisdictions in which their homes are located discreetly inquire about the potential recruits' family backgrounds among their pools of informants in those localities. Any applicants with a tainted background simply fail to pass the qualifying examination.

The recruit's religion is also investigated. The police discourage active participation by police officers in religious organizations, especially the "new religions," such as Soka Gakkai. The police feel that the activities of these religions compete with police duties for the police officer's time, and Soka Gakkai in particular has practices, such as *shakufuku* (a forceful conversion method), that are in conflict with the role of police officers. I was told that in about 1965 the Okayama Prefectural Police chief ordered all Soka Gakkai members in the police to quit either the religion or the police and that the few who were members quit the religion. I was informed that there are now no Soka Gakkai members in the Okayama Prefectural Police.[24]

Police officers are mostly high school graduates or less, but the percentage of college graduates among new recruits has started to rise sharply

22. Interview in the Fuchu Police Station, 1974.
23. See chapter five for a more detailed discussion of police and outcastes. Discrimination based on social status or origin is a violation of Article 27 of the National Public Employees Act (Kokka Kōmuin Hō), and Article 3 of the Labor Standards Act (Rōdō Kijun Kantoku Hō). This discrimination has not been a political issue, because it has never been specifically pointed out in public or proven by solid evidence.
24. Interview with a reliable Kurashiki informant.

TABLE 6. *Percentage of College, Junior College, and High School Graduates among Police Officers (1974)*

	College Graduates	Junior College Graduates	High School Graduates (or less)
Nation	8.2	0.8	91.0
Okayama	9.2	0.7	90.1

since the economic slowdown in Japan in 1974 and 1975. College graduates are beginning to find police work more attractive as a profession as the business world becomes increasingly unstable. Table 6 indicates the national and Okayama percentages, for 1974, of college, junior college, and high school graduates (or less) among all police officers.[25] As a general rule, a person must be a high school graduate to apply for the police, but a small number (0.9%) of the police officers in Okayama are graduates of postwar junior high schools. Junior high school graduates are not hired by the Tokyo Metropolitan Police Department. In 1975 the percentage of college graduates among new recruits nationally was 46 percent, up from about 10 percent in 1966, indicating that the ratio of college graduates in the police will continue to rise over time.[26]

The percentage of new recruits who have held other jobs before joining the police has decreased recently. In 1972, 47.6 percent of the 170 Okayama police recruits had held other jobs and did not join the police directly out of school. Of these, the largest percentage were company employees (53.1%), and the others were industrial workers (28.4%), civil servants (13.6%), and store employees (4.9%).[27] In 1974, previously employed recruits are said to have been closer to 10 percent, less than a quarter of the 1972 ratio.[28] Most of the group came from smaller enterprises, which

25. Figures supplied by the National Police Agency and the Okayama Prefectural Police Headquarters, 1974. College, junior college, and high school dropouts (a small number) are merged with the graduates of each group.

26. Information supplied by the personnel division, National Police Agency. In 1975, the percentage of male high school graduates who went on to advanced education was 33.8 percent (female high school graduates going on were 34.6%), indicating that the police were attracting a higher percentage of college graduates than the population average would suggest. Prime Minister's Office, ed., *Nihon tōkei nenkan*, 29th edition [Japan statistical yearbook] (Tokyo: Nihon Tokei Kyokai, 1979), p. 595.

27. *Okayama Prefectural Police Yearbook*, p. 311.

28. From an interview with an official of the personnel section, Okayama Prefectural Police Headquarters, 1974.

are the most vulnerable to economic reverses. A number join the police because they want work more active than a confining clerical or production-line position. A young patrolman of my acquaintance in Kurashiki ran a bar before joining the police and shifted at the urging of his parents to find a more respectable occupation.

The police invest considerable effort in recruiting new police officers. In Okayama, for instance, the police mount recruitment campaigns twice a year (July and October). They put posters up in front of police-boxes and police stations, they make announcements in the media, and police officers visit likely young men in their jurisdictions to urge them to join. Entrance to the police is by competitive examination. In a survey administered to 312 applicants taking the examination in Okayama in October 1974,[29] the following answers were given to the query about who had urged them to join the police:

Family	24.0%
Relative or friend	8.7%
Teacher	3.8%
Police officer	48.1%

As we can see, the largest number were urged to join by police officers who visited their homes, and the second largest number were urged by their family. Competitions are held in police stations to see which police-box can recruit the most applicants from its jurisdiction, and section chiefs from the police station frequently make follow-up visits to encourage the young men to take the examination.

The July examination is mainly for young men who will graduate from college the following April, though some high school students take it also, and the October examination is for those who will graduate from high school in April. The examination has two parts. The first part consists of multiple-choice questions that test general knowledge at the high school or college level, depending on the schooling of the individual, and lasts two hours. The second part lasts one hour and consists of an essay type of question to measure the applicant's reasoning and ability to express himself. Those who pass this examination go on to a second stage of the selection process which involves an interview, a physical examination, and an aptitude test. In 1975 there were 7.3 applicants (53,696 total) for

29. Information supplied by the Okayama Prefectural Police Headquarters, 1974.

every police officer hired in the nation (7,352 total).[30] A number of applicants, after passing the examination, do not enroll in the prefectural police school, because they were accepted at a university. They take both the police and university examinations to give themselves two options.

The reasons given by recruits for wanting to join the police are interesting. In the July examination of 1974, both college and high school graduates were applicants, and their reasons for wanting to join the police are shown in table 7.[31]

TABLE 7. *Reasons Given by New Recruits for Joining Police (in percentage)*

	College Graduates (Total 140)	High School Graduates (Total 102)	Total (242)
To serve society	20.0	15.7	18.2
Because it is a stable life	14.3	23.5	18.2
Because of an advancement examination system based on ability	25.7	8.8	18.6
Because it is a good job for a man	28.6	38.3	32.6
Was attracted by the uniform	0.7	0.	0.4
No other suitable job available	2.1	4.9	3.3
Wanted to ride a patrol car or motorcycle	0.	2.9	1.2
Other	8.6	5.9	7.4

College and high school graduates alike acknowledged, in highest proportion, the attraction of the police profession because of its masculinity; this response, of course, might preempt specifics such as uniform or motorcycle, which few respondents specified. Whereas the appeals acknowledged next most often by college graduates were achievement through merit and the altruistic opportunity to serve society, employment security appears to have had stronger appeal to high school graduates. It has been noted that civil service occupations become more desirable during times of economic crisis in Japan; the severe inflation and recession initiated by the "oil shock" of 1974 could well have influenced those answers.

In districts such as Okayama prefecture, almost all recruits come from within the prefecture. Ninety-eight percent of the Okayama police officers come from Okayama homes.[32] By contrast, police in the metropolitan areas of Tokyo and Osaka are composed to a large extent of people from

30. Information from the personnel division, National Police Agency.
31. Data supplied by the Okayama Prefectural Police Headquarters, 1974. The questionnaire involved free responses.
32. Figure given me by the Okayama Prefectural Police Headquarters, 1974.

outlying districts. For instance, in the Tokyo Metropolitan Police Department, even though the largest number of officers from any one prefecture are from Tokyo, policemen from outside of Tokyo make up 83 percent of the force of 38,420.[33] It is historically interesting that people of Tohoku (northeast Honshu) and Kyushu origin are numerous, which is consistent with tradition begun in early Meiji. As the Metropolitan Police Department grew in size in the Meiji period former samurai from Kagoshima concentrated in the higher ranks and former samurai from Tohoku filled the lower levels. The feudal fiefs from Tohoku had supported the fallen Tokugawa regime, so samurai from this area were initially barred from high positions in the army or police. The phrase "Kagoshima *keishi*/Ibaragi *junsa*" (Kagoshima superintendent/Ibaragi patrolman) was current in Tokyo police circles at the time. The large numbers from southern Kyushu and Tohoku today reflect the fact that these areas are rather isolated and economically depressed and perhaps indicate a policy of recruiting "like types" for organizational harmony—and, in this case, zealously obedient men from the most traditional areas.

Until recently, the Japanese police establishment has been almost exclusively a man's world with very few female police officers. Okayama prefecture had a few female police officers in the late 1940s but has had none since then, and there are apparently no current plans to hire any,[34] whereas there were 2,544 female police officers in Tokyo, Osaka, and fourteen other prefectural police organizations in 1974.[35] The interest by young women in becoming female police officers is apparently high, because the national ratio of applicants to available positions was 5.0 to 1 in 1974, much higher than the national ratio of male applicants to positions available as police officers (3.2 to 1) in the same year.[36] In addition, 2,786 young women work throughout Japan as "traffic inspectors" (*kōtsū junshiin*, i.e., meter maids) in every prefecture. This job is not as desirable as becoming a female police officer, as is seen by the ratio of 2.8 applicants for every position in 1974.[37] Women also work as "guidance counselors" (*hodōin*) in the youth section of the police in many prefectures,

33. Data supplied by the Metropolitan Police Department and the Okayama Prefectural Police Headquarters, 1974.
34. Interview at the Okayama Prefectural Police Headquarters, 1974.
35. National Police Agency, ed. *Keisatsu hakusho, 1974* [Police white paper] (Tokyo: Okurasho Insatsukyoku, 1974), p. 381.
36. Ibid.
37. Ibid.

including Okayama, with 227 in the nation in 1974.[38] Women employees occupy a moderate percentage of the general secretarial and clerical positions in the police as well.

TRAINING

The Japanese police have long placed importance on the training of police personnel, and the extensive training system touches both new recruits and seasoned officers. Police schools at the prefectural and regional levels and a national police college in Tokyo form the core of the system. General training at schools is given at each rise in rank through police inspector (*keibu*), and technical training is given in the various police specializations, such as criminal investigation, traffic, crime prevention, security, and communications, to police officers assigned to those duties.

The various types of training offered at prefectural police schools, regional police schools (connected to regional police bureaus), and the police college are outlined below.[39]

Prefectural Police Schools (todōfuken keisatsu gakkō)

1. Initial course for new recruits (one year if high school graduate and six months if college graduate)[40]

2. Review course for new police officers after six months to a year on the job (four months)

3. Review course for police sergeants and assistant police inspectors (two weeks)

4. Specialization course for police officers of the rank of assistant police inspector and below (two weeks)

5. Course for new police sergeants (two weeks)

Regional Police Schools (kanku keisatsu gakkō)

1. Course for policemen who will soon be made police sergeants (three months)

38. Ibid.
39. National Police Agency, ed., *Keisatsu hakusho, 1973* [Police white paper] (Tokyo: Okurasho Insatsukyoku, 1973), p. 376.
40. The National Police Agency has decided to extend initial training for new recruits who are high school graduates from one year to two years, in order to meet the criticism that new policemen under twenty years of age are not yet legally adults and are not mature enough to exercise the necessary degree of responsibility. The cost of this doubling of the preservice training period will be offset by a five-year phase-in period, and also by the fact that college graduates, who are older and will not receive longer training, are making up larger proportions of new police recruits.

2. Course for police sergeants who will soon be made assistant police inspectors (six months)

3. Specialization course for police officers of the rank of assistant police inspector and below (three weeks to one year)

Police College (keisatsu daigakkō)[41]

1. Course for assistant police inspectors who have passed competitive examination to become police executive officers (one year)

2. Specialization course for new police inspectors (two and a half months)

3. Initial training for elite-course police recruits who have passed the Higher National Public Service Examination and entered the police as assistant police inspectors (three months)

4. Technical training course for assistant police inspectors who will become instructors in judo, kendo, techniques of arrest, and other technical subjects (one year)

5. Special training course for assistant police inspectors and above in various fields of police work (three weeks)

6. Specialization course for assistant police inspectors and above (two weeks to three months)

7. Research course for advanced training for police inspectors and above (two weeks to three months)

8. Special training course for police inspectors in criminal investigation (five and a half months)

A high school graduate who advances to police inspector will automatically receive at least two years of training in police schools, apart from any specialization training.[42] In addition to these training programs, the National Police Agency operates a communications school as a part of the police college, and also special training facilities in foreign languages. An important factor in the solidarity of the nationwide police organization is the bringing together of police officials from various prefectures for extended periods of training at regional police schools or the police college. This leads to the development of strong affective schoolmate (*dōkyūsei*)

41. An interesting fact that points to the functional equivalence of the present police organization to the prewar army is that the police college occupies the same site as the old military police (*kempei*) school in Nakano-ku, Tokyo.

42. This will increase to three years total police schooling when the change in initial training is implemented (see n. 40).

bonds that help integrate the police organization in an informal and horizontal manner. Police officers frequently use the national police telephone network to request personal favors from police school or police college friends in other prefectures. In addition, informal bonds formed between students at police schools and their instructors are powerful, transcending the formal command structure, and police officers often counsel with their former instructors about problems and concerns.

The prefectural police-school experience for new recruits is a total immersion into police life, ideals, and subculture. All recruits must stay in the school dormitories, and their days are heavily structured. In Okayama recruits arise at 6:30 A.M., eat breakfast, and have classwork from 8:30 until 12:00. After an hour break for lunch, they have classes again from 1:00 P.M. until 4:00, followed by an hour for club activities or sports and two hours for a bath and dinner. They are supposed to study in their own rooms from 7:00 until 10:00 P.M., when all lights are turned out.[43] High school graduates take the one-year course and receive the following types and amounts of training in the Okayama police school:

General Education (190 hours total)[44]

Character building	50 hours
Japanese language	20 hours
History	20 hours
Economics	10 hours
Psychology	20 hours
Natural science	20 hours
Current events	20 hours
Others (e.g., how to talk to people)	30 hours

Law (158 hours total)

Constitutional law	20 hours
Police administration	24 hours
Criminal law	58 hours
Civil law	10 hours
Criminal procedure	46 hours

43. From an interview with officials of the Okayama Prefectural Police School, 1974.

44. Many instructors in general education are high school teachers whom police invite to give lectures. The various levels of police schools, including the police college, regularly bring in outside experts.

Police Activities (848 hours total)

General affairs	
Criminal investigation	436 hours
Patrol duties	
Criminal identification	48 hours
Crime prevention	84 hours
Traffic	146 hours
Communications	44 hours
Security	90 hours

Technical Training (562 hours total)

Etiquette and drill	70 hours
Firearms	60 hours
First aid	40 hours
Arrest techniques	80 hours
Judo	90 hours
Kendo	90 hours
Exercises	40 hours
Other	92 hours

Other Training (310 hours total)
Driving practice, swimming, visiting cultural exhibits, practice at police stations, role playing of investigations, etc.

College graduates receive six months of training in the police school instead of the usual year, spending the time in approximately the same proportions on the five basic aspects of training, except for less general education and more emphasis on the police activities category. Recruits participate in the tea ceremony, poetry singing (*shigin*), poetry writing (*senryū*), and calligraphy as club activities, which, as was noted earlier, follows the traditional Japanese notion that a samurai must be culturally and spiritually refined. In Tokyo stress is placed on the use of standard Japanese (*hyōjungo*) among police officers because of the tendency by recruits from different parts of Japan to use their regional dialects.[45] In

45. In Okayama, police officers use the Okayama dialect when talking to each other, and especially when interrogating suspects. This is indicative of the heavily rural origins of police officers in Okayama, as well as a general lack of college education. But local dialect as used by criminal investigators enables them to establish easier rapport with suspects in their efforts to elicit confessions.

Kendo practice in the martial arts hall of the Mizushima police station. Police officers practice almost every day.

addition, the police realize that many recruits have never had an income before, and encourage them to give part of their pay to instructors regularly for deposit in a bank. About 10 percent of the recruits who enter the Okayama police school drop out for various reasons; from 5 to 7 percent drop out in Tokyo.

There is a distinct emphasis on judo and kendo and a lack of emphasis on firearms training at prefectural police schools, as can be seen by the hours devoted to each in Okayama, noted above. Of the 170 recruits who entered the Okayama Police School in 1972, 19 already held a black belt in judo and kendo on entry; 112 held the black belt on graduation (65.9 percent of all the graduates).[46] In the Okayama police in general, 67.9 percent held black belts in judo, and 57.7 percent held black belts in kendo during the same year.[47] This expertise in the martial arts compensates for

46. *Okayama Prefectural Police Yearbook*, p. 312.

47. Ibid., p. 101. This is higher than the national police average of black belts in judo (59.9%) and kendo (53.5%). See *Police White Paper*, 1974, p. 383.

the small body-size of many police officers, as is seen by the minimum height requirement of five feet four inches and the minimum weight requirement of 104 pounds.[48] The Japanese rely on physical dexterity to subdue suspects rather than on sheer body bulk or the quick resort to firearms.

The training of police officers is a continual process. The training section of the prefectural police headquarters sends out materials to police stations for in-house training on various topics. New graduates of the prefectural police school spend their first ten days in the police station working with each section, and they are required to keep detailed diaries of their experiences during this period.[49] They are then assigned to a police box to work with a senior police officer, usually an old sergeant, for about two weeks; then they can work alone like other policemen. Younger police officers in Kurashiki, especially patrolmen, are occasionally given report forms to practice filling out as homework, but this is not usually done for older police officers. Firearms marksmanship training is infrequent in police stations; police officers practice about once a year at the prefectural police firing-range. A marksmanship competition in the prefecture is held once a year, but it does not draw interest as much as the annual judo and kendo tournament in which all police stations in the prefecture compete. A national tournament is also held annually, to which every prefectural police organization sends competitors. Police officers practice judo, kendo, or other martial arts every afternoon in the judo/kendo hall of every police station. In addition, each police station in Okayama holds a competition each year for skill in stopping, interrogating, and arresting suspects.

OTHER METHODS OF SOCIALIZATION

The police employ a number of other mechanisms in addition to formal police schools to inculcate in policemen the ideals of solidarity and loyalty that are vital in the functioning of the police organization. One such mechanism is the riot police. Young police officers can become riot policemen for a few years after serving a year or two as patrolmen in a *kōban*. In Tokyo they volunteer for the duty; in Okayama they are chosen by senior riot police officials. Besides specialized training for riot and demonstration control, the riot policemen, particularly in Tokyo, receive

48. Figures taken from police recruitment material, Okayama, 1974.
49. All police officers are required for administrative purposes to keep an account of their daily activities (*nisshi*), which is then periodically read by the police chief and other officers.

classroom instruction in law and other police matters. Police officers in police stations do not have the time for this amount of instruction. Accordingly, because rank advancement in the police is by competitive examination, riot policemen in Tokyo usually rise sooner to the rank of sergeant than do other police officers. This may also be because the Tokyo riot police are considered an elite, since their function is important to the political stability of the nation's capital, and therefore more enthusiastic and ambitious police officers volunteer for the force. In Okayama the riot police are not considered an elite, and the specialty is attractive mainly to those police officers interested in judo and kendo and in group living and work.

The riot police in Tokyo may thus be considered an instrument of socialization for young policemen who will be rising to positions of leadership within the police. It provides an intensive environment for learning the values and espirit de corps that are the ideals of the entire police establishment. The organization of the riot police is modeled directly after the abolished Imperial Japanese Army,[50] and it performs many of the functions to maintain order carried out by the army before the war.[51] The riot police also consciously inculcates prewar army values into its men, which coincide with many of the highest samurai traditions. For instance, the commander of one of the Tokyo riot-police forces spoke to his men at length, during an inspection that I witnessed, about his experiences as an officer in training in China during World War II, and how he developed total dedication to his army unit and its officers and to his duty as a soldier. He urged his riot policemen always to have a similar commitment to their riot police unit and officers and to their duty.[52] Indeed, if the prewar spirit of *bushidō* ("the way of the warrior," the samurai ethic), as found in the Imperial Japanese Army, exists anywhere in Japan today, it persists in the riot police.

The visual similarities between the equipment of the riot police and the armor of the samurai are striking. The helmets have neck protectors ex-

50. The organization of the riot police is as follows: squad (*buntai*) of eleven men, platoon (*shōtai*) made up of three *buntai*, company (*chūtai*) made up of three *shōtai*, and battalion (*daitai*) composed of three or four *chūtai*. Each prefectural riot police force and each of the ten Tokyo forces is a *daitai*.

51. The Self-Defense Forces are authorized to perform order-maintenance duties under the direction of the prime minister, but the police insist that they will never need to be called. The police often refer to the fact that Japan does not have an "army" now, reflecting their derogatory opinion of the value of the ground Self-Defense Forces.

52. Observed during a day I spent with a riot police force, Tokyo, 1975.

Riot police commander atop command vehicle at Kakumaru demonstration. He is flanked by assistants, including one carrying a lighted staff, which indicates the presence of the commander. The large 8 stands for the 8th Riot Police Unit, Tokyo. (Eight is pronounced *hachi*; a bee is also pronounced *hachi*.)

tending down from the back, giving the visual impression of a samurai helmet. Forearm protectors (*kote*), worn by the samurai and used in kendo armor today, are also worn, as well as armored vests, loin guards, and shin protectors, which further enhance the samurai appearance.[53] Officers

53. The entire riot police armor weighs about twelve pounds.

lead their platoons and companies by waving a white stick (*shikibō*) with a colored tassel hanging from the handle end, exactly in the manner of Imperial Japanese Army officers leading their troops into battle with samurai swords. Platoon and company commanders are attended by from one to three riot policemen assistants (*denrei*) during riots and demonstrations, one holding a flag (in the day) or a lighted pole (at night) aloft to identify and pinpoint the location of the officer, the others operating a two-way radio or recording events. This is similar to the attendants who accompanied samurai commanders, one of whom usually carried a banner with the officer's emblem on it.

The riot police are unique in the degree of love (*aijō*) manifested between the officers and their men, and in the comradeship (*yūjō*) found among the men themselves. This type of relationship is found to some extent among the various police units, but the group nature of riot police work and life accentuates it. Riot policemen, most of whom are young and single, live in dormitories within tightly guarded and walled compounds.[54] The demands of their work schedule allow few friendships to be formed with outsiders. These relationships of love and comradeship are usually mentioned in conversation with riot policemen about their impressions of life in the riot police. The commander always attends the weddings of his men, counsels them if they have problems, visits them when they are sick, and drinks with them off duty. The men reciprocate whenever possible. For instance, when a detachment of riot policemen is relieved in the morning after spending the night on duty, they gather below the window of the commander and sing him a police or an old army song. The closeness of the men is seen graphically when one of them is transferred: all line up and clap to martial music played over a loudspeaker as the man being transferred walks down the line shaking hands before he gets in a police car to be driven away. The strength of the bond among the men is obvious as they bid farewell to their comrade.

The police use slogans as another method of inculcating values and ideals. Like most Japanese, they seem to have a fondness for slogans, which one finds pasted or painted on cabinet doors, mirrors, or walls in police stations and police-boxes. I counted nine slogans urging kindness, in the patrol section room of the Kurashiki police station alone. The word "kindness" is painted on the mirrors of every police-box I visited in Oka-

---

54. Married riot policemen live with their families in homes nearby.

yama prefecture, demonstrating the realization by police administrators that the sometimes highhanded manner of police officers is often offensive to the citizenry.

The police also use songs to express and reinforce police ideals and espirit de corps. Each prefectural police organization has its own songs, including a police school song, and each regional police school and the police college has a song. In Tokyo many police stations have their own songs, and each riot police unit has several songs, including songs for their dormitories. Some police specializations, such as criminal investigation and crime prevention, also have their own songs.[55]

Songs, like slogans, give evidence of contrasting police images.[56] The official song of the National Police Agency, with its hymning of "rights," "democracy," and "friend of the people" that strongly hints a postwar date of composition, is in conflict with and attempts to change, the traditional samurai-like image of a haughty and authoritarian police.

ATARASHIKI HI NO WARERA

Atarashiki hi no aa warera
Aozora no chie wo kumi
Heiwa no niji wo shitaite
Tsutsumashiku kozoritatsu nari
Akarushiya minshū no shirube
Yo no michi wo mamoru ni mo, nigori naku isagiyoku
Jinken wo tōtoban ka na

Atarashiki hi no aa warera
Chi no ue ni hana hiraku
Bunka no hae wo inorite
Ono ga mi wo sasageyuku nari
Takanaruya seigi no chishio
Ōyake no shimobe zo ya, hirumu naku isamashiku
Akugyaku to tatakawan ka na

Atarashiki hi no aa warera
Soyokaze no ai mitsuru
Jiyū no hata wo kazashite

55. See two commonly used collections of police songs: National Police Agency, ed., *Keisatsu kashū* [Collection of police songs] (Tokyo: Jiji Tsushinsha, 1956), and Metropolitan Police Department, ed., *Keishichō kashōshū* [Metropolitan Police Department song collection] (Tokyo: Kasumigaseki Shuppankai, 1971).

56. See the contrasting images in the motto of the Okayama Prefectural Police ("warm and human solidarity," "kind, cheerful reception").

Utsukushiku furuitatsu nari
Kiyokeshiya chian no tsutome
Shitashimite aiyorite nikoyaka ni shinjitsu ni
Minshū no tomotaran ka na.

O WE OF THE NEW DAY

O we of the new day
Draw in the wisdom of the azure sky
Yearn for the rainbow of peace
Come together in respect
Bright guide of democracy
Gallant and pure in defending the world
Revere human rights

O we of the new day
Flowers bloom on the earth
Pray for the glory of culture
Consecrate your being
Ring high, the blood of justice
Servant of the public, undaunted, courageously
Do battle with treachery

O we of the new day
Filled with the love of a gentle breeze
Hold aloft the banner of freedom
Beautiful, flowing
Sacred, the duty of public peace
Genial, drawing close, smiling, truthful
Friend of the people.[57]

Police songs are sung mostly in police schools or at special ceremonies attended by police officers, the former reinforcing the latter's intensive socialization and indoctrination in police ideals. Riot police quarters more often echo such songs than do ordinary police settings. Police songs are seldom sung during the daily activities in a police station.

As another tool of indoctrination, each prefectural police headquarters publishes a monthly journal that is distributed to all police officers free of charge. In Okayama the journal is called *Kōraku*, a title taken from the name, meaning "pleasure after [work]," of the premodern lord's park, a centerpiece of modern Okayama City. It offers such things as news notes on personnel and police station activities, cultural articles on Okayama

57. *Police Songs*, pp. 1–3.

history and customs, articles on hobbies, articles on police topics, a poetry page (haiku), and an etiquette page.[58] The cover always has a beautiful painting of flowers or a landscape. The articles seem focused on the ideals of police work, especially the frequent articles in which senior police officers reflect on their years of police service.

Other reinforcement comes through the ceremonies and meetings that the police often hold. These include bimonthly meetings held in police stations, in which all police officers gather for instruction and encouragement (to be discussed further in chapter nine). Special meetings are also held. For example, in Kurashiki, all the police officers gather on the last regular working day of the year and again on the first regular working day of the new year and are greeted by the police chief and exhorted to work hard during the coming year. All section chiefs visit the residence of the police chief on New Year's Day to wish him greetings, and all members of each section visit their section chief's home on January second. This custom, conforming with traditional New Year's visiting in Japan, serves to reinforce the authority structure in the police.

Another ceremony that serves to strengthen solidarity and ideals is the yearly memorial service (*ireisai*) for all police officers who have died in the line of duty. It is held in October or November in every prefecture, usually in October in Okayama. The ceremony takes place at a Shinto shrine in Okayama City in front of a large memorial stone tablet set up in an open area near the shrine to commemorate the deceased police officers. All of the section and division chiefs of the prefectural police headquarters, the prefectural police chief, and the entire general-affairs section of the headquarters attend, as well as all police station chiefs. Significantly, the entire riot police and all police recruits who are attending the prefectural police school also participate. The families of the deceased are also there. All the participants are led in "venerating" (*ogamu*) the dead by a priest from the shrine, thereby reaffirming their commitment to the ideals of the police organization.

In this chapter we have looked at the backgrounds, selection, and training of police officers, and the building up within them of the subculture of the police organization and its values of solidarity and loyalty. We shall now turn to an examination of the maintenance of that subculture and unity through various formal and informal mechanisms.

58. Similarities between the police journal and the gangster magazine described in chapter six are striking.

nine

SOLIDARITY IN THE FRONT LINE

Police think of themselves as the "front line" (*daiissen*), the first line of defense in society's battle with crime and disorder. This does not imply that the police have a siege mentality, confronted with enemies on all sides, for the police enjoy widespread community support. It refers to the sense of mission with which the police are imbued and the preeminent role played by solidarity within police ranks. Solidarity entails both a strong sense of loyalty to the group and unswerving obedience to superiors in the police command structure. Group identity and obedience to seniors is strong because of active recruiting, comprehensive screening, and long and pervasive schooling and indoctrination to conform to an image of dignity, honor, competence, and loyalty. Once a man is fully socialized into the police way of life, however, the process does not end. A sense of "togetherness" and hierarchy is continually augmented by formal methods of police utilization and informal mechanisms of police life-style. Yet the police are not conspicuously unlike Japanese companies in their philosophy of employment, hence members of the police organization are, on the whole, probably predisposed to living with an all-encompassing and vertically structured system.[1]

This chapter will discuss a number of mechanisms that the police use to maintain solidarity and hierarchy. These include the promotion system, physical arrangement of the work environment in police offices, decision-making processes, transfers, police housing complexes, the pursuit of lei-

1. See, e.g., Chie Nakane, *Japanese Society* (Berkeley and Los Angeles: University of California Press, 1970).

sure by police officers, marriage and family life, and retirement assistance. These mechanisms, both formal and informal, help to reinforce the structure of police hierarchy and create the almost totally enveloping character of police life.

Solidarity and total obedience to authority are only ideals and are not fully achieved in reality. The chapter will also point to tensions and potential fissures beneath the façade of unity and allegiance to superiors, which are not completely eradicated by the pervasive socialization mechanisms described in chapter eight. The most important cleavage, and one that may prove injurious to the cultivated, samurai-like image of sacrifice of self and responsibility to leadership and policy, is a generation gap between older and younger police officers, which tends to reinforce strains inherent in the rank structure. Another factor is deviation from authority within the police and how misconduct is handled. These fracture lines within the police, as well as contrasting public images of the police (authoritarian versus "democratic" or egalitarian), may ultimately have a disequilibrating effect on both the police and their relationship with their citizen clients, law abiding and outlaw.

THE STRUCTURE AND REINFORCEMENT OF POLICE HIERARCHY

Police hierarchy is a function of both the formal rank structure and seniority among police officers. Promotion to higher ranks is essentially based on merit, but the system also takes seniority and experience into consideration to an extent. Merit is demonstrated primarily through competitive examination for the ranks of sergeant (*junsa buchō*), assistant police inspector (*keibuhō*), and police inspector (*keibu*). For the ranks of superintendent (*keishi*) and above, police officers are selected by senior police officials based on their record, their abilities, and the need for police executives. However, recognition is also given to policemen (*junsa*, the lowest rank) with a number of years experience but who have not passed the examination for sergeant, by awarding them the title of "senior policeman" (*junsachō*), which is not an official rank. Older policemen who are nearing retirement are awarded the rank of sergeant as a reward for their long years of police service and are termed "specially appointed sergeants" (*tokubetsu nin'yō buchō*).

There is a definite difference in the speed with which high school graduates and college graduates can rise through the police ranks, though schooling sets no ceiling on how far one can rise. A high school graduate must wait three years to take the examination for police sergeant, but a college graduate may take it after one year. A high school graduate must wait three years after becoming a sergeant before he can take the examination to become assistant police inspector, and another three years before he can take the examination for police inspector. A college graduate can take the first examination one year after becoming a sergeant, and the second examination two years after that.[2] Theoretically, a college graduate can become an inspector (section chiefs in police stations are inspectors) within four years after graduating from the police school, but the fastest rise I know of in Okayama required eight years. The possibility of fast promotion based on one's abilities as measured in examinations and work record—instead of being based on age and school background, as is the case in many Japanese companies—is an attractive aspect of the police for young men, especially college graduates.

The examinations are not easy. They are in two parts: the first is a one-hour multiple-choice examination that is primarily on law (about 90%) with a small portion testing general knowledge, and the second involves an interview with the senior officers of the prefectural police headquarters. The examination for sergeant is particularly rigorous, with an additional all-day essay examination on the various aspects of police work, which precedes the interview stage. A limited number of positions are open for each rank, and those with the highest scores are selected; the competition is heaviest for the sergeant examination, as is seen in the following ratios of candidates to the number of positions available (1972): sergeant, 15.4 to 1; assistant police inspector, 5.1 to 1; police inspector, 10.5 to 1.[3] Promotion does not depend entirely on examination for these ranks, however, because the evaluation of a police officer's daily work by the executive officers of the police station is given almost equal consideration.

It would not be surprising if a feeling of fulfillment in the police profession was tied to promotion. In a study of about fifteen hundred police officers in Kanagawa prefecture in 1971, the answers to certain questions indicate that this is true (see table 8). There is also an apparent link between job specialization and the answers to the questions in table 8. Security, crime-prevention, and criminal-investigation personnel gave highly

2. Figures taken from Okayama Prefectural Police recruitment material, 1974.
3. Okayama Prefectural Police Headquarters, *Okayama ken keisatsu nenkan, 1972* [Okayama Prefectural Police Yearbook] (Okayama: Okayama Prefectural Police Headquarters, 1972), p. 48.

TABLE 8. *Answers to the Question "Is Your Present Job Worth Doing?"* *(in percentage)*

Rank	Worth Doing	Indifferent	Not Worth Doing
Policeman	58.6	35.6	5.4
Sergeant	67.4	27.9	4.1
Assistant Inspector	78.5	18.6	2.8
Inspector	92.3	7.6	0.0

Answers to the Question "Do You Like Working for the Police?" (in percentage)

Rank	Like It	Don't Feel Anything	Don't Like It
Policeman	58.2	27.0	14.4
Sergeant	66.0	21.1	12.3
Assistant Inspector	70.0	20.5	9.3
Inspector	88.4	11.5	0.0

SOURCE: Kanagawa Social Psychology Research Association, *Jūmin no yōbō to kinmu kankyō nado ni taisuru keisatsu shokuin no ishiki chōsa* [Attitude survey of police employees concerning citizens' desires and work environment], n.d.

positive responses, but general-affairs and patrol personnel gave the least positive responses, while traffic personnel were distributed in between. The first three are considered desirable assignments in the police. A feeling of fulfillment is particularly high in the older men who are made "specially appointed sergeants," I was told by several such old sergeants in Kurashiki.

The promotion system based on merit and open equally to all applies to regular police officers hired by the local prefecture. The police organization, like other governmental bureaucracies in Japan, is directed at its upper level by a highly educated administrative elite.[4] They are hired directly by the National Police Agency after they pass the Higher National Public Service Examination, then are given three months training at the police college in Tokyo, and if they pass another difficult examination after the training, they begin their climb on a path separate from other officers toward the top positions in the police establishment. Fifteen young men, on the average, are hired each year in this category, twelve of whom

4. Most of the following information was given to me by a member of the administrative elite working in the National Police Agency, Tokyo, 1975.

usually are graduates of the University of Tokyo Faculty of Law, two are from the Kyoto University Faculty of Law, and one is from another university. One person in about every two years is from the Economics Department of the University of Tokyo.

Elite-course police officers enter at the rank of assistant inspector and follow a rigidly structured course of advancement during their first few years. After graduating from the police college, they spend six months as a unit head (*kakarichō*) in patrol, criminal investigation, or traffic in a large urban police station somewhere in Japan and then another six months in a prefectural police headquarters. After a year, they are promoted to inspector, and work in two different positions in the National Police Agency in Tokyo for two years and four months. They are then promoted to superintendent and are sent to another prefectural police headquarters as a section chief. It takes them three and a third years to achieve the rank of superintendent, a rank that requires twenty-five years for most regular police officers who rise that far. After their service as a section chief, the course becomes varied, with some serving as the top officers in prefectural police headquarters in the regions, some spending most of their time in the National Police Agency and Metropolitan Police Department in Tokyo.[5] Those who eventually rise to the top positions in the National Police Agency and Metropolitan Police Department spend the largest part of their careers working in Tokyo.

Able police officers hired locally occasionally become administrative elite by passing the Higher National Public Service Examination. A number of prefectural police chiefs, and section and division chiefs in the National Police Agency, had risen in 1975 to the elite from being regular policemen. These men seldom move to the highest levels of the National Police Agency or the Metropolitan Police Department, however, and are informally referred to in a train analogy as *kyūkō* ("express") when compared with those who entered directly from an elite university (called *tokkyū*, "super-express"). Those who enter the police from the University of Tokyo or Kyoto University frequently have a relative or a family member who was a police officer, and this inclines them toward the police. It is said that those who join the police are often of the second level in ability of all the University of Tokyo and Kyoto University graduates, since the

---

5. Certain police stations in Tokyo are always commanded by an elite-course police chief (Motofuji, Kanda, Seiyo, and Ushigome) because they are near the prestigious universities, and one or two of the riot police units in Tokyo are also usually led by elite-course officers.

top people prefer the Ministry of Finance or the Ministry of International Trade and Industry.[6]

Regular police officers occasionally express resentment against the administrative elite, especially young policemen who consider the practice "undemocratic" and older police officers who resent having young and inexperienced men as their superiors.[7] Most, however, do not question the system and feel that the elite officers have little relation to their own daily work or promotion. The Okayama Prefectural Police Headquarters is proud of its elite members because they frequently come directly from Tokyo and return directly to Tokyo, which shows their high stature in the ranks of the elite.[8] However, the automatic ("escalator," as the Japanese phrase it) system of promotion of elite-course officials could lead to a preoccupation with efforts to avoid incidents. An officer rises in the system unless he is knocked off the escalator by a serious mistake, and this tends to augment a lack of imagination or creativity in some of the less able elite officers.

The hierarchy of rank and seniority is reinforced by a number of mechanisms, both formal and informal. The hierarchy within police work groups, for example, is reinforced by the physical arrangement of the workplace. In a police station, the arrangement of desks serves to strengthen both the sense of hierarchy and the identity of police officers with their units. The first impression one receives when walking into a police station is of utter confusion. There is an entrance way with a reception desk, beyond which numerous desks are crowded into a large open room, with people talking, walking around, and answering telephones. A low roar of noise pervades the main floor. People are going and coming through the main entrance, and occasionally a prisoner is brought in the front door in handcuffs with a rope around his waist, the other end held by a police officer. Except for this last, the feeling is very similar to a Japanese bank or any other large office. Everyone works together in large rooms on the several floors of the police station, but with a definite order that may escape one's first glance.

6. Before the war, it was considered ideal for junior members of the elite to marry the daughters of senior elite officers. That custom has not continued after the war, as far as I can determine.

7. I was told this by two high police officials in the Kurashiki police station, 1974.

8. Elite officers in the Okayama Prefectural Police Headquarters are usually the headquarters chief, general-affairs division chief, security division chief, criminal-identification section chief, and the first driver's license section chief.

Detectives at work in the criminal investigation room of the Kurashiki police station. The section chief at the left is taking a statement from a suspect. Note the flowers and potted plants on many desks.

Each section (*ka*) within the police station occupies a large room with the desks grouped by unit (*kakari*) within the section. The seating arrangement in each section and unit reflects the rank and seniority of the members. In the Kurashiki criminal investigation section on the second floor of the police station, for instance, the commanding criminal-affairs officer (*keijikan*, who holds higher rank than other section chiefs) sits at the center rear of the room facing the desks of the other police officers, flanked by seven section and unit heads. The members of each unit have their desks grouped in front of the unit head, the most senior officers sitting nearest the head. The officers sit facing each other. There is always a small reception area for guests in every section office, usually consisting of a small table and two couches. The section chief usually has a thermos of hot water, a tea set, and a carved wooden tray, to serve his guests tea. There is frequently a bonsai or a flower arrangement on or near the table. The police seem to work well in this open office arrangement, and they comment that the American custom of separate offices must be very lonely. They regard each grouping of desks as a separate office and are not distracted by activity in other desk areas; they rely on mental and organizational, rather than physical, walls between units. The physical proximity

Formal greetings to the assistant chief of a Tokyo police station by officers after a brief meeting. Tokyo police stations tend to be more formal than those in Okayama and other more rural areas.

and the ordering of the desk assignments adds to the espirit de corps of the units and visually symbolizes the hierarchy of rank and seniority.

The strict hierarchy of the work environment in a police station is mitigated somewhat in most Okayama police stations by a pervading air of informality. Formality increases in more urban prefectures and larger police stations. In Tokyo, for instance, all police officers in police stations except detectives are in uniform and, there is a formal bowing to superiors in most interactions. In Kurashiki the patrol, traffic, and general-affairs officers are in uniform, as well as the chief and assistant chief some of the time, but the other police officers are usually in civilian clothes. In the summer, the assistant chief of the smaller Mizushima police station is sometimes found at his desk at the rear of the main room on the first floor in his underwear. If a visitor comes to his desk, he politely excuses himself and puts on his uniform from a nearby locker before greeting his guest. Needless to say, there is also less formal bowing to superiors in Kurashiki and Mizushima than in Tokyo.

The hierarchy of rank and seniority is also reinforced in decision-making processes within the police. The decision by individual line police officers of whether to formally invoke the legal system through arrest is a graphic example. The police organization and command structure, as well as the laws, are formulated so as to minimize the discretion of individual policemen in making this decision.[9] Senior police officers and police commanders are usually consulted, if possible, before the decision to arrest is made. Younger policemen frequently defer to older ones in a police-box if the decision is difficult or somewhat in doubt. For instance, one of my acquaintances received a parking violation summons and reported to the nearby *kōban*.[10] Since the no-parking area was newly designated, the young patrolman could not decide whether to write a ticket. An older police sergeant sat back and watched for awhile and then finally stepped in and told my friend that he would be issued a warning. The young patrolman acquiesced to his decision immediately.

Whenever there is an incident or a crime of any consequence in Okayama, the commanding officer—police chief, section chief, or corps commander—is always notified, even in the middle of the night, and he assumes control of the situation and makes all the necessary decisions. For instance, whenever there is a murder (there were 43 in 1974) or a robbery (there were only 34) anywhere in Okayama prefecture, the criminal-investigation section chief from the prefectural police headquarters goes to the scene and assumes immediate command of the investigation. Because senior officers are ultimately accountable for the actions of their subordinates, they frequently assume direct control to minimize possible error.

The strongly hierarchical police organization is resilient enough, how-

9. The laws governing arrests allow police officers margin in deferring the formal decision of whether to arrest. If a police officer has "reasonable ground" to suspect that a person has "committed or is about to commit a crime," or that he knows something about a "crime which has already been committed or is about to be committed," he may stop and question the person (*shokumu shitsumon*, Article 2 of the Police Duties Execution Law, 1948). The police officer may ask the person to accompany him to a nearby police station or *kōban* for questioning, but force may not be used to compel the person to go, and he may not be compelled to answer questions (Article 2, Police Duties Execution Law, 1948). The person is not under arrest at this point, and according to Koshi, "his status is technically that of a witness." See George M. Koshi, *The Japanese Legal Advisor: Crimes and Punishments* (Rutland, Vt., and Tokyo: Charles E. Tuttle Company, 1970), p. 75. The police estimate that over 95 percent of all people questioned come voluntarily to the police station or police-box. It should be noted that the authority to apply for an arrest warrant is limited by law to higher ranking officers (inspector and above).

10. A parking violation summons is a note placed on the violating vehicle by police officers asking the driver to report to a nearby *kōban* or police station. He is asked to explain why he parked in violation of the law, and if he does not have a good excuse, he is issued a citation. This system allows discretion for police officers in deciding whether to formally invoke legal sanctions.

ever, to be responsive to suggestions from below in the decision-making process concerning everyday operations. Most changes in police station operations occur, of course, through directives from the higher levels of police hierarchy. For instance, the National Police Agency issues a directive to the prefectural police headquarters, which in turn issues the directive to the police station. If it is a matter concerning the patrol section, the patrol section of the prefectural police headquarters notifies the police chief and assistant chief, who then inform the patrol section chief of the police station. Some changes, however, are initiated from the lower levels of the police station and are circulated upward. These are usually written down (*kian*, "a written suggestion") and are of two types, *ringi* and *kessai*. They are initiated only by officers holding the rank of sergeant and above, and most originate with sergeants and assistant inspectors. The upward flow in the decision-making process serves to validate the hierarchical command structure, but also relieves some of its most stifling strictures.

The *ringi* system is commonly found in Japanese companies and other organizations. It works, for example, as follows: a sergeant in the patrol section has an idea on how to handle traffic better at the city auditorium. He discusses his plan with his unit chief (*kakarichō*) and then with the patrol section chief. The chief approves it and has the sergeant write up the plan with his name on it; the sergeant stamps his *hanko* (personal seal) on the plan, as does the section chief. The plan is put in a black folder labeled "patrol section" and is circulated among the related sections (e.g., the traffic section). Each section chief places his *hanko* on it; it then goes to the assistant chief and finally to the chief for their *hanko*. If there is an amendment or a notation, it goes back to the originator, otherwise it is initiated as policy. The rotation among several involved sections in the decision-making process is the essence of the *ringi* system. The *kessai* system is a method that involves only one section and goes in a straight line through the levels of the hierarchy from the initiator to the police chief.

If a policeman (*junsa*) or senior policeman (*junsachō*) has an idea for improving police work (*nōritsu tei'an*, "efficiency proposal"), he writes it up and hands it to the general affairs section. When several ideas are collected, the efficiency committee (*nōritsu iinkai*) meets, composed of ten police officers representing all ranks and police specializations. They discuss the ideas, and if they see merit in any, they write up the proposal as a *ringi* or a *kessai* and send it to the appropriate sections and on to the assistant chief and police chief for approval. In a *kōban*, if a young patrolman has an idea for improving the effectiveness of the *kōban* operations, he informally discusses it with the sergeant who runs the *kōban* (the *kumichō*); if the sergeant approves, he puts it into action.

The work load in a police station does not necessarily increase the higher one goes up the ladder of command. Most of the work of running a police station is done by police officers below the level of section chief. Section chiefs and the assistant chief seem about equal in their burden of work, with periods of heavy activity and a few times of relative slack. The police chief handles little of the daily duties of running the police station. As in most Japanese companies and bureaucracies, the actual running of the organization occurs at the level of the assistant chief, with the chief serving mainly as the representative of the organization to the outside and also bearing the ultimate responsibility for all actions of the organization and its members.[11] The police chief is frequently found reading a book or watching television in his office (the only separate one in the station) while the assistant chief is frantically working at his desk in the main room on the first floor. The pressure of being police chief lies not in the work entailed but in the weight of responsibility.

THE ENVELOPING NATURE OF POLICE LIFE

It was noted in chapter eight that the police tend toward being a total institution. This is largely the result of social distance between "police society" and the surrounding larger society, which is created by the all-encompassing nature of police life. Police officers and their families, to a certain extent, are literally separated from other Japanese, and this limits the degree and quality of their interactions. They cannot readily build significant affective relationships with people outside the police sphere because they have little opportunity to become acquainted. The majority of their friendships and social dealings are with others within the police milieu, although most policemen probably do not consciously choose to limit their friendships primarily to police types. Formal mechanisms such as frequent transfers and police housing complexes, and such informal processes as recreation, marriage, and family life, result in isolation.

Transfers between police stations help to isolate police officers from the

---

11. The Kurashiki chief estimates that 60 percent of his time is spent meeting community representatives and government officials, 10 percent in contacts with the prefectural police headquarters, and only about 30 percent in daily affairs of the police station.

outside community. Transfers are tied to rank in the Japanese police system; sergeants and those above are usually transferred to a new police station every two or three years. This is done explicitly to prevent the formation of conflicting ties of friendship and obligation between senior police officials and local men of influence. Police officers hired by the prefectural police are transferred to positions within the prefecture only, except in occasional instances when an outstanding officer is sent to Tokyo to work in the National Police Agency or to the regional police bureau for a few years. The prefectural police headquarters determines the police station or police unit (e.g., the riot police) to which a man of policeman (*junsa*) rank is to be sent, and the police chief or unit commander decides which specialization will use him (e.g., criminal investigation). Sergeants and those above are assigned to stations and units, as well as to specializations, by the prefectural police headquarters. Individual abilities, desires, and personal and family circumstances are said to be considered in transfers.

The desirability of transfer to certain specializations is substantiated by the answers to the question "Do you want to change to another job within the police?" (see table 9). The high percentage of patrol policemen in *kōban* and patrol cars who expressed a desire to be transferred is probably due to the grueling shift system and the relatively low prestige of patrol work among police officers; and a *chūzaisho* is also not a glamorous assignment. I assume that the reason that more police officers do not want to be transferred from the general-affairs section is that they are mostly older or sick men who would not want the physical rigors of other police

TABLE 9. *Answers to the Question "Do You Want to Change to Another Job within the Police?" (in percentage)*

Specialization	Don't Want to Change	Want to Change	Other
General affairs	69.7	21.0	9.2
Criminal investigation	82.7	13.9	3.3
Crime prevention	93.7	5.0	1.2
Patrol (*kōban*)	33.5	58.3	8.0
Patrol (*chūzaisho*)	46.8	42.5	10.6
Patrol (administrative, patrol car, etc.)	37.2	55.0	7.3
Security	84.6	7.6	7.6
Traffic	75.6	17.7	5.2

SOURCE: Attitude Survey of Police Employees (see table 8), p. 79.

work. The popularity of crime prevention, security, and criminal investigation work is clearly borne out in the responses. "Crime prevention" in most prefectures means investigation of violations of the special laws (*tokubetsuhō han*) rather than strictly preventive work, and all three of the most sought after specializations involve investigation. Work that emphasizes investigation and the catching of criminals is usually thought of as "real police work" in Japan as in the United States and is considered very desirable duty.

Transfers are a subject of keen interest and rumors within the police because of the uprooting and isolating effect they have on the lives of police officers and their families. Transfers occur en masse in the spring, and tension mounts as the time approaches. Police officers speculate whether they will be transferred and try to read meaning into new assignments. An old sergeant, for instance, who was switched from criminal investigation to patrol work a couple of years before retirement, was certain it was a punishment for some mistake, but was perplexed as to what he did wrong. Normally, police officers are never assigned to their town or village of origin—it is feared that conflicts of interest in enforcing the law will arise out of "human bonds" (*ningen kankei*) with their relatives or friends—but this rule has been relaxed recently in Okayama prefecture. When transfers are announced, those who are to remain make individual gifts of cash to those who are to leave, usually of between three and ten dollars (the amount depends on personal closeness) in envelopes used by Japanese on festive occasions. The police privately complain sometimes about the expense of this custom, called *o sembetsu*, but continue it because of its instrumental role in the perpetuation of "human bonds" of friendship.

Many police officers do not like the inconveniences and unsettling effects of a transfer and purposefully fail the examination for sergeant or simply refuse to take it. Specially appointed sergeants are not subject to frequent transfers, as are the ambitious young men who pass the competitive examination, and thus they end up staying far longer in one police station than any other rank grouping of police officers. Table 10 gives the average number of years served in the Kurashiki police station by rank in 1974.[12] The specially appointed sergeants all work in key positions in the various sections, providing continuity and wide knowledge of the police

12. Figures computed from data supplied by the Kurashiki police station, 1975.

TABLE 10. *Number of Years Spent by Officers in Kurashiki Police Station, 1974*

Rank	Number of men	Average Number of Years in Kurashiki
Senior superintendent	1	1.0
Superintendent	2	1.0
Police inspector	5	2.0
Assistant police inspector	17	2.5
Police sergeant (exam)	29	2.1
Police sergeant (special appointment)	15	18.6
Senior policeman*	28	8.7
Policeman	55	3.3

*Senior policemen usually become specially appointed sergeants.

station jurisdiction, which is vital to effective police work. Although their rank may not reflect it, they are in reality the key personnel in local police operations.

Police officers are further separated from other Japanese because most of their recreation is taken with other policemen. The police have most of their friends within the police station or the police apartment complex, and they are specifically centered on the *kōban* or police station section workgroup. The evening mood in a police station is relaxed, and many police officers remain until late at night simply chatting with their work mates. Several police officers told me they would rather be at the police station than at home because it is more interesting. Police officers on their days off frequently drop in at their *kōban* and spend hours chatting with the same men they work with the rest of the week. Young bachelor policemen often go to the homes of the married officers in their *kōban* or section for dinner and recreation, and develop close relations with the families.

The police station organizes recreational activities for police officers, which serve to enhance the unity and morale of the men. Most sections of the police station and some *kōban* have year-end parties (*bōnenkai*) at restaurants and the men all become gloriously drunk. Such parties foster communication between ranks, because the Japanese accept the convention that they may drop all pretense and speak from the heart when they are drunk. In Japan whatever one does or says when drunk is usually forgiven. The police stations also hold an athletic meet (*undōkai*) once a year to which married police officers bring their families, and everyone (married officers, single officers, and family members) participates in games and contests. Competition is usually based on sections of the police station, and they have organized cheering, banners, and the like. The police station has a baseball team, which plays with local high school and company teams, and the police also participate in daily judo and kendo practice in the police station judo/kendo hall.

When policemen seek leisure on their own or in small groups, they frequently go to bars or cabarets. Police officers enjoy pachinko and Mah-Jongg, and I have seen them on several occasions in such establishments. Because of potential conflicts in later law-enforcement situations, police officers usually frequent only places where they do not know the owner, so they often go to a neighboring city for recreation. Policemen sometimes go to a nearby prefecture for a day or two at a hot springs spa for extended drinking and relaxation because no one knows them there.

The demands of police work often limit opportunities for extended leisure. Police officers had twenty days of paid vacation a year in 1974, but this is usually given only one day at a time. Long vacations are rare, and workers everywhere in Japan use their leave only a day or two at a time. Section chiefs and other command officers in police stations find it difficult to take time off, and they must get permission before they can take a trip that requires more than one hour of travel time. The station must be able to reach them at all times in case of an emergency. Several police officers commented that they feel like physicians because of their lack of freedom to travel.

The all-encompassing nature of police life affects even the courtship and marriage of policemen. Police officers in Okayama are said to marry younger than the population at large because of the stress command officers put upon early marriage to bring stability to the lives of young policemen. For example, only 28 police officers out of the 152 in the Kurashiki police station in 1975 (18.4%) were not married, and every police officer above the rank of policeman (*junsa*) was married.[13] Significantly, the overall incidence of arranged marriages is said to be higher in the police than in the general population, older police officers having such marriages almost entirely, with only a few younger men having "love marriages." The demands of police work and the lack of women in the work group limit the opportunities of police officers to meet girls.[14]

13. Figures obtained from the Kurashiki police station, 1975.
14. Opinions on the desirability of marrying police officers vary, with some observers commenting that "salarymen" (*sarariman*, the Japanese word for middle-class office workers)

Older police officers frequently act as marriage go-betweens (*nakōdo*) for the younger men, or introduce them to girls if they are not formally the go-between. This functions as a powerful informal reinforcement to the rank and seniority hierarchy. A few marriages occur between police officers and the civilian "meter maids" (*junshiin*) or the clerical staff who work in police stations, but typical marriages are with girls outside the police structure. As an example, when a house within the jurisdiction of a certain *kōban* in Kurashiki was broken into by a burglar, three young policemen from the *kōban* went to investigate. The daughter of the family liked one of the policemen, so her mother called the old sergeant in charge of the *kōban* to discuss the matter. The young policeman had to go back to the house on numerous occasions during the investigation, and he was always given lots of cakes and tea. The mother finally asked the sergeant to act as the marriage go-between. The sergeant agreed, investigated the girl's family background, and then visited the policeman's home in the rural northern portion of the prefecture to discuss the marriage with his father. After the policeman's family investigated the girl's background, they too asked the sergeant to be the go-between. The young people were married in 1972 with the old sergeant acting as the *nakōdo*. The personal relationship of the young policeman with the go-between lasts a lifetime, for if problems arise in the marriage in the future, the couple will come to the go-between for counsel and assistance.

One aspect of police utilization with a profound effect both on police officers and on their families is the wide use of police apartment complexes and dormitories. Most police stations have at least one, usually several, housing areas provided for married police officers (Kurashiki has nine of varying ages and size) and a dormitory for single policemen. In Okayama there is no rent charged for these facilities, though a small amount is paid for utilities. In the dormitory, no meals are provided for policemen, who eat at the police station or *kōban* or at restaurants in the neighborhood. The dormitory has an 11:00 P.M. curfew, which is not strictly enforced because of the constant comings and goings of the policemen. It is difficult for friends of young policemen to visit them in the

---

do not like their daughters to marry policemen. Several police wives commented that they hated the police or were afraid of them before they married. Once policemen do marry, however, most families of the bride do not worry about the policeman's family background, because of the thorough screening that police officers usually receive before joining. One police officer's wife said that when she became engaged, the local *chūzai san* went around the village inquiring about her family.

Bachelors' dormitory, Kurashiki.

dorm. Married officers in Okayama usually live in the apartment complexes until they can afford to buy a home of their own, which is often shortly before or after retirement. In Kurashiki about 70 percent of the 124 married police officers live in the police apartment complexes, and when those living in the *chūzaisho* are added, about 80 percent of the married police officers were in police housing.[15] Single policemen are strongly encouraged to live in the dormitories, and most of those in Kurashiki do (all but one of the 28 single police officers in 1975).[16] Police housing facilities concentrate police officers in several locations for quick mobilization, but also isolate them and their families from the community contacts they would have if they lived in normal neighborhoods.

Police apartment complexes intensify the sense of togetherness of police families but also their separation from the rest of society.[17] Most police wives say that the majority of their friends are other women living in police apartments. They get together during the day and talk, but they say

15. Data provided by the Kurashiki police station, 1975.
16. Ibid.
17. The following information is based on three interviews with groups of wives in police apartment complexes in Kurashiki and Mizushima, 1974.

that their husbands seldom go to each other's apartments for recreation after work (most of their recreation is away from home). Some wives of police officers are occasionally involved in activities outside of the apartment complex, such as serving as officers in the PTA of their children's schools, but this is not common, because of their frequent relocations. Police families seem to realize that others are watching them; wives sometimes mention that they must keep their children from misbehaving so they will not reflect badly on the police. A sense of mission apparently often permeates to the family level.

The pressures of police work affect the families of police officers, and this indirectly influences police solidarity. The family life of police officers, especially the older ones, is often almost matrifocal because of the infrequency with which husbands are home; younger police officers seem to make greater efforts to be involved with their families. Wives sometimes complain, when asked, that they can never take family trips because of their husbands' work, and that when other families are enjoying themselves during holidays, their husbands are busier than usual. Husbands are frequently working when their families need them the most, such as during natural calamities like typhoons. Wives say that when their husbands are home they spend most of their time sleeping because of the exhausting nature of their work. Life in police apartment complexes also has both good and bad points: the families help each other when there are transfers, but some wives feel uncomfortable about the awareness of husbands' ranks when they are with other police wives.

Some aspects of police life are considered very desirable by families. Wives most often mention economic factors: that they do not have to pay rent in police apartments, that their husband's clothes are provided free of charge, that retirement benefits are good, and that they have financial security even during periods of economic decline. The wives I talked with usually noted that police can buy household items at discounts at designated stores. Police wives almost always do the family budgeting and give allowances of spending money to their husbands, as is usually the case in Japanese society. Very few wives of Japanese policemen work outside the home (I know of none), which may reflect the financial security of police officers. By contrast, families in which the husband and the wife both work are not at all rare in Japan in recent years.

Children of police officers have varying reactions to their father's job, and their age is a major factor in determining their attitudes. Young children, especially boys, are often proud that their fathers are policemen; they want to become police officers also. When they are about middle-school age, their attitudes often shift, and they become embarrassed to tell their friends their father's occupation. One girl I met tells her friends simply that her father is a civil servant. Children and mothers often complain about the frequent moves the family must make with transfers (the children of one command officer I know have had to change schools seven times between elementary and high school). Children complain that their fathers always break promises to take them places, because of the demands of their work. Some wives say they do not want their sons to be police officers, and many police officers themselves also share this sentiment. Indeed, the police profession often acts as a bridge by which men with poor rural backgrounds and little education are able to move their children up to high-status jobs in industry or the government bureaucracy. A large number of sons of police officers in Okayama are in the best high schools in the prefecture and will be able eventually to go to the University of Tokyo or other prestigious universities.

Traditionally, policemen, like schoolteachers, had pride but were not well compensated, as we see in the oft-cited phrase "Pay is low but life is correct." That has changed now, and compared with other occupations in Japan at least, the police are often well paid, a significant economic incentive for solidarity and loyalty to the organization.[18] For example, in April 1974, a twenty-six-year-old college-graduate police sergeant in Okayama with three or four years of experience in the police earned $362.00 a month as basic salary, whereas a college graduate of the same age working in the office of an average-sized company earned $334.02 a month basic salary.[19] With numerous allowances and bonuses the actual total salary is nearly double that figure. If this hypothetical sergeant was married, had one child, and worked in the patrol section, he would get the following additional monthly allowances.[20]

18. Police salaries, like all salaries in Japan, are difficult to compute because they are composed of a basic salary and numerous allowances and bonuses. The police also receive fringe benefits that make their apparently low salaries by American standards somewhat deceptive.

19. Based on figures supplied by the Okayama Prefectural Police Headquarters and the *Jinjiin geppō* [Monthly report of the National Personnel Authority], September 1974, p. 34. Computations are based on ¥ 300 = $1.00.

20. Figures supplied by the Okayama Prefectural Police Headquarters, 1974. Other allowances include those for special or dangerous work, housing if the police officer rents, com-

Wife allowance	$16.67
Child allowance	5.00
Patrol allowance	11.00
Night work allowance	18.27
Overtime allowance	34.67 (average)
	$85.61

This amounts to a total of $447.61 per month for the police sergeant, but the office worker would earn only $372.84 per month with overtime and other allowances added. If the yearly bonus is added to this pay, which in 1974 was equal to 4.8 times the monthly basic salary for police but 4.5 times the basic salary for most companies, the sergeant earns $7,108.92 and the office worker earns $5,977.17 per year.[21]

Salary helps to reinforce the rank and seniority hierarchy because pay increases are based mainly on promotions in rank and years of service in the police. The schooling of a police officer, however, does establish a differential in the level of starting pay and the speed of possible promotion. For instance, in 1974, a college graduate began at $277.00, a high school graduate at $236.66;[22] the college graduate could expect a faster pay rise if, as would be expected, he moved up in rank faster; and even if he did not move up faster, he would probably stay in advance. However, years of service in the police seems to have a greater influence on the level of pay than does rank; for example, a forty-year-old policeman (*junsa*) in the Kurashiki patrol section in 1975 with two children made more money ($10,462.60 per year) than a thirty-five-year-old assistant inspector in the same section with the same number of children ($9,676.80).[23] The money for salaries of police officers between the ranks of policeman and superintendent is provided by the prefecture, but salaries for senior superintendents and above, who are national civil servants, are paid by the national government. Since the prefectural police usually pay higher salaries than the national civil service scale, prefectural police officers who are promoted to senior superintendent (*keishisei*, the highest rank prefectural police officers usually achieve) actually take a cut in salary. This is compen-

---

muting, and one for the wives of criminal investigators because their husbands are so frequently gone at night.

21. Based on a recruitment brochure from the Okayama Prefectural Police Headquarters, 1974.

22. Figures supplied by the Okayama Prefectural Police Headquarters, 1974.

23. From a small survey administered for me in the Kurashiki patrol section, May 1, 1975.

sated for, however, in prestige and benefits after retirement (as we shall see below).

There are various fringe benefits that make police work additionally attractive. The virtually free housing provided in police apartment complexes and dormitories is a major fringe benefit. The prefectural police provide low-interest and long-term loans for police officers who want to build their own homes, which is particularly difficult in Japan because of the skyrocketing cost of land. Many retiring police officers use their savings and retirement pay (a large percentage of which is paid in one lump sum) to buy their home. The police also provide loans to buy furniture when police officers get married.[24] Police families can buy items at stores designated by the prefectural police headquarters that sell to police at discounted prices, as was noted earlier. The police also have a nationwide chain of attractive police hotels in sixty-four locations, frequently at spas or other tourist centers, where police officers and their families can stay at a nominal cost; a nationwide police telephone network allows police officers to make reservations without the expense of long distance calls. The police also have two hospitals in Tokyo for use in treating injuries and certain illnesses of police officers.

There are no labor unions, policemen's benevolent associations, or any other type of organization to represent the police officers to police management in Japan. The police organization is paternalistic, and the welfare section of the prefectural police headquarters handles most of the health and working-condition matters that would be of concern to a police union. For instance, it administers the "mutual benefit association" (kyōsai kumiai) that does such things as build police hotels, run police hospitals, and build police housing complexes, and it also is in charge of pensions for police officers. Money for the support of the mutual benefit association is deducted from the paychecks of all police officers. The welfare section and the mutual benefit association are parts of the police organization and do not serve the representative functions of labor unions.

In recent years, the Japan Communist party and the militant and leftist General Council of Labor Unions (Sōhyō) have agitated for the formation of labor unions in the police, but there has been no movement in that

---

24. The prefectural police in Okayama in 1974 provided loans up to $11,666 for buying a home, repayable at 5 percent interest in twenty years.

direction by the police. The police hierarchy is adamantly opposed to labor unions within the police and will undoubtedly prevent their formation as long as possible. The chief of the Okayama Prefectural Police Headquarters visited every police station in Okayama in the summer of 1974 and talked to all the police officers after the Communists distributed a paper to the residences of police officers in the prefecture urging them to form a labor union because of their difficult working conditions.

There are irritations within the police organization that work against police solidarity and could well tempt some to press for collective representation. One of these is overtime pay, which is not based strictly on hours worked, but is apportioned to police stations and divided among police officers according to a set pattern. Younger police officers, as we shall see, are particularly bothered by the amount of overtime demanded in police work. However, the police organization seems to be responsive to the desires of police officers. For example, the police will soon shift to a five-day work week from the present five-and-a-half-day week, owing mainly to pressures for change from young policemen. The lingering ideas of *bushidō* ("the way of the warrior," the samurai ethic) in the police organization, such as long-suffering and self-sacrifice, as well as no sense of being blue-collar workers, prevent the unionization of police officers.

The supportive nature of police life continues to a limited extent even after one leaves the police. Mandatory retirement in the police is at age fifty-seven. The retirement benefit is based on salary at time of retirement and involves monthly payments in addition to the large sum of money paid in one lump sum. Like salary, police retirement benefits are usually larger than those of companies, as is true of all civil service in Japan; 4.8 percent of the salary of assistant inspectors and below goes to retirement benefits, whereas only 3.8 percent of the salaries of most company employees is deducted for retirement.[25] The fact that retirement benefits are good may be one factor in the relatively low rate of quitting the police.[26]

The desire to quit the police and get another job seems to be related to

25. Interview at the Okayama Prefectural Police Headquarters, 1974.
26. Those that leave the police through quitting are not very numerous. Among the four one-year classes that entered the Okayama police school between October 1971 and October 1972, 12.8 percent of the recruits dropped out before graduation. (*Okayama Prefectural Police Yearbook*, p. 310.) It is estimated that the first-year quit-rate in companies of over 500 employees is 25 percent, twice as high as the first-year quit-rate of Okayama police. See National Police Agency Personnel Management Council, ed., *Seinen keisatsukan: sono rikai*

TABLE 11. *Answers to the Question "If You Could, Would You Like to Change to Another Occupation?" (in percentage)*

Age	Do Not Want to Change	Want to Change	Other
Below 29	74.3	14.2	11.4
30–39	78.0	13.7	7.6
40–49	83.6	11.3	4.3
Over 50	88.0	7.7	4.2
Totals	78.6	12.7	8.3

SOURCE: Attitude Survey of Police Employees (see table 8), p. 80.

age, as is seen in the answers to the question "If you could, would you like to change to another occupation?" (See table 11). The percentage of those who express a desire to change professions is roughly equivalent to the percentage that dropped out of police school in Okayama. (I was told that up to 30% of all police officers in Okayama had wanted to quit the police for one reason or another during their careers.)

Most police officers, like workers in many firms in Japan with an early retirement age, secure other employment after retirement from the police. Aid from the police in this respect, however, goes mainly to those of higher rank. The early retirement age keeps the promotion system operating by continually thinning out the upper ranks of the police hierarchy. In Okayama in 1975, 80 percent of the fifty-two police officers who retired got another job, usually related to police work in some way. Of those who were reemployed, one-third got jobs in some sort of automobile-related work, such as driving schools, traffic-safety associations, and taxi companies, and 26 percent were employed as guards for shopping centers, banks, or department stores. The other 40 percent returned to farming, took office-work jobs, and such.[27] The general-affairs section of the prefectural police headquarters finds jobs for police officers with the rank of superintendent and above, but those of inspector and below (who constitute nearly the entire prefectural police force) must find their own jobs. Often the local police chief assists them in their search for employment,

---

to shidō [Young police officers: understanding and leading them] (Tokyo: Keisatsu Kyokai, 1970), pp. 44–45. When police officers quit, it is usually for personal reasons, such as the need of eldest sons to care for aging parents or to inherit the family farm. Between 1968 and 1972, only two police officers were fired from the Okayama prefectural police. (*Okayama Prefectural Police Yearbook*, p. 46.)

27. *Kōraku* (Okayama), April 1975, pp. 71–72.

but many secure positions through contacts they developed themselves in the course of their police service. Police chiefs frequently get administrative jobs, most often as the head of a local driving school.[28] Police officers hired by companies are sometimes assigned to labor relations duties and are in charge of monitoring leftist workers. Police officers in the lower ranks usually work as guards, an unprestigious occupation.

Retired police officers become members of a Police Friendship Association (*keiyūkai*) that meets about once a year for fellowship purposes. The associations are organized within the jurisdictions of police stations. The associations in Okayama are not very active, however, but they help and give money when a member dies or is hospitalized. The prefectural association publishes a newsletter that appears periodically with police news, activities of local chapters, and obituaries of members.

POTENTIAL CLEAVAGES IN POLICE SOLIDARITY

Misconduct by police officers and their deviation from the norms established by the police leadership is a potential fissure in the solidarity of any police system. For the Japanese police, however, the problem is minimal.[29] A major reason for this is that public expectation of exemplary behavior by police officers is strong, perhaps stemming initially from the samurai origins of early Meiji police officers and also from the relatively high esteem enjoyed since then by the police.[30] Accordingly, the police are concerned about propriety and are sensitive to public criticism. When-

28. The police, who administer the driver's license examinations, also staff (with retired police officers) the driving schools that most drivers go to for practice in order to pass the examination.

29. If a problem occurs, it is either discreetly handled through negotiations with the parties involved or transfer of the offender or officially disposed of through the inspector's office (*kansatsukan shitsu*) of the prefectural police headquarters, with various warnings or punishments meted out. Official sanctions are applied to only a small portion of the cases involved. Of 71 cases officially reported in 1971 in Okayama, 44 involved policemen (*junsa*), 6 involved sergeants, 9 were assistant inspectors, 7 were inspectors, and 2 were superintendents. The inspectors and superintendents were probably among the 14 who received warnings because of their responsibility for misbehaving subordinates.

30. Japanese police officers are not easily identified as individuals by the public, unless they are personally known, because they do not wear name plates or badges with numbers (their police identification is kept in a wallet in an inside pocket). Thus, if misconduct occurs, it reflects on the police as a whole, not merely the individual officer. This may be a factor in the police sense of responsibility to the entire organization for their conduct. It also reflects the primacy of the group over the individual in the Japanese police, a characteristic not unlike other Japanese organizations.

ever an act of deviation by a police officer becomes publicly known, it makes prefectural and frequently national news. The same is true with schoolteachers, and this may indicate similar public expectations from the two professions. The news value of crimes committed even by former policemen is indicative of the commonly held assumption of high character for anyone who has qualified to become a police officer.[31]

Drinking can cause severe embarrassment for the police, and is a problem because of the role that sake plays in Japanese society. Informal get-togethers, as well as more formal year-end and going-away parties, almost always entail drinking sake, and policemen seem to be involved in numerous such occasions. I went to a patrol-section year-end party (bōnenkai) in Kurashiki in 1974 at which most of the police officers became very intoxicated; it came to an end when two of the old sergeants became violent and began throwing and smashing glasses. Police officers sometimes get into brawls when drunk, as happened in 1975 when two inebriated Osaka police sergeants, stumbling into an election campaign headquarters, assaulted two campaign workers. A few commit even more heinous crimes, as in 1974 when a Niigata chūzai san beat his wife to death in the chūzaisho when drunk.[32]

Traffic accidents form the largest category of police deviation reported in Okayama. For instance, there was public uproar in 1973 when an Okayama police officer was killed when he was driving while drunk, prompting the chief of the prefectural police headquarters to send a letter to every police officer urging him to exercise caution in his behavior. An even greater shock occurred in 1974 when a traffic policeman in Okayama hit a woman pedestrian early one morning and fled from the scene, parked his damaged car behind the police station, with a cover over it, and participated in the investigation of the hit-and-run accident before confessing later in the day. He was arrested and immediately fired from the police.[33]

31. I was riding in a patrol car in Mizushima one evening in 1974, when we got a radio report of a thief apprehended by citizens. We rushed to the scene, where the young man was put in the patrol car and taken to the station for questioning. As it turned out, he was a former policeman from Kanagawa prefecture, and his arrest was reported in the national newspapers and on television.

32. San'yō shimbun (Okayama), 12 April 1975, p. 18, and San'yō shimbun, 7 September 1974, p. 15.

33. Ibid., 18 September 1974, p. 19. The head of the prefectural police has the authority to fire police officers. There are no hearings held, and the decision is seldom appealed. Investigations of misbehavior are made not at the police-station level, but in the prefectural police headquarters (specifically by the inspector's office—kansatsukan shitsu).

Many police chiefs and other high police officials never drive, even if they own a automobile, but have a subordinate chauffeur them, for fear of being fired if they should cause a traffic accident.[34]

Misuse of weapons by police or other censurable violence against suspects is rare, to judge from all available testimony. Violence by police officers in making arrests or during interrogations, though not unknown, has seldom been reported in postwar years.[35] Police officers use martial arts or adroit wielding of a nightstick to disarm and subdue suspects, who are seldom armed with more than a knife. Police can be victims in the context of firearms, as was seen in the devastating incident in Osaka in 1974 in which the revolvers of two sleeping police officers were stolen from their *kōban* one night, one being used later in an assassination attempt by a Korean resident of Japan on the life of Korea's President Park (the assailant missed Park but killed Park's wife).

A case involving a police officer who gets a girl pregnant is usually handled with utmost discretion. If marriage does not ensue, settlement with the girl's family is attempted by the police, and the officer is usually transferred. A doctor I know in Kurashiki was once asked by the police if he could "handle" such a situation—that is, he was requested to discreetly perform an abortion (which is legal and frequently performed in Japan).[36]

Bribery is highly unusual in the Japanese police. I talked to newspaper reporters and to a former Communist member of the prefectural assembly, people who would know and would probably tell me if such problems existed; they all agreed that police officers are usually above bribery attempts. This probably is because the police, like gangsters, are moved more by bonds of indebtedness (*giri*) and by personal influence than they are by bribery with money. Recall the Japanese notion that "face is more powerful than money" (*okane yori kao ga kiku*).[37] Police recognition of the power of human ties (*ningen kankei*) underlies the policy of frequent transfer of command officers to lessen this influence. Indeed, one of the chief complaints by present police officials about the decentralized post-

34. This was told to me by a riot police commander who always had a riot policeman drive him places in his privately owned automobile.

35. A female cab driver, mistaken for a man, was beaten by three traffic policemen in Osaka for refusing to surrender her driver's license when they stopped her. She was awarded damages in court in 1975. See *Japan Times* (Tokyo), 21 March 1975, p. 2.

36. An official of the public relations section of the Okayama Prefectural Police Headquarters told me categorically that no police officers in Okayama had gotten girls pregnant in the past five years; he either was badly misinformed or was lying.

37. See chapter six on the police relation with gangsters.

war police was that small-scale municipal and town police departments were very susceptible to control by influential locals because of over-powering "human ties."

The power of local men of influence is still felt in the police. In Kura-shiki, for example, the most powerful individuals are said to be members of the Rotary Club, some of whom describe themselves informally as the main behind-the-scenes power brokers (*kuromaku*) in Kurashiki, (candi-dates for public office in the city usually visit them before starting their election campaigns). Although these local bosses probably do not influ-ence policy because of the prefectural (and ultimately national) organiza-tion of the police, they do seem to have a degree of influence over the decisions of individual police officers as to whether to enforce the law. Several influential club members told me of instances in which they com-mitted traffic offenses near their homes and were quickly released when the officers recognized who they were. They said that cars parked in front of their homes are never ticketed by police officers, even if in no-parking areas, unless they call the police to have one ticketed (when the response is quick). The Kurashiki police chief plays Mah-Jongg with a group of local bosses in an inn in town one evening a week. Although it is impos-sible to determine whether improper influencing of the police chief occurs in this group, binding ties of obligation and friendship are undoubtedly formed. This is of special significance because such men of influence sometimes run for political office, and the police are in charge of making arrests for election violations.

Another possible source of undue influence of local bosses on the police is an organization in Tokyo known as the Police Social Group (Keisatsu Konwakai), made up of company presidents and other influential individu-als in each police station jurisdiction who meet periodically with the police chief, the assistant chief, and all the section chiefs in a restaurant for drinking and discussion. Their primary function is to donate money to the police station for use in aiding injured police officers, in meeting the edu-cational expenses of the children of policemen, as gifts for meritorious service by policemen, as loans for policemen to help build their homes, and in other police-support activities. In Fuchu there were a hundred mem-bers in 1974, and they donated $5,000 to the police station in 1973. Oka-yama prefecture used to have the same organization in each police station jurisdiction, but it was abolished because of the difficulties that arose when the police attempted to enforce the law when members of the asso-ciation were violators.

Although actual bribery is rare, acts that approach petty bribery are widespread among the police. In Okayama, many police officers constantly receive free tickets to bowling alleys and movie theaters (especially those specializing in pornographic films), free meals or reduced prices on food, and items from many stores either free or very cheaply. Because of gratuities, gifts, and cash payments on transfer, "local identity" of the police may seem to be equated with the provision of goods and services by the locals in return for favors by the police. What may appear to be a series of endless payoffs, however, must be evaluated in the context of Japanese culture before it can be labeled as bribery.

Japanese society is marked by extensive institutionalized gift-giving. Besides gifts when someone is moving or being transferred, gifts are given twice a year to one's associates and to people to whom one feels indebted, during the midyear gift-giving season in July (*o chūgen*) and also at the end of the year before New Year's (*o seibo*). Souvenirs from a trip are expected to be brought back to friends and work mates, and a gift is a necessity when visiting someone's home. As in gift-giving everywhere, reciprocity is the essence of the transaction—a gift of like value is later returned to the giver or a service or favor is performed. The Japanese say that gifts are the "oil that lubricates society" (*junkatsuyū*) and view them as smoothing the complex web of human relations in which they are enmeshed. However, the line between a gift and a bribe is, indeed, often a very fine one.

In Japan, a bribe can usually be identified if it is an event-specific quid pro quo, or if the value of the gift is unusual for the particular situation. When I questioned police officers about some of the gifts they received, they insisted that they could distinguish an attempted bribe from a gift given by one of their *kyōryokusha* ("cooperators"). If the gift is intended to pervert their judgment or prevent them from enforcing the law, then it is a bribe; otherwise it is a gift.[38] Local officials, such as those in the city office, also receive numerous gifts, whereas judges and prosecutors and

---

38. I may have witnessed a case of quid pro quo petty bribery. I was with a police officer when he was told by the police station to leave his *kōban* and check on some reported net-fishing by members of a fishing cooperative in an illegal location on a nearby river. He investigated and saw that the fishermen were at that time in a permitted area; the policeman said he would return later to check again. Before we left, the head of the cooperative gave the policeman eight cans of cold soft drinks, which he took and put into his car. He became busy with other matters and never went back to the river that day. The Japanese Supreme Court recently held that a seasonal gift to a public school teacher is not a bribe as long as it is within the reasonable scope of social intercourse. ——— vs. Japan. 744 *Hanrei jihō* 119 (April 24, 1975). (In some Japanese court cases, the parties wish to remain anonymous.)

officials assigned to local offices of national bureaucracies seldom receive them. This is because police and local officials, and not the others, are perceived as very close to the daily lives of people, and relationships with them must be well "lubricated." The Japanese also say, somewhat disparagingly, that police and Buddhist priests will take almost anything that is free.

There is historical precedent of a sort in Japan for police taking gratuities. The police of Edo, *okappiki* and *meakashi*, who were actually gangsters working for the authorities, received only nominal amounts of money from the government for their work and were paid primarily by residents of local neighborhoods for protection. The samurai traditions and expectations mentioned earlier, and the "bottom-of-the-barrel" traditions noted here, indicate a diversity in the historical origins of the Japanese police. The samurai tradition and values compose the official police ideology (the *tatemae*) and are personified most clearly in command and elite-course officers, reminiscent of the exclusively samurai status of police commanders in Edo (e.g., *machi bugyō*, or "town magistrates") and early Meiji. Line officers were of samurai origin only in the beginning years of Meiji. The continued existence of *okappiki* notions points again to the incomplete merging of traditions through police socialization.[39]

When clear deviations occur, the repercussions are often felt high in the police hierarchy because of the idea that command officers are responsible for the actions of their subordinates. For instance, after the Korean assassination attempt with one of the revolvers stolen from the *kōban* in Osaka, the two police officers whose guns were taken were suspended for three months (the heaviest punishment ever meted out to Japanese police officers short of firing them); the sergeant who supervised them was suspended for ten days; the assistant inspector over them and the chief of the patrol section of the police station received cuts in salary; the assistant chief of the police station was reprimanded; the police station chief received a cut in salary, as did the assistant chief of the Osaka Prefectural Police; the patrol division chief of the prefecture was reprimanded; the

---

39. Any police system, because of its position between law-abiding and law-breaking society, exposes its members to "criminal socialization" as part of the required expertise. Some systems recruit pretrained experts, such as the gangsters and criminals who served as policemen in the Edo period; Japan today appears to avoid this. The evidence suggests that the system does exploit the criminal-like image positively, such as through use of criminal language (it reinforces special police identity and helps to establish rapport with gangsters and other criminals), yet the system is not co-opted by it.

chief of the prefectural police resigned; and the head of the National Police Agency received a warning from the National Public Safety Commission.[40] In a rare case of suspected corruption in Okayama in 1968, the traffic division chief of the prefectural police headquarters committed hara-kiri when the news broke that numerous Koreans who could not read Japanese, and thus could not pass the examination, had somehow received driver's licenses. The fact that he committed suicide meant that he took personal responsibility, and the matter was pursued no further in the prefectural assembly.[41]

Japanese police officers take their work very seriously, and it is not unknown for them to commit suicide when suffering from sickness, fatigue, or discouragement over poor performance in their police work. A promising young Okayama patrolman whose father is a police officer and who graduated first in his police school class had frequent bouts with illness, became despondent, and shot himself in a police-box in Okayama City in 1974.[42] An investigator in a large bombing incident in Tokyo complained to a fellow investigator of exhaustion because of the grueling pace, and then hanged himself in a darkroom in his police station a few days later. He left a note in which he apologized to the police chief and his section chief and asked them to care for his family.[43] Another incident in Shizuoka prefecture involved a criminal investigator who shot himself one night in a room of his police station because he was having little success in his work. A note addressed to the police station chief expressed his "apologies for 'a poor performance' in arresting suspects."[44] These suicides illustrate the total devotion that Japanese police officers give, or are expected to give, to their work, and in each instance the policeman was trying to shoulder responsibility for what he considered to be his failures.

We turn now to a cleavage within the Japanese police organization that has potentially far-reaching implications. This is a division between generations, essentially between "prewar" and "postwar" types. This generational cleavage is manifest in the larger Japanese society. While it is often

40. *San'yō shimbun*, 4 October 1974, p. 19.
41. I was told this by a very reliable source in the Okayama Prefectural Assembly, 1975.
42. *San'yō shimbun*, 23 December 1974, p. 15. The article shows a good example of deferment to superiors in the decision-making process in a *kōban*. The other *junsa* tried to talk the policeman into putting down his revolver, but he did not listen. While they were calling their superior at the police station to ask what to do, he shot himself. There was apparently no attempt by the other policemen to disarm him by either stealth or force.
43. Ibid., 7 September 1974, p. 14.
44. *Japan Times*, 13 February 1974, p. 2.

attributed to differences in schooling, it is apparent in attitudes and world view. As for the police, a large influx of police recruits to increase the total number of men occurred immediately after the war and throughout the period of independent municipal and town police departments (1945–1954) as young soldiers returning to Japan joined the police when other work was scarce. Another influx of recruits occurred in the early 1960s and has continued to the present. There are, thus, two distinct age groupings in the police, those between the ages of twenty and thirty-five and those between forty and fifty-five. The accompanying age-distribution graph illustrates this phenomenon (see figure 19). There is a smaller percentage of police officers between the ages of thirty and forty-five than in the general population, especially in the thirty-five and forty age group. The consequence of the notch in age-distribution resulting from bimodal

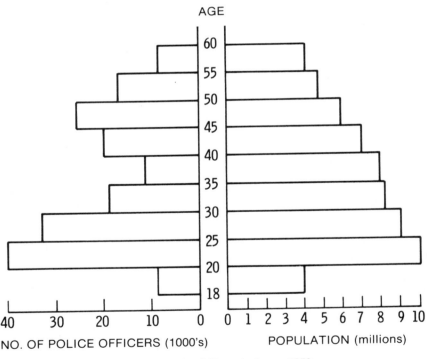

FIGURE 19.   Age Structure of Police Officers in Japan, 1972
SOURCE: National Police Agency, ed., *Keisatsu hakusho, 1973* [Police white paper] (Tokyo: Okurasho Insatsukyoku, 1973), p. 374.

recruitment is that bottom-rank patrolmen are, of course, mostly young, while all higher ranks have mainly much older men.

Older police officers usually complain that the young policemen (twenty-five and younger) are egotistical and calculating, do not recognize traditional authority or defer to elders, are poorly versed in manners and etiquette, lack patience and endurance, and are "dry" (i.e., they ignore *giri* and *ninjō*).[45] They are also said to lack a sense of mission or devotion to their work and tend to look at the police as simply a means of earning a living. In the Kanagawa prefecture police study the question was asked "Does it bother you to get home late because of work?" (see table 12). The percentages of those who do not mind and those who really dislike returning home late show a sharp contrast between the oldest and the youngest men (a generational phenomenon perhaps true anywhere). The answers according to rank show the same differential, for 37.3 percent of the policemen (*junsa*) and 88.4 percent of the inspectors say they do not mind a late return.

TABLE 12. *Answers to the Question "Does It Bother You to Get Home Late Because of Work?" (in percentage)*

Age	Do Not Mind If It Is Late	Will Not Say Either Way	Really Dislike It
Below 29	32.9	31.6	35.5
30–39	49.4	23.9	25.5
40–49	55.9	20.7	22.4
Over 50	60.5	18.3	21.1

SOURCE: Attitude Survey of Police Employees (see table 8), p. 76.

Older police officers, after a lifetime of service, seem to have more pride in their police occupation than younger police officers. In a question about how police officers feel when someone asks their occupation, the answers pointed to a definite age differential in the policemen's reactions (see table 13). Many older police officers still believe that the police organization is accorded a relatively high prestige position as agents of the emperor, whereas younger officers seem to share the current view that policemen occupy a middle range of social status. The high percentage of young officers who replied that they feel nothing in particular when asked about their work indicates that they look at the police as simply an ordinary occupation.

45. *Young Police Officers* (n. 26, above), pp. 34–35.

TABLE 13. *Attitudes of Police Officers toward Their Occupation (in percentage)*

Age	Feel Proud	Do Not Feel Anything in Particular	Feel Embarrassed
Below 29	33.2	62.9	3.9
30–39	34.6	59.6	5.1
40–49	38.4	57.4	3.7
Over 50	43.6	52.8	3.5

SOURCE: Attitude Survey of Police Employees (see table 8), p. 81.

TABLE 14. *How the Police View the Public's Understanding of Police Work (in percentage)*

View of the Public's Understanding	Age of Police	
	Under 25	Over 25
Understand well	4	8
Pretty much understand	30	46
Cannot say	20	14
Do not understand well	39	30
Understand hardly at all	7	2

SOURCE: National Police Agency Personnel Management Council, ed., *Seinen keisatsukan: sono rikai to shidō* [Young police officers: understanding and leading them] (Tokyo, 1970), p. 47.

An age differential is also seen in how policemen view the general understanding by the public of the hard work and sacrifices made by police officers (see table 14). Combining the two categories at the top and the two at the bottom, we see that 34 percent of the young officers felt they were more or less understood, and 46 percent felt they were not; 54 percent of the older officers felt that the police were more or less understood, and 32 percent felt they were not. This indicates a greater feeling of isolation from and hostility toward the community by younger police officers than by older ones, which is reflected in worse language used by younger police officers in dealing with offenders (especially traffic offenders), and is perhaps also seen in the style of patrol work done in *kōban*. Younger police officers patrol by merely walking or bicycling around their jurisdiction and returning immediately to the *kōban*; older police officers often use a form of patrol that combines visiting homes (*junkai renraku*) with patrolling, by going from house to house (or store) of acquaintances in the jurisdiction and chatting with them and gathering gossip and other information. Young patrolmen often complain that patrol and the required home visiting are uninteresting and that they would rather be criminal investigators doing "real police work" by catching criminals.

The ability to communicate with direct superiors seems to increase with age among police officers. See table 15 for answers to the question "Can you say whatever you are thinking to your directly superior officers?" The large percentage of those below twenty-nine who felt that they could not talk to superiors probably reflects the tension and distance that is sometimes seen in *kōban* between young patrolmen and the old sergeants in charge. Older policemen and younger ones patrol together and work together for hours, yet often have very little conversation. The older men usually sit at desks at the rear of the *kōban* office, and the younger patrolmen have desks near the front door where they must assist people with street directions and go outside to direct traffic. The younger men are also usually given the tedious and complicated paperwork for crimes that occur in the jurisdiction because they "need the practice," while the older men sit at the rear of the police-box and chat. Several young policemen complained to me of this work imbalance.

TABLE 15. *Answers to the Question "Can You Say Whatever You Are Thinking to Your Directly Superior Officer?"*

Age	Can Talk Freely	Normal	Cannot Talk Freely
Below 29	20.9	49.0	30.1
30–39	24.4	52.5	22.4
40–49	35.5	44.6	19.5
Over 50	42.9	40.8	16.2

SOURCE: Attitude Survey of Police Employees (see table 8), p. 72.

These generational variations in attitudes and perceptions of police officers may be simply a product of age differences and may have no implications for the future of the police. Similar generational differences may have existed in the Meiji or Taisho periods, but we have no data on these periods. However, the watershed in values and education that occurred after World War II would probably lead one to conclude otherwise. The magnitude of the variations point to changes in attitudes and world view that are deep-rooted and significant. The traditional model of the police is in flux as Japanese society and young police officers who come newly from it change toward more individualistic and ego-centered notions of purpose.

Within the police, the official samurai model, which perceives the police as a hierarchical, authoritarian, and somewhat elite entity and which stresses loyalty, patriotism, and a sense of mission, is embraced mostly by older police officers with prewar educations, many of whom served in the imperial army or navy. Younger police officers seem to share what can be called a "salaryman" model of the police that views police work as merely another occupation. They do not think of the police as occupying as high a social position as do older officers and seem less willing to sacrifice in terms of long working hours without corresponding overtime pay. The police employ extensive formal and informal mechanisms to inculcate the samurai model in new recruits, but generational cleavages persist. The altered milieu from which new officers come is not fully overcome in the socialization processes in the police.

Outside the police, this changing model is similarly blurred by two conflicting perceptions or models of the police in the eyes of the public. A samurai model is evident to citizens when the police function in an authoritarian and haughty manner, as in their handling of traffic law violations and their practice of "guidance" (shidō). On the other hand, an egalitarian, or "nice guy," model is projected by the various service activities that police engage in for "community relations." This latter approach was adopted after World War II under American tutelage and serves merely to cover the persisting hierarchical and authoritarian samurai model (in this case the honne) with a more palatable façade, or tatemae.

Yet the two public images are inimical, and further weaken the basic samurai model in the eyes of young people in Japan, both lawful citizens and outlaws. As we have seen in earlier chapters, young people appear to find the samurai model less compelling, with ordinary youths openly confronting police authority and gangsters seeming to be less cooperative with the police than before the war. This may unbalance the entire system of police relations with the community.

A question for the future is whether young police officers will eventually internalize the official samurai model of the police organization or alter it as they increase in rank and maturity and assume top police leadership roles. The samurai model will probably persist as long as it is useful as a symbol to both the police and the community. We can safely say, however, that as Japanese society changes, so will the police whose job it is to control it.

ten

CONCLUDING REMARKS

As we have seen, the present police establishment in Japan is an imperfectly blended amalgam of the authoritarian, powerful, and highly centralized prewar police system and the "democratic" and decentralized postwar system. The prewar system was based on a continental German and French model of a national police force on a level above the people, and the postwar system was patterned after an American or British model of small-scale police forces on the same level with the people. The former is closer to the *honne* (reality) of the police system, and the latter is ultimately a mere *tatemae* (façade).

The hierarchical severity of the basic structure and orientation of the police has a demeanor of openness and kindness. This duality of the police often leads to conflicting reactions toward the police by the public. Although people respond to the small kindnesses done by police officers, they also fear the police and usually meekly obey police orders and directives. The police are often referred to as *okami*, signifying someone with total authority who is above the people. The tax office is another authoritative—and often feared—government organization referred to by this term. A fear of police officers is inculcated early in children, whose mothers, to curb their misbehavior, threaten to call a police officer to take them away.[1]

The question of who formally controls the police is the key to understanding that the hierarchical, centralized, and authoritarian model more closely approaches reality. Therefore, we shall look at the division of

---

1. I saw numerous instances of mothers threatening their children with this remark as I walked with police officers through residential neighborhoods and shopping areas.

funding and control between the prefectural and national police organizations.

The prefectural police have a dual status. They are an operational agency responsible for police matters in a prefecture (an autonomous body) and are under the supervision of the prefectural public-safety commission, which is under the jurisdiction of the prefectural governor; as such, they are an autonomous and local police force. Yet they are nationally controlled in leadership and in matters handled by the National Police Agency, and this leads to a high degree of uniformity in the various prefectural police forces. Everyday decisions on the functioning of the prefectural police are made at the prefectural level; Tokyo is involved only in affairs of national scope and in the expenditure of funds on matters under the jurisdiction of the National Police Agency. This distinction is highly significant. Police officials frequently insist that the prefectural police are autonomous forces (a *tatemae*); but they have a national outlook and are thus not autonomous in the parochial sense of the word (the *honne*).

The chief of the prefectural police is always a national civil servant, sent by the National Police Agency. Several of the other top police officials in every prefecture are also sent by Tokyo, almost always including the assistant chief (formally, the chief of the police administration division (*keimubuchō*)) and the chief of the public security division (*keibibuchō*).[2] The chief and the assistant chief are the highest police officials in the prefecture. The security division chief is the third man in the hierarchy; he also handles all incidents of a national nature, such as the activities of Communists and student radicals and riots.

Police finances are divided between prefectural funds and national funds. In 1973 two billion dollars was spent by the National Police Agency, which was one-tenth of the total amount spent by all of the prefectures for police protection.[3] The National Police Agency provides the prefectural police with funds for and coordinates and supervises nationally the following: salaries of senior superintendents and above;[4] police edu-

2. Tokyo usually sends five top police officials to Okayama: the chief (*hombuchō*); the chief of the police administration division (*keimubuchō*); chief of the security division (*keibibuchō*); chief of the identification section (*kanshiki kachō*); and chief of the second driver's license section (*menkyō daini kachō*).

3. National Police Agency, ed., *Keisatsu hakusho, 1974* [Police white paper] (Tokyo: Okurasho Insatsukyoku, 1974), p. 388.

4. In addition to the five men sent from Tokyo (n. 2 above) seven high police officials of Okayama origin are senior superintendent (*keishisei*) in rank and are national public servants

cational and training facilities; communication equipment and systems; criminal identification facilities; compilation of criminal statistics; police vehicles, boats, weapons, and other police equipment; reimbursement for expenses involved in escort and guard duty of VIPs, disasters, and riot control, including all expenses of the riot police; and reimbursement for expenses involved in investigating offenses against the internal safety of the state, or serious offenses affecting several prefectures. The prefectural police finance all other expenses, mainly salaries of police officers below the rank of senior superintendent, police buildings, uniforms, and gasoline for patrol cars. Prefectural police have the option of supplementing funds in certain categories covered by the National Police Agency, if the prefecture provides such funds. For example, Okayama prefecture bought about half of its own patrol cars, and it could also purchase other equipment with National Police Agency approval.

The financial arrangement is of particular interest because of the independence it gives the police in the sensitive area of internal security. With the increase of leftist governors in recent years, this is of added significance. The prefectures, in effect, pay for the patrolman on the beat, traffic control, criminal investigation, and other daily police functions.[5] They have little or no control of the riot police or the security police, units that are used to control leftists. A high official in the National Police Agency told me that finance and the movements of high police personnel are the most important factors in police operation, and the National Police Agency controls the critical aspect of both.[6]

The nationwide unification of the important police functions of security, communications, and the training and transfer of command-level officers enhances police dignity and insures some uniformity in police operations in various regions. The prefectural basis of most of the police funding and the prefectural scope of operations allow for a degree of local identity with

---

(*chihō keimukan*) who are appointed by the National Public Safety Commission and receive their salaries from Tokyo. The chief of the Kurashiki police station, as well as the chiefs of two in Okayama City, are among the senior superintendents.

5. The closest contact between the police and the prefectural government is in the annual formulation of the prefectural portion of the police budget. The police prepare the estimated budget (and say that they usually pad it by about 20% to allow for expected cuts by the prefectural government). The prefectural finance section considers it and forwards it to the prefectural general affairs section, which in turn passes it to the governor. The budget in final form is presented to the prefectural assembly, which usually passes it with little debate or opposition.

6. Interview with a high official in the National Police Agency, Tokyo, 1974.

the police and a prefectural level of control over day-to-day activities. The division of funding and control between the central government and the prefectures according to the type of police function is a skillful method of retaining all the key and potentially problematic police duties in the hands of the National Police Agency, yet avoiding the inevitable social distance that would result from a completely national police force.

Perhaps more basic is the problem of public control and accountability of the police. Formally, the national and prefectural public-safety commission system, one of the main remnants from the immediate postwar period of decentralized police, is supposed to guarantee democratic control of the police (the *tatemae*). In many ways, however, the public-safety commission system serves to mask the total independence of the police and the almost complete lack of formal checks on the power and operation of the police establishment (the *honne*). The prefectural and national public-safety commissions ostensibly function as buffers between police and politicians to prevent bias and untoward influence, yet they do not insure public control over the police organization.

Prefectural public-safety commissions (*todōfuken kōan iinkai*) are composed of five members in prefectures with large metropolitan areas, and three members in other prefectures. Okayama has a three-member commission. The members are appointed by the prefectural governor with the consent of the prefectural assemblies. Prefectural public-safety commissions approve the chiefs of the prefectural police, who are sent by the National Police Agency after formal appointment by the National Public Safety Commission (Kokka Kōan Iinkai). Yet there has never been a case in which a prefectural public-safety commission did not approve an appointment. Prefectural public-safety commissions "supervise" the prefectural police through the chiefs of the prefectural police. "Supervision" (*kanri*) does not mean enforcement or control of daily affairs, however, for this function is exercised solely by the prefectural police chief.[7]

The National Public Safety Commission is composed of six members, including the chairman, and is under the jurisdiction of the prime minister. The chairman is a minister without portfolio in the prime minister's cabinet. The members of the commission are appointed by the prime minister with the consent of both houses of the Diet. The National Public Safety

7. Ralph J. Rinalducci, *The Japanese Police Establishment* (Tokyo: Obun Intereurope, Ltd., 1972), pp. 139 and 167.

Commission in particular is supposed to ensure the political neutrality of the police by insulating the National Police Agency from the influence of national politicians. However, because the chairman is a cabinet member, he passes on the ideas of the ruling (conservative) party to the National Police Agency.

Most members of public-safety commissions, both national and prefectural, are old and very conservative men. Limitations on membership on a commission include a prohibition on a member's serving within five years after retiring as a police officer or public procurator, and on all members having affiliation with the same political party. This last requirement is frequently given by members of public-safety commissions and by police officials as evidence of their political neutrality, but this claim is really meaningless (a *tatemae*). Political party membership does not have the same connotation as it has in the United States, because Japanese political parties, on the whole, are not mass membership parties, and usually only professional politicians join them. In Okayama, for instance, the three members of the prefectural public-safety commission in 1974 included two doctors aged seventy-seven and sixty and a building-materials dealer aged sixty-eight, none of whom is formally a party member. Yet the two doctors were active in conservative politics and were both purged as rightists during the American occupation after the war. All three are members of the Rotary Club, the fraternity of the conservative local elite in Japan. Besides approving the appointment of the head of the prefectural police headquarters, they are also supposed to counsel the headquarters chief if they feel the police are in error. This has never happened in Okayama, however.[8]

The question remains as to who controls the police. The answer is simply that the police are totally autonomous in a formal organizational sense; they control themselves and are ultimately responsible only to the head of the National Police Agency (the *honne*). This can be seen in the selection of the heads of the National Police Agency and the Tokyo Metropolitan

8. The head of the National Public Safety Commission reprimanded the chief of the Metropolitan Police Department for laxity after Prime Minister Miki was assaulted by a right-wing extremist during the funeral of former Prime Minister Sato in Tokyo in 1975. This was the first time the head of the commission ever reprimanded the superintendent general of the Metropolitan Police Department, and he was said to have done it so that he himself would not have to resign, as had been the custom when such an incident occurred. The head of the National Public Safety Commission wanted to run for the Diet, and his resignation would have damaged his chances of election.

Police Department.[9] The head of the National Police Agency usually retires at age fifty-five (he decides when he wants to retire), and he chooses
his successor without consultation with others in the police (he probably
has informal consultations with the prime minister and other ministers
influential in the conservative establishment). He notifies the head of the
National Public Safety Commission of his choice, and the commission
appoints the new director general. He also selects the head of the Metropolitan Police Department after consulting with the assistant chief of the
National Police Agency and former superintendents general of the Metropolitan Police Department. The prime minister must formally approve the
appointment of the superintendent general of the Metropolitan Police Department, but not that of the director general of the National Police
Agency. The National Police Agency stands absolutely independent, formally, from all other bureaucracies and branches of government.

The independence of the police is for the stated purpose of preventing
untoward political manipulation. The police are by and large immune to
overt pressure from the prime minister, for example, to take or abstain
from specific actions. The head of the National Police Agency has been
known to refuse to comply with pressure openly exerted by the prime
minister in the past, and he was backed up by the head of the National
Public Safety Commission. There have been no known cases of such pressure in the past ten years. If such a case were to become public, the press
would invariably devote large coverage to the issue, embarrassing both
the police and the national government.

The police, however, are usually responsive to the desires of the prime
minister in subtle ways that do not require the obvious application of du-
ress. The prime minister has three secretaries from the ministries: one
from the Foreign Ministry, one from the Finance Ministry, and one from
the National Police Agency. Police officials who are on the track toward
becoming head of the National Police Agency almost always serve as a

9. The headships of the National Police Agency and the Metropolitan Police Department
have traditionally alternated between veterans of the security police and the criminal police;
security police have been appointed more often in recent years because criminal investigators
have not been solving major and heavily publicized crimes to the extent that they once did.
For example, the statute of limitations expired in 1975 without an arrest in the infamous
Fuchu (Tokyo) robbery case of December 1968, in which a robber posed as a police officer
and stole nearly a million dollars from a car carrying year-end bonuses to a nearby factory.
This competition for top positions in the police hierarchy partially accounts for the rivalry
between detectives and security police, who both have jobs that involve investigative work,
a rivalry that permeates down to the police-station level.

secretary (*hishokan*) to the prime minister for a period of time. The secretary is aware of the desires of the prime minister on various topics and informally passes the information on to the head of the National Police Agency. The National Police Agency head, thus, has no need to talk directly with the prime minister and destroy the *tatemae* of complete political independence, because he is aware of his wishes through the human connection of the police secretary to the prime minister.[10] This is an example of the importance of informal personal bonds which interconnect the various segments of the Japanese government.[11]

The police have informal relationships with other politicians as well. For example, if the police have a matter they wish to raise in the Diet, they must first explain it to the various political parties. If the ruling Liberal Democratic party opposes the idea, it is usually abandoned because it would have little chance of being passed through the Regional Administration Committee (Chihō Gyōsei Iinkai) of the lower and upper houses, which handles police-related matters.[12] Police officials and Liberal Demo-

10. The centralized police system facilitates the investigation of local corruption because the investigating officers are controlled from afar. But this makes it easy to stop probes into corruption of national governmental officials, by informal pressure from high levels. The quashing of such investigations has been known.

11. Elite-course command officers of the National Police Agency often serve for periods of time in various governmental bureaucracies. Police personnel serve in all ministries of the government except the Ministry of International Trade and Industry and the Ministry of Agriculture and Forestry. In some agencies, like the Japan National Railway and the Ministry of Posts and Telecommunications, the police usually serve in police-related jobs, such as head of the railway security division or chief postal inspector (who also handles labor problems within the postal ministry). Police personnel in the Finance Ministry, Foreign Ministry, Transport Ministry, and Prime Minister's Office perform duties not usually related to police responsibilities. Police officials on loan to the Foreign Ministry often serve as first secretary of Japanese embassies abroad, a position held before the war by army officers. Other ministries also send elite-course bureaucrats to the police to serve, usually as general-affairs division chiefs in prefectural police headquarters. This top-level interchange of personnel creates bonds between the police and various governmental bureaucracies, which facilitates communication and cooperation and counteracts the tendency of Japanese organizations to emphasize internal solidarity at the expense of external relations; it also serves to broaden the vision of top police personnel to incorporate a national scope and to overcome the tendency to protect narrow police interests and ignore the wider needs of the government as a whole.

12. Few large-scale debates about the police have taken place in these committees recently. The committees in both houses are staffed by a majority of conservatives (in 1975, 17 out of 29 in the lower house and 11 out of 20 in the upper house), and the only party to consistently raise objections to police matters is the Japan Communist party. The assistant chief of the National Police Agency and the various bureau heads attend when police matters are to be discussed. Questions addressed to the police are answered by the appropriate bureau heads, and if their answers are not satisfactory, the question is asked of the head of the National Public Safety Commission, and if he fails, the prime minister is requested to answer. There is, thus, an effort to select bureau heads of the National Police Agency who are skillful in answering inquiries, in order to prevent questions from becoming political problems.

cratic members of the Diet develop personal bonds because of this process of explaining desired legislation to the party. Bureaucrats in some ministries, such as Finance and Construction, are said to develop close ties with powerful Diet members, who exert political pressure on their ministries to help them rise within the bureaucracy. The bureaucrats, in turn, then support the Diet member in his struggle for power within the Diet. All indications point to the fact that similar Diet-police relations are rare, although they do exist.

At the prefectural level, the police budget and police activities are supervised by the Commerce, Industry, and Police Committee of the prefectural assembly.[13] In Okayama in 1975, six of the nine committee members were conservatives.[14] I was told that many prefectural assemblymen hope to serve on this committee because of the personal benefits that accrue from it. Opposition party assemblymen change committee assignments every two years, but the Liberal Democrats shift every year to give more people opportunities to serve on desirable committees. Liberal Democratic assemblymen usually feel that membership on this committee will ingratiate them with the police, and they hope it will soften police stringency regarding their election law violations during future campaigns. The commerce and industry aspect of this committee is also beneficial during elections because assemblymen can approach small businesses for election contributions in return for helping them obtain prefectural guarantees on bank loans. Thus, committee membership can help an assemblyman both in respect to election law violations and in raising financial support for election campaigns.[15]

An even more vital issue than informal ties between police and politicians is the political neutrality of the police. This comes to a focus most clearly in the enforcement of the election laws. The election laws in Japan

13. Few controversies or debates centering on the police are raised in the Okayama prefectural assembly (which was 64% controlled by conservatives in 1975—36 out of 56 assemblymen). An exception occurred in 1974, when a Communist assemblyman questioned the headquarters chief about why the security police gave a washing machine to a young Communist party member to elicit information on the party from him. This issue was raised in two different sessions, the last one in early 1975, and it led to a recess of the session when the Liberal Democrats called the Communists liars and a heated argument broke out.

14. Five Liberal Democrats, one conservative independent, and one member each from the Japan Socialist, Komei, and Democratic Socialist parties.

15. Members of this committee frequently drop in on sections of the prefectural police headquarters on business or simply for a chat, and I was told by a high official of the police headquarters that they often make personal requests of the police on such matters as parking violations.

are complex and strict, and it is said that almost all successful candidates must violate them to be elected. For instance, the spending ceiling for candidates in the national constituency of the House of Councillors is the equivalent of $60,000, but observers felt that candidates who spent only $1,300,000 in the 1974 election would lose, and those who spent $1,700,000 would probably win.[16]

There are various types of offenses, but the most frequent ones are literature or poster violations (too many posters or handbills, posted or distributed too early or in the wrong locations, too many sound trucks and such) and bribery (usually offering food, drink, or gifts to people at gatherings, or simply paying them money for their support). The police admit that they do not enforce all aspects of the election law or investigate violations of all elections with the same vigor.[17] Lower-house elections, which influence the composition of the cabinet and the premiership, and prefectural assembly elections, which influence the control of the prefecture, are watched the most strictly for violations, and bribery cases are said to be relentlessly investigated. A high prefectural police official told me that many aspects of the election laws are enforced loosely, like traffic laws, except for bribery cases, which would "rot the nation and destroy it, like narcotics, if left unchecked."[18] He went on to say that elections affect the police directly, as well as the political complexion of Japan, and the police must watch election violations closely. Of the 297 violations investigated in Okayama after the 1971 unified regional elections, 280 were for alleged bribery.[19] Bribery is particularly serious in Japan because of the traditional influence of local bosses on voting, especially in rural areas. Campaigners for candidates ply these bosses with sake and gifts in attempts to obligate them to the candidate and thus acquire a block of votes.

Election violations by conservative candidates are the most prevalent, and almost all bribery arrests involve conservatives. Opposition party candidates are frequently guilty of literature violations, and these are usually handled with warnings and fines. I was told that the reason conservative

16. *Japan Times*, 17 June 1974, p. 2.

17. When elections occur, the second criminal investigation section, which handles "crimes of intellect," is in charge of election violation investigations, but police officers from every section are mobilized to help. During the 1974 lower-house election, 25 of Kurashiki's 150 police officers were temporarily assigned to full-time investigation of election violations. All police officers in *kōban* and *chūzaisho* are issued handbooks on election law violations, but several surmised that few had ever read them.

18. Interview at the Okayama Prefectural Police Headquarters, 1975.

19. Ibid.

candidates are most frequently arrested for bribery is that they often run as independents with the backing of their own personal support groups (*kōenkai*) rather than that of the Liberal Democratic party per se, and their lack of expertise leads to clumsiness in their attempts to bribe bosses. A Liberal Democratic party official in Okayama insisted that the leftists are also paying bribes, but they have close ties to their parties and are advised how to do it in such a manner that they will seldom be caught.

Because of the large number of conservative candidates or their supporters arrested for violations during each election, we can probably conclude that the police are formally neutral in the enforcement of the election laws (the *tatemae*). But this does not negate their ideological leaning toward the right (the *honne*). For instance, former high police officials occasionally run for office, but always as candidates of the Liberal Democratic party. A heated campaign took place when a former head of the Metropolitan Police Department recently ran unsuccessfully as the Liberal Democratic candidate for governor of Tokyo. Yet, even the former police officials or their supporters are sometimes arrested for flagrant election violations. The former head of the National Police Agency, Masaharu Gotoda, lost an election for a seat in the House of Councillors in 1974, and a number of his local campaigners were arrested for violations in Tokushima prefecture.[20] In a rural area of Aomori prefecture, a former police chief was arrested for election violations in the 1971 mayoral election in a small town.[21] A Socialist party official in Okayama told me that he felt the police are now usually fair in making arrests for election law violations, but he expressed a significant anxiety. He wondered if the police would continue to arrest conservative violators if the conservative majority were on the verge of falling before leftist parties in the national elections.

There are concerns other than political neutrality about the Japanese police system. A major issue in the Diet in recent years is the increasing number of police officers. The authorized national strength of police officers in 1975 was approximately 197,000, up from 137,710 in 1963.[22] Police strength increased by an average of more than 4,500 men a year over the thirteen-year period. Critics feel that the increase in the number

20. *Japan Times*, 17 July 1974, p. 2.
21. Ibid.
22. National Police Agency, ed., *Keisatsu hakusho, 1976* [Police white paper] (Tokyo: Okurasho Insatsukyoku, 1976), p. 319, and National Police Agency, ed., *The Police of Japan* (Tokyo: National Police Agency, 1974), p. 45. This is about a 3 percent annual growth rate.

of police officers is unwarranted. The police counter by pointing out that Japan has the heaviest population burden per police officer (568 people per policeman in 1975) of the major non-Communist industrialized countries, yet they fail to note that Japan also has the lowest crime rate and the highest arrest rate of those countries, as is shown in table 16.

TABLE 16. *Rates of Crime and Arrests in Industrialized Nations, 1972*

	Population per Police Officer (1975)	Crime Rate (per 100,000) (1972)	Arrest Rate (%) (1972)
Japan	568	1,140	57.2
England	413	2,803	41.4
West Germany	405	4,171	46.5
United States	385	2,829	20.6
France	298	3,227	52.4

SOURCE: *Police White Paper, 1976*, p. 319, and *Police White Paper, 1974*, pp. 95 and 102.

The goal in increasing the police manpower has been to create a strong police force capable of dealing with crimes or disorders of almost any scale. The need was particularly evident in the late 1960s when the police were faced with massive radical-student violence. The largest proportionate increases in manpower during this period were among the riot police and security police. The police are now confident of the strength of their organization, as was illustrated by the director general of the National Police Agency when he stated:

The National Police Agency of Japan has been developed into a highly mobile organization capable of mustering large numbers of well-trained officers anywhere in Japan in a few hours to cope with major crimes, public functions, or civil disorders.[23]

The massive violence of the 1960s is now a thing of the past, but the police are still pressing the Diet to increase their authorized strength.

Many fear a strong police force and a possible revival of the vast octopus-like duties and powers of the prewar police. Although it would require legislation to increase the range of responsibilities of the police, their actual power even under the present system is enormous. For instance, the police seem to be highly effective in suppressing certain target groups perceived as threats to society. Their power has many sources. One is the

23. *The Police of Japan*, p. 3.

centralized direction and control of the police system, which allows the focusing of the police resources of the entire nation, if necessary, on specific targets of concern. Another important factor is the degree to which the police are able to use their intimate ties to various segments of the community to elicit tips and other forms of formal and informal assistance. Older, stable citizens, who usually serve as leaders of neighborhood police-support organizations, function as the core of the extensive police network of local informers and readily pass on information about targeted groups. In addition, the police can glean a wealth of information on virtually every individual in Japan from the vast amounts of data available in every *kōban* and *chūzaisho* collected from the daily rounds of home visiting (*junkai renraku*) by patrolmen. The potential certainly exists for abuse of these and other means of police power.

Although there are few formal controls on the independence of police, they are remarkably restrained in the use of their power and are generally responsive to public demands. The reason for this is in part societal: there are informal and indirect mechanisms inherent in Japanese society that are ultimately relied on to control governmental excesses (this is an even deeper *honne*). One of the most important is public opinion. The density and homogeneity of Japan's population, and the traditional system of reciprocal obligations that still has wide currency today, result in a tendency for group conformity and responsibility to take precedence over individuality. In many ways Japan resembles a sort of village community on a national scale, in the webs of interrelations, mutual awareness, and concern that tie its people. In this milieu, aroused public opinion has effectively served as one of the primary means of influencing the conduct of those in authority. Thus, the legislation of formal organizational checks to counterbalance possible police bias and to assure accountability, which is unlikely in the present political and social climate of Japan, would be of doubtful efficacy in any event. The informal mechanism of public opinion is fundamentally relied on.

Public opinion is most powerful in an urbanized nation like Japan when it is focused through the mass media, and Japan's media is highly developed. Japan has the largest per capita newspaper circulation of the world's major countries.[24] All of the principal newspapers (Japan has five national

24. E. O. Reischauer, *The Japanese* (Cambridge: Harvard University Press, 1977), p. 198.

newspapers) are slightly left of center in political orientation and tend to be critical of the government. Yet they are not merely editorial voices for their owners or of political parties, as in many other countries.[25] Television, with two government networks and five private networks supported by advertising, diffuses information throughout Japan. Practically every urban and rural home has a television, and there are actually more color televisions than households in Japan.[26] Television tends to be politically uninspired, but its news programs make citizens dramatically aware of any police wrongdoing.

The most effective check on police impropriety in Japan is thus an unfettered and aggressive press. The police establishment has the potential of great power and abuse, but it is sensitive to public desires and criticisms as articulated in the media. This responsiveness is perhaps tied to the Japanese notions of "face" (*kao*) and "humaneness" (*ninjō*). The Japanese police are, after all, themselves Japanese. They dread loss of face (*kao*) through embarrassment, and their excesses are tempered by a feeling of common humanity with other Japanese (*ninjō*). This latter point is also expressed in the phrase *ware ware Nihonjin* ("we Japanese"—an almost familial notion). The responsiveness of the police to public opinion indicates, at least at present, that a powerful bureaucracy can be susceptible to the demands of the public. But the future is not at all certain. As Japanese society continues to change and perhaps to become impersonalized through urbanization, the restraining force of public opinion may lose much of its efficacy.

The police are by no means swayed by every current of public sentiment. The goal of the Police Law of 1954, under which the police are now organized, was to create a strong and efficient police force impervious to overt political pressure. This goal has largely been achieved and the police actually view their strength as being partly due to their stability in the face of societal vicissitudes. Yet the police and other segments of the criminal justice system, notably the public procurators, are responsive to public censure through informal channels of demand and not formal systems of checks, like public-safety commissions. As we have seen, the *tatemae* of formal control institutions patterned after an imported and externally imposed model is merely a smoke screen for the *honne* of a powerful and

25. Ibid., pp. 199–200.
26. Ibid., p. 197.

independent police organization controlled only by informal mechanisms compatible with the traditional structure of Japanese society.

The police, of course, are not wholly responsible for social control in Japanese society. The public is actively involved, because the demarcation between citizens and official police authority in law enforcement is not sharp. Mutual aid organizations of citizens that function to maintain social order were formed throughout Japanese history both at the decree of the governing elite and also spontaneously at lower levels of society where the authority of the government did not seek to reach. The Japanese have long believed that the primary responsibility for social control lies with the community and that citizens must discipline themselves to maintain order. Japanese society, in effect, polices itself. Citizen involvement in policing in Japan does not resemble vigilantism, which is a symptom of insufficient police power and has the undesirable connotation of people taking the law into their own hands. Widespread community participation in police-support activities is undoubtedly one of the main reasons that Japan enjoys declining crime totals.

There are trade-offs in the maintenance of social order and the prevention of crime, however. Western concepts of the right to privacy and self-fulfillment are sometimes abridged in Japan, as is seen in the effective recent police program of publishing in the morning newspapers the names, addresses, and companies of people apprehended for driving while drunk the night before. The method quickly eliminated the problem of drunk driving in several regional cities because of the social pressure brought to bear on the offenders by their families, neighbors, and employers; but it can be argued that the privacy of those caught was infringed. The head of the criminal investigation division of the Okayama Prefectural Police Headquarters pointed to a basic reason for Japan's low crime rate and the impressive cooperation between the police and the community when he said that the Japanese are still somewhat "feudal" (*hōkenteki*).

Indeed, as we have seen, Japanese society places emphasis on intertwining bonds of human relations to maintain the societal fabric and to prevent crime and disorder. These age-old social constraints limit individuality and often hamper self-fulfillment, as does life in a village, though they are effective mechanisms of social control. Japan is politically one of the freest nations on earth, but this does not necessarily equate with societal freedom. The alternative may be that in societies where the rights and liberties of the individual take precedence, the possibility of a relatively high level of crime and disorder will increase.

GLOSSARY OF SELECTED TERMS

Bōhan kumiai - a crime-prevention association (also known as a *bōhan kyōkai*)

Bōhan renrakusho - a crime-prevention checkpoint; neighborhood homes selected by police and neighborhood leaders to act as a crime-prevention liaison between the police and the citizenry

Bōnenkai - a year-end party

Burakkai - a village residents' organization

Burakumin - a formerly outcaste group still subject to severe social and economic discrimination

Chōnaikai - an urban neighborhood association, which functioned as the basic level of local government before World War II

Chūzai san - the police officer who lives and works in a *chūzaisho*

Chūzaisho - a residential police-box, found in rural areas, in which a police officer lives with his family

Daikan - Edo-period lower-level officials in the shogunal hierarchy who performed law enforcement, judicial, and other administrative functions in the shogun's private rural domains

Danchi - a housing complex (usually a number of apartment buildings)

Dōshin - unmounted Edo-period police officers of samurai status

Eta - meaning "filthy," the term formerly used for *burakumin*, or outcastes

Fūzoku eigyō - businesses affecting the public morals, such as bars, cabarets, and pachinko halls

Gaikin keisatsu - outdoor-duty (or patrol) police

Giri - obligation and loyalty (usually linked with *ninjō*)

Gonin gumi - five-family associations of the Edo period which performed social-control functions through mutual responsibility among neighbors

229

Gumi - a group, association or gang (from the word *kumi*)

Gurentai - youthful street hooligans

Hashutsusho - the correct name for a *kōban*, or urban police-box

Hinin - a type of outcaste of the Edo period

Hogoshi - voluntary probation officers

Honne - one's real intention or true motive; the essence or substance of reality; usually contrasted with *tatemae*

Hyakutō ban - Emergency 110, in which citizens summon police assistance by dialing 110 on their telephones

Ingo - "hidden language" argot used by criminals

Jingi - a code of conduct or morality, including formalized words or actions of greeting (as among gangsters)

Junkai renraku - the practice of visiting homes and businesses in a jurisdiction twice a year by police officers in *kōban* and *chūzaisho*

Junsa - the rank of policeman (the lowest in the police command structure)

Kanku keisatsu kyoku - regional police bureaus (seven in Japan) which function as liaisons with the prefectural police; the lowest level of the National Police Agency

Keiji - a detective

Keisatsusho - a police station

Keishichō - the Tokyo Metropolitan Police Department

Kempei - the feared prewar military police

Kenkei hombu - a prefectural police headquarters

Kidō keisatsutai - the mobile police force; a specialized vehicle unit of the prefectural police which backs up the local police by providing rapid mobile response to incidents

Kidōtai - the riot police

Kikikomi - a tip (police have traditionally relied upon *kikikomi sōsa* (investigations based on tips) to solve crimes in Japan)

Kōan iinkai - public-safety commissions, found in all prefectures and nationally (*kokka kōan iinkai*), with the function of supervising the police

Kōban - a police-box, or "mini-station," in urban areas in which police officers work in shifts

Kobun - literally "child role"; a gangster linked to a gang boss (*oyabun*) through fictive kinship ceremonies

Kokka chihō keisatsu - the immediate postwar National Rural Police who functioned in towns and villages of less than 5,000 population (abolished in 1951)

Kokka keisatsu yobitai - the National Police Reserve, later the *jieitai*, or Self-Defense Force, formed in 1950 after occupation troops began to leave

Kōtsū anzen kyōkai - a traffic-safety association

Kōtsū kyōjoin - volunteer citizen "traffic assistants"

Kyōaku hanzai - "atrocious crimes": murder, robbery, arson, and rape

Kyōryokusha - a "cooperator" or tipster of the police

Machi bugyō - Edo-period magistrates of samurai status who functioned as chiefs of police, prosecutors, and judges in criminal and civil matters both in Edo and in most castle towns

Machi hikeshi - Edo-period firemen, the spiritual ancestors of modern gangsters

Meakashi - semi-official detectives of the Edo period, often former outlaws of low-class or outcaste origin, who served the feudal government to save themselves from execution

Metsuke - Edo-period inspectors who ferreted out cases of misrule by officials and who spied on samurai or groups who were thought to be menaces to the government

Minseiiin - voluntary welfare-case workers

Naimushō - the prewar Home Ministry

Nakōdo - a go-between in marriages and in gangster fictive-kinship ceremonies

Naniwa bushi - long ballads, often with gangster protagonists

Ningen kankei - "human relations"

Ninjō - humanity and compassion (usually linked with *giri*)

Ninkyōdō - the "way of chivalry"; the term used by gangsters to describe gangster-ism

Okami - "one who is above"; a term for a powerful official

Okappiki - low-class semiofficial detectives of the Edo period (see *meakashi*)

O mawari san - "Mr. Walkabout"; a patrolman in a *kōban*

Oyabun - literally "parent role"; a gang boss linked to his underlings (*kobun*) through fictive kinship

Shōbōdan - a volunteer fire brigade

Shōnen kyōjoin - volunteer citizen "youth assistants" who aid the police by counseling youths

Sobōhan - crime of "violence": assault, battery, intimidation, extortion, and possession of a dangerous weapon

Tatemae - a superficial rule or principle describing how something should be ideally, but which does not coincide with reality; usually contrasted with *honne*

Tekiya - street-stall vendors, often with links to gangsters (*yakuza*)

Tokkō - an abbreviation for *tokubetsu kōtō keisatsu*

Tokubetsu kōtō keisatsu - Prewar Special Higher Police who regulated publications, motion pictures, associations, political meetings, and election campaigns, and who investigated political crimes

Yakuza - a gangster

Yoriki - mounted Edo-period police sergeants of samurai status

BIBLIOGRAPHY

General References

English

Ames, Walter L. "Police and Community in Japan." Ph.D. dissertation, University of Michigan, 1976.

Bayley, David H. *Forces of Order: Police Behavior in Japan and the United States*. Berkeley and Los Angeles: University of California Press, 1976.

Clifford, William. *Crime Control in Japan*. Lexington, Mass.: Lexington Books, 1976.

Dando, Shigemitsu. *Criminal Procedure*. Translated by B. James George, Jr. South Hackensack, N.J.: Fred B. Rothman and Company, 1965.

DeVos, George A., and Hiroshi Wagatsuma. *Japan's Invisible Race*. Berkeley and Los Angeles: University of California Press, 1972.

DeVos, George A., with Keiichi Mizushima. "Organization and Social Function of Japanese Gangs: Historical Development and Modern Parallels." In *Socialization for Achievement*, edited by George A. DeVos, pp. 280–310. Berkeley and Los Angeles: University of California Press, 1973.

George, B.J., Jr., "Impact of the Past upon the Rights of the Accused in Japan." *American Journal of Comparative Law* 14 (1965–66): 672–685.

Hodge, Robert W.; Siegel, Paul M.; and Rossi, Peter H. "Occupational Prestige in the United States: 1925–1963." In *Class, Status and Power: Social Stratification in Comparative Perspective*, 2d ed., edited by Reinhard Bendix and Seymour Martin Lipset, pp. 322–334. London: Routledge and Kegan Paul, 1967.

Kerr, Clark, et al. *Industrialization and Industrial Man*. Cambridge: Harvard University Press, 1960.

233

Kirk, Donald. "Crime, Politics and Finger Chopping." *New York Times Magazine*. 12 December 1976, pp. 60 ff.

Koshi, George M. *The Japanese Legal Advisor: Crimes and Punishments*. Rutland, Vt., and Tokyo: Charles E. Tuttle Company, 1970.

Nakane, Chie. *Japanese Society*. Berkeley and Los Angeles: University of California Press, 1970.

Parsons, Talcott. *The Social System*. New York: Free Press, 1951.

Reischauer, Edwin O. *The Japanese*. Cambridge: Belknap Press of Harvard University Press, 1977.

Rinalducci, Ralph J. *The Japanese Police Establishment*. Tokyo: Obun Intereurope, Ltd., 1972.

Wallace, Samuel E., ed. *Total Institutions*. Chicago: Aldine, 1971.

Yamagiwa, Joseph K. "Language as an Expression of Japanese Culture." In *Twelve Doors to Japan*, edited by John Whitney Hall and Richard K. Beardsley, pp. 186–223. New York: McGraw-Hill Book Company, 1965.

Yazaki, Takeo. *Social Change and the City in Japan*. Tokyo: Japan Publications, Inc., 1968.

Japanese

"Bakudan jiken omowanu hamon [Unexpected ripple of the bombing incident]." *Shukan Bunshun*, 11 June 1975, pp. 144–151.

Daikasumikai, ed. *Naimushōshi* [History of the Home Ministry]. 4 vols. Tokyo: Chiho Zaimu Kyokai, 1970.

Hironaka Toshio. *Sengō Nihon no keisatsu* [Postwar Japanese police]. Tokyo: Iwanami Shoten, 1968.

———. *Nihon no keisatsu* [Japanese police]. Rev. ed. Tokyo: Tokyo Daigaku Shuppankai, 1958.

Ino Kenji. *Yakuza to Nihonjin* [Gangsters and Japanese]. Tokyo: Mikasa Shobo, 1974.

Iwai Hiroaki. *Byōri shūdan no kōzō* [The structure of pathological groups]. Tokyo: Seishin Shobo, 1969.

Japan Sociological Society, ed. *Nihon shakai no kaisōteki kōzō* [Status structure of Japanese society]. Tokyo: Yuhikaku, 1958.

Metropolitan Police Department, ed. *Keishichō kashōshū* [Metropolitan Police Department song collection]. Tokyo: Kasumigaseki Shuppankai, 1971.

Mugishima Fumio. "Sōshiki hanzai [Organized crime]." In *Hanzai shinrigaku*: *hanzai kōdō no gendaiteki rikai* [Criminal psychology: a modern understanding of criminal behavior], edited by Ako Hiroshi and Mugishima Fumio, pp. 295–307. Tokyo: Yuhikaku, 1975.

Mugishima Fumio, Hoshino Kanehiro, and Kiyonaga Kenji. *Bōryokudanin no danshi to shisei* [Tattooing and cutting off of finger joints by members of criminal gangs]. A pamphlet published by the National Institute of Police Science, n.d.

National Police Agency, ed. *Keisatsu kashū* [Collection of police songs]. Tokyo: Jiji Tsushinsha, 1956.

National Police Agency Personnel Management Council, ed. *Seinen keisatsukan*: *sono rikai to shidō* [Young police officers: understanding and leading them]. Tokyo: Keisatsu Kyokai, 1970.

Nieda Rokusaburo. *Tatemae to honne* [Form and essence]. Tokyo: Daiyamon-dosha, 1973.

Nihon rekishi daijiten [Dictionary of Japanese history], 1969 ed. S.v. "Gonin gumi," "Jishinban," and "Meakashi."

Supervisory Committee for Commemorative Activities for the Hundred Year Anniversary of the Founding of the Metropolitan Police Department, ed. *Keishichō hyakunen no ayumi* [Hundred-year progress of the Metropolitan Police Department]. Tokyo: Keishicho Soritsu Hyakunen Kinen Gyoji Un'ei Iinkai, 1974.

Takahashi Shoki. *Kōban to seishun* [Police-box and youth]. Tokyo: Tachibana Shobo, 1973.

Yamamoto Noboru, and Nakagawa Kiyoko. "Daitoshi ken ni okeru kaisō kōsei to seikatsu ishiki [Status composition and life consciousness in the area of metropolises]." *Toshi mondai kenkyū*, vol. 25, no. 6 (n.d.): pp. 1–15.

Documents

English

National Police Agency, ed. *The Police of Japan*. Tokyo: National Police Agency, 1974.

Japanese

Criminal Investigation Bureau, National Police Agency. *Shuto ken ni okeru hanzai no ansū nado chōsa kekka* [Survey results on unreported crimes, etc., in the metropolitan area]. Tokyo: National Police Agency, 1974.

Kanagawa Social Psychological Research Association. *Jūmin no yōbō to kinmu kankyō nado ni taisuru keisatsu shokuin no ishiki chōsa* [Attitude survey of police employees concerning citizen desires and work environment]. A classified study published by the Kanagawa Prefectural Police Headquarters, n.d.

Kōraku (Okayama), April 1975.

Metropolitan Police Department, ed. *Keisatsu ingo ruishū* [Collection of police secret language]. Tokyo: Criminal Investigation Division, Metropolitan Police Department, 1956.

National Personnel Authority. *Jinjiin geppō* [Monthly report of the National Personnel Authority], September 1974.

National Police Agency. *Gaikin tsūhō* [Patrol bulletin], vol. 12, no. 3 (n.d.).

National Police Agency, ed. *Keisatsu hakusho*, 1973 [Police white paper]. Tokyo: Okurasho Insatsukyoku, 1973.

———. *Keisatsu hakusho*, 1974 [Police white paper]. Tokyo: Okurasho Insatsukyoku, 1974.

———. *Keisatsu hakusho*, 1976 [Police white paper]. Tokyo: Okurasho Insatsukyoku, 1976.

Okayama Prefecture, ed. *Okayama-ken tōkei nempō*, 1971 [Okayama prefecture statistical yearbook]. Okayama: Okayama-ken Tōkei Kyōkai, 1974.

Okayama Prefectural Police Headquarters, ed. *Bōhan-hoan keisatsu no ayumi*, 1974 [Activities of the crime-prevention and safety police]. Okayama: Okayama Prefectural Police Headquarters, 1974.

———. *Hanzai tōkeisho*, 1973 [Criminal statistics]. Okayama: Okayama Prefectural Police Headquarters, 1973.

———. *Okayama-ken keisatsu nenkan*, 1972. [Okayama prefectural police yearbook]. Okayama: Okayama Prefectural Police Headquarters, 1972.

Prime Minister's Office. *Keisatsu ni kansuru seron chōsa* [Public opinion survey concerning the police]. Tokyo: Prime Minister's Office, 1974.

Yamaguchi gumi jihō (Osaka), 5 January 1973.

Newspapers and Ephemerals

English

Ann Arbor News, 20 October 1975; 18 February 1976.

Asahi Evening News (Tokyo), 15 March 1974; 4 April 1974.

Japan Times (Tokyo), 13 February 1974; 17, 23 June 1974; 17 July 1974; 17 September 1974; 16, 22, 28 November 1974; 1 January 1975; 21 March, 1975; 14, 25 May 1975; 2 June 1975; 16 April 1977; 30 June 1977.

New York Times, 17 March 1977.

Pacific Stars and Stripes (Tokyo), 9 July 1975.

Time, 17 October 1977.

Japanese

"Aa kidōtai [O riot police]." Roon Record Company. RD-5007.

Asahi Shimbun (Tokyo), 19 May 1975; 9, 14 June 1975.

San'yō shimbun (Okayama), 10 December 1973; 7, 18, 28 September 1974; 4 October 1974; 23 December 1974; 28 March 1975; 12 April 1975.

Sankei shimbun (Tokyo), 1 August 1974.

Yomiuri shimbun (Tokyo), 8, 18 July 1975.

INDEX

Abortion, 205
Access to the police, x–xii
Adaptation by the police, 1–2; to changes, 31–33; to juvenile crime and delinquency, 78–93; in rural communities, 14, 17–33; to social outcastes, 95–104; strategies for, 1, 9; in urban areas, 34, 46–55; via specialization, 130–148; versus police solidarity and loyalty, 3
Administrative elite, 183–185
Administrative Police Regulation, 10
Age: of arrested juveniles, 79–80; of police officers, 32, 181, 188, 210–211; for retirement, 201, 202
Ainu, 95n
American police system: and gangsters, 107; influence on the Japanese police system, xiv, 11, 71
Apartment complexes, 140; for police officers and their families, 195–197, 200; police visits to, 37n, 52–54
Arrests: decision-making process for, 188; of juveniles, 79–80
Arrogance of police officers, 160–161
Asama Sansō incident, 159
Asia and Far East Institute for the Prevention of Crime and Treatment of Offenders (UNAFEI), xi, xiv
"Atrocious crimes," 61, 66; by juveniles, 80
Automobile gangs, 84–85
Automobiles of gang bosses, 115

Ballads, 159–160; with gangster protagonists, 121. *See also* Songs
Bars, and gangsters, 116, 125–126
Bicycles, theft of, 79, 80

Bōhan kumiai, crime prevention associations, 25, 41–43, 53, 124, 125, 141–142
Bōhan renrakusho, crime-prevention checkpoints, 27, 42–43, 45, 46, 48, 50, 53, 97
Bonds: among gangsters, 108–109, 112; among the riot police, 176; formed during police training, 170. *See also* Human relations; Obligations
Bootlegging, 98
Bowing to superiors, 187
Bribery of the police, 30, 205, 207; and election violations, 223–224
Brothel areas, 51–52
Brother-brother bond among gangsters, 108–109, 112
Buddhism, 100, 101
Burakkai, village residents' organization, 25, 41, 42
Buraku Liberation League, 102
Burakumin, 2, 45, 99–104, 120n; defined, 95; future of, 99–100, 103; in gangs, 112, 113; origins of, 95, 100–101; and police recruiting, 45, 163; police relations with, 102–104; political activities of, 102, 145

Calligraphy, 158
Ceremonies: for bonds among gangsters, 108–109, 122; for police solidarity, 179
Children of police officers, 197–198
Chivalry, 120, 121
Chōnaikai, urban neighborhood associations, 41–42, 44, 48, 49, 50, 56; relations with security police, 146–147
Chūzai san: community activities of, 24–28, 31–32, 74; compared to urban police officers, 34, 40, 41; defined, 20,

Kurashiki Spinning Company, 23, 27
Kyoto University Faculty of Law, 184

Labor unions, 200–201
Language: training in, 171; used by the police and criminals, 161–162
Law enforcement: and power of local
bosses, 206; in rural areas, 28–30; of
"special laws," 138
Laws, Japanese, 11, 12, 207; on arrests,
188n
Leftists, 217; activities among the *burakumin*, 102; centralized police structure opposed by, 12; confession of crimes by,
137, 143; formation of police labor
unions encouraged by, 200–201; and
gangsters, 107, 123–124; police attitudes
toward, 93, 143, 144; student organizations of, 78
Leisure time of police officers, 142; cultural
interests pursued during, 157–158; recreational activities at police stations,
193–194; in rural areas, 31–32
"Letter strategy," to control auto gangs, 85
Liberal Democratic party, 102, 123,
221–224
Licenses: for business, 141; for driving,
209; for firearms, 140–141
Lie detectors, 99
Lockheed bribery scandal, 123n
"Lock patrols," 43
Loyalty among gangsters, 111, 120
Loyalty and solidarity among police officers, 2, 151, 152, 153, 159–160, 173;
conflicts in, 181, 185, 203–214; methods
to obtain, 180–181, 197

Machi hikeshi, and modern gangsters,
109–110
Mafia, American, 107, 114, 117
Magazines: for gangsters, 118–120; for po-
lice officers, 178–179. *See also* Media,
the
Mah-Jongg parlors, 141, 142, 194, 206
"Mama police," 82
Marriage: ceremony for, 108; and social
outcastes, 101
Marriage of policemen, 194–197 *passim*;
go-betweens for, 195; and promotion,
185n
Martial arts, 172–173
Masaharu Gotoda, 224
Masculinity in police work, 154–155, 157,
158–159, 166
Media, the: magazines for gangsters,

118–120; magazines for police officers,
178–179; and police public relations,
72–73; and public opinion, 226–227; social control augmented by, 73–74. *See
also* Newspapers
Meiji period: gangsters in, 113, 122; police
system in, 9–10, 154, 203, 208
Meter maids, 169, 195
Military Police, 10–11
Minorities, police relations with, 95–104
Misconduct by police officers, 203–204
Mizushima industrial complex: described,
6–7; gangsters in, 125; industrial pollution in, 139–140; investigation of industrial accidents in, 132–133; Korean population in, 96, 98, 145; police response
time in, 69; police work in, 47, 52–54;
rate of crime solution in, 64
Mizushima police station, xiii; informality
at, 187; number of patrol cars for, 67–68;
organization of, 19
Mobile police force, 68–69
Money: donated to the police, 206; given to
transferred police officers, 192; lent by
police officers, 74; obtained by gangsters,
116–120
Morality among gangsters, 110–111
Mothers, traffic-safety associations formed
by, 44
Motivations for police work, 166, 201–202
Motorcycle policemen, 154–155
Motorcycles, 68; theft of, 79, 80
Murder, 188
Mutual benefit associations, 200

Naked Festival, 156–157
Nation, Japanese word for, 104
"National Narcotics Banishment and Purification of the Homeland League," 119
National Police Agency, ix, x, xi, xiv, 13,
141, 147, 209; administrative elite hired
by, 183; directives issued by, 189; functions of, 12, 14; head of, 220, 221, 224,
225; official song of, 177–178; in police
organizational structure, 216–217,
218–220; posters of criminals issued by,
73; role in police training, 169, 183, 184;
survey by, 31, 32
National Police Reserve, 11–12
National Public Safety Commission, 209,
218–219
National Rural Police, 12
National Tax Agency, 127
Neighborhood police-support organizations,
226; bonds with the police, 45; historical

formers in, 44–46; citizen support groups
for, 41–44; compared to rural police
work, 32–33, 40, 61–62, 65–66, 187;
crime rate in, 58–62; gift-giving in,
45–46; police adaptation to, 46–54. See
also *Kōban*

Vacations, 194
Valentine, Lewis J., 11
Values: of gangsters, 120–124; of police of-
ficers, 201, 203, 208, 214
Violence: crimes of, 61–62; by gangsters,
124, 126; by police officers, 205; by stu-
dents, 86–87
Voluntary police-support groups, 41–44.
See also Neighborhood police-support or-
ganizations
Volunteers: to prevent juvenile delinquency,
83; for traffic control, 44

Wealth, and crimes by juveniles, 80–81
Wives of gangsters, 116

Wives of policemen: courtship of, 194–195;
role in rural police work, 30–31; social
life of, 196–197
Women: in police work, 167–168, 195; traffic-safety associations formed by, 44
Work environment in police stations, 180,
185–187
World War II: crime rate after, 58, 78; gang
membership influenced by, 113; Koreans
in Japan after, 95–96

Yakuza. See Gangsters
Yamagiwa, Joseph K., 94n
Yamaguchi *gumi* (gang), 105, 118–119,
124n; boss of, 126; ideology of, 121
Year-end parties, 193, 204
Young police officers: compared to older
policemen, 209–214; complaints of, 201
"Youth assistants," 83. *See also* Juvenile
crime and delinquency